SHAKESPEARE'S PUB

BY WALTER KERR
The Theater in Spite of Itself
The Decline of Pleasure
Pieces at Eight
How Not to Write a Play

PETE BROWN

SHAKESPEARE'S
PUB

A Barstool History of London as
Seen Through the Windows
of Its Oldest Pub ~ The George Inn

ST. MARTIN'S GRIFFIN ✿ NEW YORK

www.stmartins.com

The Library of Congress has cataloged the hardcover edition as follows:

Brown, Pete, 1968–
    Shakespeare's pub : a barstool history of London as seen through the windows of its oldest pub – the George Inn / Pete Brown.
        p. cm.
    ISBN 978-1-250-03388-8 (hardcover)
    ISBN 978-1-250-03387-1 (e-book)
    1. George Inn (Enfield, London, England)—History. 2. London (England)—Buildings, structures, etc.—History. 3. Bars (Drinking establishments)—England—London—History. 4. Enfield (London, England)—History. 5. Great Britain—History. I. Title.
    TX950.59.G7B77 2013
    647.95421—dc23

                                                                        2013010139

ISBN 978-1-250-04902-5 (trade paperback)

St. Martin's Griffin books may be purchased for educational, business, or promotional use. For information on bulk purchases, please contact Macmillan Corporate and Premium Sales Department at 1-800-221-7945, extension 5442, or write specialmarkets@macmillan.com.

First published in Great Britain under the title *Shakespeare's Local* by Macmillan, an imprint of Pan Macmillan, a division of Macmillan Publishers Limited

First St. Martin's Griffin Edition: June 2014

10 9 8 7 6 5 4 3 2 1

For Liz,
Of course

CONTENTS

Would I were in an alehouse in London! I would give all my fame for a pot of ale, and safety.

(William Shakespeare, 1564–1616, *Henry V*)

Were I to choose a place to die in, it should be an inn. It looks like a pilgrim going home, to whom the world was all an inn, who was weary of the noise and confusion of it.

(Archbishop Robert Leighton, 1611–84,
who had his wish granted and died in a London inn)

The Public House represents what should be the hub of our wheel of Life, essential to our material need and second only to the Church that stands and represents our spiritual necessity. The Church is to the spirit as the Inn is to the flesh and, if good and well designed, they baulk the Devil himself.

(Sir Edwin Lutyens, 1869–1944)

The George Inn, circa 1870.

The George Inn, 2012.

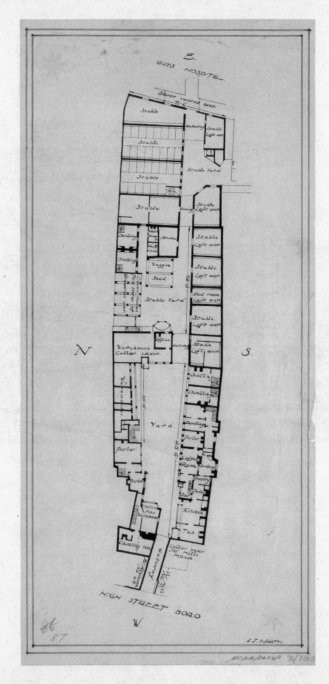

The George Inn in all its glory – ground-floor plan from 1849.

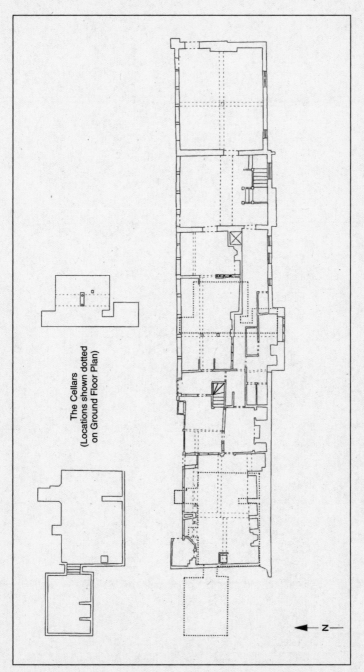

The Cellars
(Locations shown dotted
on Ground Floor Plan)

N

The somewhat reduced but still impressive George Inn today – ground-floor plan from 2009.

SHAKESPEARE'S PUB

PROLOGUE: CONCERNING SCANDAL, MURDER, SMUGGLING, HIGHWAYMEN, COFFEE, &C.

Or to some coffeehouse I stray
For news, the manna of a day,
And from the hipp'd discourses gather
That politics go by the weather;
Then seek good humour'd tavern chums,
And play at cards, but for small sums;
Or with the merry fellows quaff,
And laugh aloud with them that laugh

('The Spleen: An Epistle to Mr Cuthbert Jackson',
Matthew Green, 1737)

ROBBERIES. MUGGINGS. Fatal Accidents. Interest rates.

It's always the same old stories, the same sensationalism, every day in the newspaper. Every day you tut and shake your head. And every day you read it anyway. Because while the world gets seemingly wilder and more incomprehensible with each passing hour, sitting down with the paper and a good cup of coffee is one of life's enduring pleasures.

Today, April the nineteenth in the Year of Our Lord 1737, is no different.

You quickly scan the front page news of shipping lost on its way to the colonies and elsewhere, pausing only for a sorrowful wince at the loss of twenty-four cases of Rhenish wine that went down with the *Hector*, bound for Dublin.

Out of habit, you flip over to the back page. Here are the usual notices of new books published today: a history of Rome; a 'Defence of natural and reveal'd Religion'; a military history of the Duke of Marlborough; and – huzzah! – the fourth edition of the *Practical Farrier*.

Here's one that looks interesting, towards the foot of the page: *The Ladies Physical Directory*, seemingly 'a treatise on the Weaknesses, Indispositions, and Diseases peculiar to the female sex, from 11 years of age to 50 and upwards', which includes advice on treating 'the Green Sickness, Obstructions, Immoderate Fluxes, Hysteric Affections, the Piles, and every other Disorder or Distemper the fair sex are peculiarly liable to'.

You like the *London Evening Post* for its politics. The paper hates Walpole and his Whig government, and you enjoy its scathing attacks on him. But it's good for news of London as well, devoured eagerly when it reaches the provinces by the stagecoach, and it is that news which predominates today. Having done with the formalities, you open the single folded sheet to its densely packed centre pages, where the good stuff is.

A customs man seized 1,545 gallons of spirits from smugglers ''Tis almost incredible to believe what considerable Seizures are daily made in many Places of the Country, notwithstanding the severe laws against the Smuggling Trade', says the *Post*.

Mr Quill's house was raided by two chimney sweeps. He managed to shoot one of them, but the other scuttled back up the chimney down which he had arrived.

Mr Vaitier, a weaver, was with his family in Spitalfields when he was attacked 'by three Ruffians arm'd with Pistols, who with execrable Oaths threaten'd them with Death and Destruction'. The paper warns, as papers always do, that 'such a knot of rogues infest Spitalfields that 'tis dangerous to stir out of doors after Sun-set'.

A drunk who bought a pint at a pub in Petticoat Lane refused to leave, and was found dead, head first in a grate, the following morning. He joins the rest of this week's fatalities, duly listed on page three: 'Consumption 66, Convulsion 134, Dropsy 19, Fever 51, Smallpox 18, one man excessive drinking [our man above], one falling off a horse, one from a cart, 2 drowned and three murders'.

One of those drownings happened not far from the coffee room in which you sit. One of the Fellow Apprentice Butchers from across the road was rowing some meat out to a vessel lying just off Pickle Herring Stairs, when he was run down by a barge. Neither the fellow, nor his boat (nor his meat presumably) were seen again.

But here, in the dead centre of page two, is a story that interrupts your musings and hits even closer to home:

> On Tuesday the Body of a Female Infant new-born
> was found in a Ditch behind the George Inn, South-
> wark. There were apparent Marks of Violence upon
> it, but the Mother has not as yet been discover'd, tho'
> diligent search is making after her.

As you happen to be sitting in that very same George Inn, it makes you stop and think.

There are those who believe London's poor are inferior beings, incapable of feeling pleasure or pain the same way others do. But a female infant is a female infant, and surely nobody deserves such an awful premature end as this. It appears to be a growing problem – according to the paper, this infant is the third found murdered this week, after the discovery of two tiny bodies stabbed to death near an alehouse in Whitechapel a few days ago.

And yet, this is a crime almost unknown in the rest of Europe. As the *Post* says, 'In Great Britain . . .'tis thought more Murders of this Nature are committed in one Year, than in all Europe besides in Seven.'

Such is the extent of the problem that eight years ago there was a plan to build 'an Hospital for the maintaining of unfortunate women in their Lying in', but for some reason, despite £500 having been raised for the venture, it never came to anything. Now there are rumours that the Queen herself is getting involved, and is pressing her husband for the building of a foundling hospital like the one she is known to have seen on a recent trip to Paris.

But for now, the problem of dead babies is an everyday occurrence that clearly plays on the conscience of all levels of society. It bothers you, as surely it must bother the other regular customers who gather here in the coffee room of the George to read their newspapers and discuss events.

The room you are in is bustling with people, for as Matthew Green's new poem acknowledges, coffee drinking has become one of life's greatest pleasures, with more than three thousand coffee houses now scattered across London alone. As 'M.P.' wrote in a famous pamphlet some years ago, coffee is 'extolled for drying up the Crudities of the Stomack, and for expelling Fumes out of the Head. Excellent Berry! which can cleanse the English-man's Stomak of Flegm, and expel Giddinesse out of his Head.'[1]

So if an inn such as the George – an inn described by the clergyman and historian Mr John Strype in his *Survey Of The Cities Of London and Westminster* in 1720 as 'very large, with a considerable trade' – wishes to remain in such a position, it must now compete not only with the other inns and alehouses of Southwark, but with the coffee shops as well.

The coffee room at the George is the best room in the

---

1. But not everyone is a fan: in 1674, the anonymous 'Women's Petition Against Coffee' declared that, 'The Excessive Use of that Newfangled, Abominable, Heathenish Liquor called COFFEE . . . has . . . Eunucht our Husbands, and Crippled our more kind Gallants, that they are become as Impotent, as Age.'

whole inn. Light and airy, it's the perfect place to relax, read and gossip, and you are joined in doing so by local business-men and gentlemen and the inn's residents, visiting London from Kent, Surrey, Sussex and further afield. The taproom next door is similarly busy, albeit populated by waggoners, ostlers and labourers who are smoking, drinking ale, and swapping news and gossip in their own fashion.

Here in the coffee room, you're not the only person reading the *Post*, and there is a low murmur of speculation surrounding the story of the dead infant. Who could do such a thing? With absolutely no hope, perhaps the poor mothers believe it is a kindness to kill their offspring rather than let them starve. It's probably one of the local whores – for even after the closure of the infamous Bankside brothels or 'stews', this is still where Londoners come for such pleasures. Or maybe it was just one of the many poor wretches driven half-mad by gin. Last year's Gin Act seems to have done little to deter the craze for drinking the stuff by the pint; all it has done is put the trade into the hands of criminals, driving it underground.[2] After all, isn't Madam Genever also known as Mother's Ruin?

You pause and look out through the panelled windows of the coffee room, into the cobbled yard outside. The huge waggons are just starting to arrive, heavily laden for the Borough Market tomorrow. Horses are untethered and taken through an archway at the back of the courtyard into the cramped confines of the stable yard, where there are sufficient

---

2. The 1736 Gin Act was the second of what would eventually be five Acts attempting to control the gin epidemic by applying punitive taxes and expensive licences. In response the gin trade merely became criminalized and even harder to govern, and the damage done by gin carried on getting worse. (Those who continue to believe today that the answer to the supposed 'binge-drinking epidemic' is to massively raise the price of alcohol, please take note.)

stalls to accommodate up to a hundred animals. Past these, and past the long lines of warehouses, waggon sheds and lodgings which accommodate the waggoners and their trade within the inn-yard, three hundred feet back from the inn's main entrance onto the Borough High Street, there is a small back entrance that opens out onto a narrow drainage ditch, partially covered, which separates the inn from its easterly neighbour, the newly built Guy's Hospital. This ditch, originally dug to drain the stinking swamps upon which Southwark is built, is now nothing more than a semi-enclosed sewer. It's an unimaginably bleak end for an innocent child.

So in some ways, it's something of a relief when you look back down to the *Post*, and a story at the top of the page, directly above the sad tale of the infant, catches your eye and offers you – for a moment at least – some relief, a frisson of dark excitement:

> On Saturday last as a Gentleman of West-Ham, and others in a Coach, were going to Epping to Dinner on the Forest, the famous Turpin and a new Companion of his, came up and attack'd the Coach, in order to rob it; the Gentleman had a Carbine in the Coach loaded with Slugs, and seeing them coming got it ready, and presented it at Turpin on stopping the Coach, but it flash'd in the Pan; upon which says Turpin, 'G— D— — you, you have miss'd me, but I won't you', and shot into the coach at him, but the Ball miss'd him, passing between him and a Lady in the Coach; and then they rode off towards Ongar,' and din'd afterwards that Day at the Hare-Street, and robb'd in the Evening several passengers on the Forest between Loughton and Rumford, who knew him; he has not robb'd on that Road for some Time before.

This is news indeed! Since the break-up of his gang of house robbers two years ago, and the subsequent apprehension and transportation of his first accomplices in highway robbery, little has been heard of Dick Turpin these last twelve months. Some say he has been spotted in Holland, while others believe he has adopted an alias and disappeared from public view. Since last month, however, there have been a string of robberies involving one – and it seems, now possibly two – new accomplices.

These revelations stir mixed feelings in your breast. On the one hand, Turpin's return signals a real threat to the customers at the George. Though the rogue seems to confine himself mainly to the roads and forests northeast of London, safely on the other side of the river, he has been known to venture south, with reports of him having struck in Croydon and Blackheath, each a short distance to the south of Southwark and a stopping point on some of the coaching routes that begin in this very inn.

And Turpin is hardly the only highwayman on the roads, even if he is the most notorious. Streatham Common – much closer even than Blackheath – is known as one of their regular haunts. The George may have been a little behind other Southwark inns, but it has become a popular hub since the coaches started calling here back in thirty-two. Here is a stark reminder that this desirable new mode of travel, which makes it possible to reach Dover or Hastings in under ten hours, is not without its risks.

Then again, you can't deny that the story thrills you. You couldn't explain why, but part of you admires Turpin's exploits. And it seems you're not the only one. Turpin is, clearly, recognized wherever he goes. Look – here in this very story, it says he was spotted in an inn or tavern in Ongar having dinner between robberies, and was left unmolested. The *Post* reads more like one of Fielding's plays than a factual account. Although the newspaper would never admit such a thing, it seems there is something of the folk hero starting to emerge around the villain's exploits.

This is hardly surprising, given the way popular entertainments have taken to romanticizing such figures. John Gay's *Beggar's Opera* – performed just next door in the Tabard a few years ago – at once glamorized highwaymen and likened them to First Lord of the Treasury Robert Walpole, now mockingly referred to as the 'Prime Minister'. In *Tom Thumb* and the *Covent Garden Tragedy* Henry Fielding's attacks on Walpole were far more barbed and personal, clearly suggesting he was behaving as if he were King, and you hear that Walpole is now seeking revenge.[3]

Theatre is for the most part regarded as a base and disreputable form of art. It's still less than a century since the Puritans outlawed it altogether, pulling down the playhouses just over on the Bankside, flogging the players, and fining those who dared watch them.

Once again, your thoughts carry your gaze to the courtyard outside the window. For was it not courtyards such as this that gave their inspiration to the designers of those theatres? This is where players would gather before those first permanent playhouses were built: an enclosed courtyard surrounded on three sides by two tiers of wooden balconies or 'galleries', leaving one side free for a stage to be erected, with the means to charge admission to the yard, or pit, and a little extra for a better view from the galleries.

It's a long time now since plays were staged here in the yard. But maybe they will be again, in some currently unimaginable future when people will seek to re-establish a link with this and previous centuries in the face of incomprehensible change and progress.

Of course, that's assuming the George will survive into the future, though something tells you it will. After all, people will

---

3. Later this year the Licensing Act will become a landmark piece of censorship, requiring all plays to be approved by the Lord Chamberlain before they are staged. It will remain in place until 1950.

always want food and drink, and entertainment. They'll always want a quick passage to Dover too. And what quicker, finer passage could there ever be than the stagecoach?

And now, despite the coffee, you start to feel drowsy. Maybe it's the warmth of the fire, or the close fug of pipe smoke and the smell of the roasting meat on the spit. You doze, and you start to dream. In your dream, you drift through the wall and out into the courtyard, a ghost, invisible and silent, but still alive. You must be – you can smell the horseshit, see the brightly painted coach, and hear the trumpet that announces its departure.

Now you're floating upwards, up past the galleries where the maids are busy cleaning the bedrooms and making up the vast four-poster beds for new guests; past the bootblack delivering boots and shoes to those doors behind which the more fortunate residents are only now rising. You can see the barrels of ale from the famous Anchor Brewery, just across the road, being delivered to the cellars, and the haberdashers and merchants in their offices and warehouses around the inn's interlocking courtyards. You see the goods being loaded and unloaded from waggon to warehouse, and the odd piece of semi-legal trading between people who think no one is watching them.

As you rise still further, you can see the entirety of the inn, a massive 21,000-square-foot, three-tiered business concern. Still further, and you can see more of Borough High Street, and that this is merely one of seven or eight great coaching inns, all similar in design but not quite identical, all standing shoulder to shoulder, each extending back from the street a hundred yards or so in a twisting maze of yards and stables. And that's just the big ones: the countless lesser inns and alehouses squeezing in where they can, mean that this hectic, noisy borough extending from the foot of London Bridge is home to the highest concentration of inns in all London, which makes it the largest in the newly formed United Kingdom, and therefore, in all likelihood, the whole world.

And now, something strange begins to happen (as if hanging suspended in mid-air over Southwark on a Tuesday morning isn't strange enough). Time begins to accelerate. As you watch, people and coaches become a blur. Your vision flashes as day follows night follows day follows night in fractions of seconds. You can't follow events any more, or even the seasons of the years as they fly past. It's all moving so fast now, the only narrative you can follow is that of the buildings. What you had until now thought of as permanent structures start to change and evolve at alarming speed. You see them grow higher, stand around for a bit, then disappear. A brief flash here and there and some are reduced to piles of blackened ash, only to be replaced by something bigger an instant later. Now, a great metal road sweeps in from the horizon, cutting swathes through the streets and filling the air around you with steam. Tall chimneys thrust up along the riverbank, spewing smells and gouts of noxious gas, and for a while the air is hazy and choking. Then, you sense objects whizzing past you in the sky, and for half a second it seems the entire city is in flames. Most of your reference points disappear, and then the building materials start to change, and the buildings rise higher than you thought possible, all glass and steel, until one particularly large and pointy one shoots up past you, almost taking your eye out, and everything stops and you're here, now, in the twenty-first century.

Along with everything else you know, much of the George Inn has disappeared. But incredibly, the wall you drifted through just a minute or two ago is still there, as are the galleries, the coffee room and all the rest of the main, south wing of the inn. One by one, its neighbours fell away, but in the blizzard of time travel you have just endured, the George was a constant. Around it, everything rose and fell, higher each time, before crashing back to earth again, countless times, while somehow the George remained there, fixed, unmoving, though not unchanging.

On the day we left it in 1737, the George was not the most celebrated of Southwark's inns. It wasn't the biggest, or the oldest, the most beautiful or the most important – even though it was very large, old, beautiful and important. Now, 275 years later, if we want to understand why this inn survived out of all of them we will have to employ even greater mental gymnastics than it just took us to get here.

People often tell you every good story should have a beginning, middle and end. OK, but no one said they necessarily had to come in that order, and we seem to have started somewhere in the middle. We must attempt to retrace our steps. But the story of the George has more than one beginning and, as yet, no end. It begins, enticingly, on a swampy riverbank two thousand years ago, and also in a school-hall lecture in 1858, and on a London bus in 2011.

And after that – well, it goes all over the place. As all good stories should.

CHAPTER ONE: IN WHICH WE MAKE THE PERILOUS AND EVENTFUL JOURNEY TO THE GEORGE INN, SOUTHWARK. FROM MY HOUSE.

> A man who, beyond the age of twenty-six, finds himself on a bus can count himself as a failure.
>
> (Margaret Thatcher, 1986, although the quote is apocryphal, unverified, and quite possibly just made up)

A CENTURY AND A HALF, or thereabouts, after the last stagecoach thundered under the arch and out of its yard, the George Inn can be reached easily via the number 149 bus.

It can also be reached in a number of quicker, more convenient ways. Trains into London Bridge Station (which killed off Southwark's coaching inns as quickly and as finally as the Xbox killed teenage ambition) will bring you almost to the George's door within the hour from such diverse and exotic places as Brighton, Tunbridge Wells, Dover, Luton and Bedford. London Bridge is also a stop on the Northern Line, which is handy, because as soon as you're on the Northern Line, you're looking for an excuse to get off again. Also, since its extension in the 1990s, the Jubilee Line passes through on its way to Canary Wharf.[1]

---

1. The archaeological excavation that took place before the line could be built gave us much of what we know about the Roman settlement that stood here two thousand years ago.

But for me, it's the 149 bus every time. I don't have much choice, living as I do in Stoke Newington, a part of London that's north of the river, quite close to the old City, yet lacks a tube station within what most people would think of as walking distance. (South of the river this is quite common, but it's an odd state of affairs north.) While the characteristically compassionate and understanding quote attributed to Margaret Thatcher at the beginning of this chapter may be bunkum, its snappier version – 'only losers take the bus' – was a familiar refrain uttered in all seriousness in the corridors of advertising, where I used to work, as well as in finance and management consultancy, by people who find the idea of travelling by bus even more abhorrent than being courteous to strangers.

The 149 takes people from London Bridge Station, just south of the river, all the way up to Edmonton, North London, and back again.[2] In doing so, it echoes the path that has faced many new arrivals to London from Europe and southeast England over the last two millennia. Because since the days the Romans built Watling Street from Dover to London, all the way through to the middle of the eighteenth century, all roads led to Southwark, or more precisely, to London Bridge. This is where you crossed into the City, and the rest of England beyond.

Famously, London is a city of twists and turns and corners and angles that make it a waking nightmare for tourists more accustomed to grids, freeways and bypasses. And yet, after kinking east from London Bridge, the A10 heads due north in a remarkably straight line for an unfeasibly long distance.

---

2. OK, it doesn't take the *same* people all this way – people get on and off at different parts. Or rather, most people do. Occasionally I've seen a comatose tramp who seemingly does the whole journey round. Once, when I was really busy and stressed, I found myself feeling perversely envious that he could do this. Then he woke up and told everyone to fuck off.

Eventually it clears London and carries on indefatigably, becoming the Great Cambridge Road, and finally ending up in the old port town of King's Lynn. When the Romans built it, it then joined what is now the A1, and ran all the way to York.

Going the other way, after a dalliance with Stoke Newington's one-way system the A10 runs past Dalston's exotically coiffured web designers, Caribbean fruit-and-veg vendors and Polish-delicatessen owners, and thrusts (well, crawls in a straight line) over the Regent's Canal towards the City, entering via Shoreditch. For centuries this district just outside the London city walls was home to the kind of people who wanted to be close to the action, but either didn't want to be or weren't allowed to be conventional citizens inside – just like Southwark outside the City's south side. In Shoreditch today, this non-conformist attitude is echoed by a profusion of Banksy stencils and bars that pretend to be shoe shops.

As Shoreditch High Street becomes Norton Folgate and then Bishopsgate, the road takes us between tower and gherkin, where ancient street names are the only indication of the version of the city that stood here between the Great Fire of London in 1666 and the Blitz of 1941. As Bishopsgate and Gracechurch Street, the A10 takes us to the Monument of the Great Fire, a tall plinth topped by a blazing golden orb, peeking through the buildings to let you know the tedium is almost over, and then you're round the corner and on to the southern tip of King William Street, and finally out on to the wide, gentle slope of London Bridge.

This is the special bit. Whenever you hit the Bridge, you stop whatever you're doing. If I'm doing this journey with my wife, whether we're joking (somewhat likely), arguing (just as likely) or having an in-depth conversation about hops or wool (we're a strange household) we both stop, and look, and fall silent.

To our left, looking east, HMS *Belfast* lies hard by the

redeveloped wharves where the Empire's tea was once unloaded and which are now – because it is, seemingly, the LAW – a collection of shops, cafés and fashionable eateries. Sometimes there'll be another navy ship, or even a cruise ship, moored alongside the retired Royal Navy cruiser. Behind it Tower Bridge stands proud. Next to it the Tower of London, for centuries the dominant feature of the London skyline, now snuggles almost cosily on the riverbank, struggling even to rise above the trees that almost obscure it from this angle. The towers of Canary Wharf, faded to blue-grey, shimmer hazily in the distance.

Out of the other side of the bus, looking west, the first thing we see is the tower of Southwark Cathedral poking above the riverside buildings on the South Bank. Further along, the brightly painted stern of the Golden Hind, an exact replica of Francis Drake's famous ship, pokes out from St Mary Overy Dock, its front hidden, looking from this angle as if it's playing hide and seek, its head buried, unaware that its fat rear end is giving it away. Successive wharves run away along the bank, fifty feet below the Bridge's artificially elevated height. And behind them looms the tower of Tate Modern, a building once considered hideous, now one of the top tourist attractions in the UK. The river curves in a mighty arc to the southwest, towards Waterloo and Westminster, and as we approach the middle of the bridge the north side comes into clear view: the twin towers of Cannon Street train station, then St Paul's Cathedral, and beyond that, dotting the view to the west, the brutish skyscraper of Centre Point and the spindly Telecom Tower, looking from this distance like it's been built from cotton bobbins. This is where we remember, every time, something the city itself once tried its best to forget: London was built around the river, and owes its existence to the river, and is defined by the river.

At the southern tip of the bridge on each side of the road stand two rampant silver dragons, atop plinths inscribed

'CITY OF LONDON'. They carry shields emblazoned with the red-and-white cross of St George, and above these they claw and spit at approaching road users. They're on every major road in and out of the historic City, marking the boundary where the walls (or in this case, the southern Bridge Gate) once stood.[3] If you do one of the riverboat tours up and down the Thames, the guides will inevitably point out that, symbolically, these dragons protect the City from invaders and undesirables. Just as inevitably, the guides will follow this with a quip about how they should turn the dragons around to face inward now, to protect the rest of us from the rapacious bastards of London's financial district.

And then it's a sharp swing left, up into London Bridge Station. Here, tumbling from the bus, or shot out from the train station's long, nasty, overcrowded access tunnels, or climbing up gratefully out of the tube, you stagger out and find yourself near the foot of the bridge, at the top end of Borough High Street.

And it's like having your nerve endings peeled and dipped in amphetamine.

Don't stop. Don't blink. Don't look down. If you're on the phone, hang up, because you need to concentrate. And any-way, the din means you can't hear yourself speak, never mind the person on the other end of the line. If you don't focus your entire attention on the immediate space around you, you will be hit by a bus, or a speeding ambulance, or a suicidal pavement-mounted bicycle courier, or a phalanx of commuting city workers who would not stop or deviate from their path if their own mothers were lying trampled before them.

The sound of jackhammers assaults you from all sides, drowning out the constant beeping of noise-to-tail traffic and wailing of emergency vehicles, all doing their best to keep it

---

3. I forgot to mention that we passed two more of these when we came into the City at Norton Folgate.

together in the face of eternal road works, and failing. Trains thunder across the rail bridges from London Bridge to Charing Cross and Cannon Street. The earth rumbles. The air feels thick with noise.

When I first arrived in London, I was eager to see how the city would look when the giant cranes had finished their work. I soon realized they never will. The cranes are more permanent than some of the structures they create, in a city that never stops being rebuilt.

In the summer of 2011, when I make this commute from Stoke Newington to Borough on a weekly basis to research this book, a second railway bridge is cutting a swathe of devastation through Borough Market, lurching over the High Street and into the busy station, as brutally pigdog-ugly in its modern way as the first bridge was in its day. This is the most congested stretch of train track in the whole of Britain, and drastic measures are called for.

The bridges swing close by what was recently a massive hole in the ground, is now a concrete slab, and will soon be The Place – yes, not just any old place – THE Place – The Definitive Place, The Place that clearly envies the City's capitalization across the river, The Place that, according to its website, is 'A GROUND-BREAKING NEW BUSINESS DESTINATION THAT MAKES A STRONG AND COMPELLING CORPORATE STATEMENT IN LONDON'S NEWEST COMMERCIAL QUARTER'. Those capitals leave you in no doubt just how STRONG that corporate statement is going to be. The 'newest commercial quarter' is London Bridge Quarter, a just-made-up name for a district of new offices, shops, housing, piazzas, roof terraces, and the mandatory coffee shops and fashionable eateries.[4]

---

4. I love it when property developers and estate agents try to make up these new names for districts, when they're the only people who will ever call them that. It's like those awkward lads who try to up their credibility

Central to this, rising above all, is the Shard. I didn't want to mention it when we were crossing the bridge because I didn't want to spoil the rest of the view, but by the late summer of 2011 it is so tall it blocks out the sun. The new tallest building in Europe will be complete by the time you read this, but as I come down here, week by week, it rises above us without pause, its future ghost already imprinted on the retinas of every passer-by who gazes up at it, filling in the blank sky with their image of the finished structure.

The Borough is being rebuilt. Again. Perpetually.

But while the size of the buildings may grow, and the source of the constant noise might change, alight at this spot at any time in its history, and the assault on your senses would have been just as intense.

As you stepped from a steam locomotive a hundred years ago, your nose would have borne the brunt of it; the mingled aromas of vinegar manufacturing, leather tanning, glassmaking and ale brewing adding a unique local pungency to London's overall choking, sooty miasma. A century and a half before that, stepping from your stagecoach, you'd have been pressed back against the wall by the thundering horses of mail coaches racing for the turnpikes, and the post-chaises and broughams rushing important passengers to and from the longer-distance coaches, before being accosted by mountebanks promising to show you such things as you have never seen: bearded ladies, the man with no head, the smallest person in the world, if you would only step into the back of this caravan and allow yourself to be relieved of a few coins. And a century or two before that, perhaps coming ashore from one of the thick mass of ships anchored in the 'Pool' immediately downriver of London Bridge, you'd have found the same streets crowded with market traders selling food,

---

when they introduce themselves by saying, 'Hi, I'm Steve, but everyone calls me Animal.' They don't, do they Steve?

clothes and leather goods, actors exhorting you to come and see their new comedy, a hideously scarred bear, muzzled and chained, being led to the pit for its next bout against a pack of hunting dogs, men sporting jewellery and exotic clothing, some with dark complexions, eyeing you suspiciously from the door of a dank and dirty alehouse, puppet shows satirizing the government, huge waggons on thick wooden wheels blocking the road as they slowly manoeuvred off the street and into an inn-yard, vagabonds, almost naked but for a few rags, begging for money or food, and Puritan preachers yelling that every single person noted above – yourself included – was certain to burn in hell for all eternity.

This patch of land south of the Thames has been a frenetic, hyperactive melting pot of the dirtier, baser, more hard-nosed, pragmatic, venal, speculative and lucrative aspects of humanity for a thousand years. For this is the Borough, where all human life comes to London, and tries to get in.

London's 'newest commercial quarter' my arse.

*

The last twenty years have seen enormous regeneration in Southwark, and the strip along the river, commonly known as Bankside, is now a succession of tourist attractions, cafes, markets and restaurants that hit every point on the scale between tacky and classy – sometimes simultaneously. But head down the High Street instead of along the Bankside, and it feels grittier, less compromising, than the shiny retail ideal offered in most high streets and malls.

Borough High Street doesn't feel downmarket and seedy, like some other parts of London still do; it just feels harder, more physical. The newsagents, curry houses and off-licences know the score; veterans of the scene. It's the sort of place where you can always get a seat in the Pret A Manger, but where the queue for Giuseppe's Luncheonette on the corner of King's Head Yard stretches out of the door and down the street every lunchtime. The new Starbucks – which sits in a tiny gap with the furtive air of someone who has nicked your seat when you'd just popped out to the shops for something you'd forgotten – with its smiling baristas out on the pavement giving away creamy little concoctions to passers-by, feels as uncomfortable and out of place as a hedge-fund manager at a dinner party when the conversation turns to, 'So, what do *you* do?'

There are signs of beauty here too, if you know where to look. Near Stoney Street at the bottom end of Borough Market the road forks, with Southwark Street curving away to the west and Borough High Street vaguely to the south. On the right-hand side of the fork, at the top of Southwark Street, the old Hop Exchange is a magnificent building denied the vista it deserves. If it were in Paris, or even the centre of London, it would be on tourist postcards. Its long, colonnaded frontage curves almost imperceptibly along the street, its magnificent main entrance resembling the gateway to a Napoleonic palace. It should be overlooking gardens with fountains, giving you enough space to step back and gaze on its filigree and carvings of hop pickers filling their baskets from heavy hop bines. Instead it overlooks City Tandoori, Santander and Harper's Cafe, and probably the only people who ever stand and gaze at its filigree and carvings are those waiting impatiently at the bus stop across the road for the 381 to Waterloo.

On the left leg of the fork, the view is dominated by Elephant and Castle's 42-storey Strata building. This eco-friendly apartment block, winner of the 2010 Carbuncle Cup awarded to Britain's ugliest building, looms up over everything, its petal-shaped walls holding three massive turbines like flowers at its peak. It doesn't belong – not here, not yet. It just looks wrong, as if it has somehow slipped through a dimension portal from Judge Dredd's Mega-City One.

Walking further down busy Borough High Street, the line

of shops on the left is punctuated periodically by narrow, furtive alleyways that broaden out a little if you look down them, each one stretching back a hundred yards or so, then terminating before the implacable bulk of Guy's Hospital. Only someone with an unhealthy interest in pub history would know that the names of these alleys – White Hart Yard, King's Head Yard, Talbot Yard, Queen's Head Yard – reveal that they were never built as streets at all, but as inn-yards, and that they're named and laid out for Borough's great coaching inns. They remain almost the only surviving evidence of them, save for the odd filthy local-history plaque here and there.

King's Head Yard still has a low arch, and a pub called The Old King's Head, next to the Italian restaurant linked to Giuseppe's famous luncheonette. The Old King's Head was built in 1881, after the big old inn that used to fill this entire yard, also known as the King's Head, was demolished. So I guess to avoid confusion we'd have to call the original inn The *Really* Old King's Head.

You can walk all the way to the back of King's Head Yard, where there's a staff entrance to Guy's, and the alley loops around to join the back of White Hart Yard. Walking past more offices back to the High Street this way, you pass a plaque by the entrance which tells you the White Hart Inn, immortalized by Shakespeare and Dickens, once stood here.

But tourists don't come here in search of ghosts of old buildings. They come to this very business-like street to visit the last living survivor. Finally then, if you know where to look, here's the hanging sign, an ornate, curlicued iron bracket extending out over the pavement from another narrow alley between buildings. Hanging from this bracket is a curious, painted oval sign depicting Saint George slaying the dragon, and in gold lettering, 'THE GEORGE'.

Today, the George is the last man standing of all London's great, galleried coaching inns. And it's debatable if we can even say that, really: the surviving southern wing of the old main courtyard consists of one partly galleried range stretching over 125 feet, a fifth – if that – of the complex that once stood here.

But imagine a busy modern-day coach station, such as that at London Victoria, a bustling hive of vehicles coming and going, packed with bored, open-mouthed passengers staring through the windows as they barrel in and out of the entrance. Inside, the station is a mess of luggage being loaded and unloaded, the atmosphere a cocktail of anxiety, excitement, uncertainty, regret and longing, overlaid with the stress of getting on or off the right coach at the right time.

And imagine that this busy coach station is also, at the same time, a large luxury hotel, an office block full of businesses where people work daily, a warehouse complex, a branch of Starbucks, a few shops and private houses, and one of the biggest pubs you've ever seen.

That was the George Inn in its prime.

It's still one of the most famous pubs in the world. It's in every guidebook to London pubs, a Grade One listed building protected by the National Trust, and is visited by people from across the globe.

And yet, at the same time, it's largely forgotten. Many of the regular visitors to nearby Borough Market, the swarms of city workers who flood across the bridge twice daily on their commute via London Bridge station, even the people who come here to drink in Southwark's other excellent pubs, are unaware it exists, hidden from view down a little alley between Lloyds TSB and Paddy Power.

Only a hundred years ago these two shops were both tailors – for centuries, one of Borough's main trades, now gone without trace. A hundred years from now who knows what they'll be? The online world will surely have killed off bricks-and-mortar banks and bookies by then. But the George will still be there, looking pretty much as it does now, serving a similar purpose. I feel sure of this, even without putting you through another time-travel sequence.[5]

These shops on either side each have a hanging sign extending out over the pavement, after the fashion of traditional inn signs, parenthesizing the sign for the George and quite possibly mocking it. These two buildings are linked by a wrought iron arch that spells out the name of the George again, and supports a cosy, Victorian-looking lantern at its apex, tossing out a weak orange glow into the Borough's perpetually watery sunlight. Below this arch, heavy, black wooden gates topped with spikes are permanently open onto the George Inn yard.

Pass through those gates, into the cobbled yard, and the noise and aggro of the High Street fall away. A hush soothes your battered senses and shredded nerve endings. And there stands the George – or at least, what remains of it.

The cheap, plasticky offices of the London School of Commerce stand where part of the inner yard once held capacious stabling and warehouses. This modern building also extends around the east and north sides of the yard, tracing the floor plan of the long-gone north and east wings of the inn.

If this building were simply horribly featureless, you could just about forgive the architect. But around the first floor, outside an open-plan office overcrowded with people in shirt-sleeves and ties, runs an imitation of the George's famous galleries, a modern, white design feature that's neither one thing nor the other, that evokes a sense of mocking imperson-ation: 'Ooh, look, I've got *galleries*! Look at me everyone, look at my galleries!' The sense that the new building is a grotesque parody of the George is completed by the Heel Tap, a disposable corporate pub – no, sorry, a 'Venue, bar and

---

5. Which I can't afford to do anyway – the prologue cost me millions in CGI and blew my special effects budget before I'd even got started.

eatery' – standing like a warped, funfair mirror on the ground floor of the north wing, directly opposite the George, trying to look classy and upmarket and succeeding only in resembling a Wetherspoon's trying to put on a posh accent.[6]

But on the south side of the yard, London's only surviving galleried coaching inn remains open for business. And it does more than that: for a lot of people, it takes the breath away.

It's an impressive building even now, when, sagging slightly with age, it's starting to resemble a party balloon the morning after. A century ago the American writer F. Hopkinson Smith visited the George while working on *Dickens's London*, a travelogue around the real places that provided the backdrop for Dickens's fiction. We'll come back to precisely what Dickens did and didn't write about the George later on, because it's a surprisingly contentious subject. But for now, Smith's reaction to his first sight of the George upon entering its yard, which would be shamelessly plagiarized by countless hacks over the following century, works as well in 2012 as it did in 1912:

> Seen from one end, in foreshortened perspective, it presents a continuous wobble from sill to eaves, its roof-line sagging, its chimney out of plumb, the shorter flues climbing up on the taller ones as if struggling for better air, the wonder being that it had not long ago lost all heart, and sunk into hopeless ruin.
>
> Looked at close by, however, say from beneath the chambermaid's gallery, it resolves itself to your glad surprise into quite another kind of rookery, putting to flight all your first conclusions; the same sort of surprise that comes to a man who, having made up his mind to ignore some approaching shabby person, finds himself bowing and scraping when he gets near enough to look into the kindly eyes and reassuring face of the

---

6. Places that give themselves names like 'Venue, Bar and Eatery' or 'Bar and Kitchen' strike me as talking out of their arse and rectum.

  misjudged individual. It did not take me many minutes
  to change my own opinion of the 'George Inn.'

The surviving range is 125 feet long, with three storeys and a
gabled roof. The walls on the ground floor are painted a very
dark olive green, framing an almost continuous run of windows made up of rows and columns of small, white-framed
panes. The uneven brickwork of the first and second floors
inverts the colour scheme, with pale cream walls and dark
frames around the windows. This basic design alone suggests
immediately that the building is old, and ensures that someone
within earshot will start uttering words like 'Dickensian' and
'heritage' within seconds of arriving.

  But you hardly notice any of this the first time you look at
the George. The main attraction is the pair of wooden
galleries that run, one tier above the other, along the first
third of the length of the building.

  There's something about those galleries. They draw the
gaze upwards, as compelling in their own way as the Shard,
now looming over the northeast corner of the yard. If you're
standing on one of the galleries looking down into the courtyard, you can watch the steady stream of sightseers and
pub-goers walk through the gates, look up, stop and gasp.

  On each, a series of carved wooden balusters holds a solid,
chunky handrail, periodically punctuated by slender Tuscan
columns that support the gallery above, and then the gabled
roof. The columns divide the galleries into six roughly equal
segments, each with hanging baskets of flowers and ivy. The
slight wonkiness of the lines of the galleries, which is noticeably
but only slightly more pronounced now than it was in photos
taken 125 years ago, adds to the overall charm.

  Some architectural forms are just inherently pleasing.
You've probably heard of the golden section, the seemingly
magical formula that excites mathematicians, artists, architects and even musicians which, when applied to geometry,

means one side of a rectangle is 1.61 times the length of the other. That may sound inconsequential, but the algebraic formula that expresses this relationship is itself aesthetically pleasing.[7] Since the time of the ancient Greeks it's been hidden in the proportions of many buildings we consider beautiful, and it's there – or thereabouts – all over the front of the George, in the proportions of the galleried sections and the size of the windows.

This is interesting, but actually I think the core of what makes the George so aesthetically appealing is much simpler than algebra: I think that, as a species, we just really, *really* like balconies.

There's something in their access to views and the little thrill of the alfresco blurring of lines between inside and outside that seems to do it for us. We pay substantially more for hotel rooms or cruise-ship cabins with balconies than those without. The most famous scene in Shakespeare revolves around one. When middle-class people have extensions done to their Victorian houses, their friends come round and coo, 'Ooh, you've got a *balcony*!' and then argue with each other on the way home about why they didn't get one when they had their house done up.

Yet the galleries at the George were not designed for lounging, or sunbathing, or leaning against and feeling superior while twirling a chilled glass of white wine by the stem. They were designed to allow a combination of light and physical access into the bedrooms behind. In a long, thin building such as the George, which directly backed onto other, similarly long, thin buildings, whose occupants wanted to be able to get to and from the yard quickly and conveniently, the choices were a passage at the front that blocked out the light; internal doors leading from one room to the next (which did

---

7. $\dfrac{a + b}{a} = \dfrac{a}{b}$ You must admit, it's pretty, even to someone with no interest in algebra.

happen in some inns, and even in the George in later eras); or this elegant, pretty, rewarding compromise. When galleries like this ran around the sides of an enclosed courtyard, they created a satisfying aesthetic that somehow combined majesty and cosiness, scale and intimacy, to form an open, friendly, practical, classy space.

But if to gaze upon the George in this way is to fall in love on the first date, as the affair gets under way you quickly realize the object of your affections is a little high-maintenance, even eccentric. Because the George doesn't quite conform to your idea of how a pub today should behave.

For a start, you're not quite sure where to go in. There are three entrances, two of which have their own hanging signs in addition to the one on the street outside. The nearest one to the street depicts St George on horseback, fighting the dragon again. Further away in the distance (it really is a very long pub, even in its diminished state) is a similar scene rendered in stained glass.

Most first-timers choose the nearest entrance, because it seems like the obvious thing to do. This door leads you into the old taproom, now known as the Parliament Bar. It's so called because the far wall as you go in is dominated by what is commonly referred to as a 'Parliament Clock', one of the most notable features of the inn. In 1797, after raising new taxes on horses, tea, sugar and spirits, Pitt the Younger, then Prime Minister *and* Chancellor of the Exchequer, had a fit of dazzling fiscal creativity and attempted to tax time itself. Undeterred by the impossibility of taxing an abstract but inexorable fourth dimension, he settled for placing a tax of five shillings on watches and clocks instead.

The more I learn about this, the more I slip into thinking of it as some kind of old fairy tale, but the tax was very real. Clockmakers and watchmakers were hardly the powerhouses of the late-eighteenth-century economy, but if fairy tales and costume dramas have any basis in fact – and we must assume they do – they were all wiry, lovable, excitable men with wild hair, breeches and half-rim glasses, a bit like Doc in the *Back to the Future* movies, and they did not deserve to have their livelihoods destroyed in this way.

'Ha ha!' cackled the wicked little Prime Minister. 'Now the poor watchmaker is out of work, he will have no option but to let me marry his pretty young daughter! And no one will know what time it is, so everyone will be late for work! No work will get done anywhere! The economy will collapse! Hang on, have I thought this through properly?'

Fortunately the day was saved by wily publicans and their famous 'tavern clocks'. These clocks were large and bold, usually designed with dark faces and white hands, and were popular in inns and taverns from the early eighteenth century. When Pitt's tax came in, these clocks surged in popularity and became known as 'Act of Parliament clocks', to such an extent that later generations, including most writers on the George, would wrongly assert that they were invented in response to Pitt's tax. They weren't – the George's clock dates back to around 1750 – but 1797 was their finest hour, so to speak. Saintly publicans selflessly installed these clocks in their inns, taverns and alehouses, so that people could pop in at frequent intervals during the day to check what time it was. And if they divined that the time was beer o'clock – well, surely that was Pitt's fault too, wasn't it?

The tax was astonishingly unpopular. 'Anything would be better than this!' cried the populace.

Pitt listened. 'Anything?' he asked.

'Yes!' cried the populace.

'Anything . . . at all?' persisted Pitt.

'Mm-hmm.' The populace nodded.

'OK, well, if you're sure . . .' said Pitt, and he repealed the clock tax after only nine months, and replaced it with Britain's first ever permanent, universal income tax, and we all lived happily ever after.

So the Parliament Bar is thus named because it is home to a Parliament Clock, which dates back even further than Pitt's tax, to the mid-eighteenth century. The clock has only been in this bar a few decades, having spent most of its life next door. But it's here now. And that's a good enough reason for this room, which has been called many things over the centuries and had many functions, to be called the Parliament Bar for the time being.

This is the people's bar, the old taproom where coachmen and waggoners drank from foaming tankards and smoked clay pipes, where even today it's still easy to visualize drinkers with whiskers, breeches and big hats. Market gardeners up for the Borough Market chatted here with watchmen from neighbouring business premises when they retired for the night. Dark and gloomy, every surface patched and painted and built over and repaired and uneven, it feels older than any other part if the inn, even though it isn't. The uneven, mismatched furniture was like this decades before such a look became fashionable for gastropubs and venues, bars and eateries. It looks like it's been here for centuries, and in the case of a few seats worn by countless bums, it has: a pair of fixed benches with curved ends and armrests are thought to date all the way back to the seventeenth century.

The low-beamed ceiling and the horizontal planks that form the western wall behind the clock give the fleeting illusion that you're on board an old galleon. This illusion is dispelled however by the two very solid fireplaces, one small, one huge, on the south wall. While this room was originally built as the single space it is today, for years it was subdivided into the taproom, or snug, and a kitchen. The small fire to the right heated the taproom, the big one to the left was the heart of the kitchen. When B.W. Matz, one of the founders of the Dickens Fellowship, visited in 1918, this big fireplace had a huge joint of meat suspended from an old-fashioned roasting jack, cooking in front of the fire.

As it is now, the taproom (look, I've done my best to call it the Parliament Bar, I've really tried) is seen by many fans of the George as the real heart of the pub. F. Hopkinson Smith observed that it was 'made bright with pewter and glass, and inviting easy chairs one or two; a table, and a barmaid, the whole redolent of the fumes of old Pineapple rum. The snuggery, of course, not the barmaid.' The old wag. It is, without doubt, a bar so snug, cosy, homely, characterful, timeless and cheery, the only thing that could improve it would be a group of hobbits singing to each other in the corner.

Well, that and an actual *bar*.

There is a bar, sort of, and it's lovely. In fact, as we'll see when we start digging further into the history, it's a very important bar, an example of the oldest kind of bar there is. It's a tiny room, entirely separate from the taproom, with panelled glass windows on three sides and a parlour behind it, which now serves as the manager's office. Here Matz described 'arrays of pewter pots of ancient lineage, tankards, glasses, mugs, bottles of wine, and spirits and appetizing liqueurs'.

Today, it's hard to believe that much has changed since Matz was here, apart from the selection of drinks becoming a little less interesting. The beer engine he observed is still here, although its four pumps no longer dispense ale. A little bronze sign says it was made by *South, 21 George Street, Blackfriars*. It dates back to around 1900, and is listed in the National Trust's inventory of interesting and historical knick-knacks, if that's the correct term for it. A set of modern beer pumps face the outside window, so that if you wanted to have a proper look before making your choice, you'd have to go outside into the courtyard and look in from there.

The problem is, the preserved feel of this bar, and the total absence of staff behind it, make it feel more like a mini-museum than a working part of the pub. I've been in the taproom several times for private functions, and at these, beer has been dispensed through the windows as if it were a boozy little Victorian post office, and it's still used the same way on Thursday, Friday and Saturday evenings. But on a week day, the tiny bar area is silent and deserted. So having entered uncertainly through the nearest door when you come in from the yard, and having found people sitting inside drinking pints, you stand around uncertainly for a while, and then, believing you must have missed something, go back out into the yard, and re-enter the pub through the second door.

Here is a small entry hall, with the museum/gift shop/post office-type bar to your right, a winding staircase up to the galleries in front of you, and a door to your left into another bar. Immediately, you realize this – probably – is the main bar. It's got that busy sense of purpose about it, modern beer fonts lining the bar, and most importantly, living, working members of staff behind it. It still feels slightly wrong because if this is the main bar, it doesn't seem to have an awful lot of seating. But worry about that later – clearly, this is where you can get a pint in your hand. Once that's sorted out, you can go back outside and back into the taproom (there's no internal public access from here, naturally) or push on and explore the inn a little further.

This was the old coffee room from back in 1737, now better known (officially at least) as the Southwark Bar. But a time-travelling coffee drinker would hardly recognize it now. For a start, while we're obviously very grateful that the bar is here and serving drinks, it's only been here since the late 1970s. Before then, right back before Dickens, this old coffee room was used as a restaurant. There are the remnants of a chimneystack on the wall behind the bar, which used to house yet another blazing fire. On the other side of the room, high-backed benches stuck out perpendicular to the windows, creating a series of semi-private snugs around the dining tables. In 1918, Matz delighted in the 'old box compartments with their mahogany tables, seats and high-backed partitions, mahogany sideboards and occasional tables, where the joints are placed at meal times; mahogany chairs with horse-hair seats to pull around the fire; casement windows, T-shaped gas jets, old prints and a red cord bell rope still in working order by the side of the fireplace', while in 1912 F. Hopkinson Smith loved the 'white-clothed tables, framed in settles, with pew backs so high that the fellow in the next pew could by no possible stretch of his neck discover what the fellow in the adjoining pew was having for dinner unless, of course, he stood on the settle and looked over the top – an unheard of liberty in so well-bred an inn as the "George".'

The fireplace, 'before whose cheery blazes hundreds of thousands of shivering shins had been toasted; and a mantel scratched by the bottoms of countless Tobys that had awaited the thawing out of the countless shins' and the 'big easy, fiddle-backed chairs' completed a perfect place that was 'so cosy and comfortable that once you were inside you would never want to get out, and once you were out you would be unhappy until you could again order "a fresh mug of 'alf-and-'alf, my dear, a brace of chops, with a kidney, and, if you don't mind, a mealy with its jacket on."'

Yes, this is the room the George's more literary fans fell in love with, the room that makes serious American men of letters turn into Dick van Dyke in *Mary Poppins*, the room where even Dickens is reputed to have kept a regular seat.

One of the old high-backed settles is still around some-where. According to the National Trust the design is definitely eighteenth century, but the wood is much newer. They also note that the beams across the roof are made of Baltic pine, which suggests they are from the nineteenth century. But engravings and paintings of this room from the nineteenth century (and there are more of those than you might think) show no heavy ceiling beams at all. The former coffee room and restaurant reminds us that our idea of what is old and traditional changes over time, and even the authentically ancient sometimes changes its appearance in arguably inauthentic ways.

A door at the far end of the room leads through into another small section whose comfortable, secluded booths recall the former layout of the coffee room. Beyond that, there's the ante-room where the third and final external door – the one with the stained-glass sign above it – comes in from the courtyard. Opposite the door there's another staircase leading upstairs to function rooms, flanked by comfortable sofas. And to the left – or straight ahead if you're coming out of the main bar – is a doorway into yet another bar area. This pub seems to just keep going on and on. But while these days the succession of bars all perform a similar function, this wasn't always the case. This, the furthest bar from the taproom, was formerly part of a private dwelling. It was pretty much rebuilt in the 1930s and served as a suite of offices, completely unrelated to the workings of the George, until the mid-1960s.

You'd never guess that now. This is a peaceful bar, set up as a dining area with soft lighting and patterned rugs over the floorboards. Even an untrained eye can see that the heavy beams across the ceiling are very new.

The best things about these last few rooms though are the walls. Framed pictures of the George – some of them still new to me even after months spent in various archives – evoke the history of the pub and its surroundings. There are odd photos of the George's late neighbours too. Customers hardly get as far as shedding their coats and taking the first sip of their drinks before they're out of their seats again and pacing around the walls reverentially, as if this were a museum or art gallery. In the far corner, shot in the same saturated black-and-white style as the early Victorian inn photos, is a succession of pictures of the half-built Shard, already being incorporated into the long and winding heritage of the Borough.

And possibly the best prize: a life-insurance policy from Sun Life Assurance, made out in the name of and signed by Charles Dickens. The legend is that Dickens brought it in and left it as surety after borrowing money from the landlord, and he never came back to collect it. This legend would be a lot more convincing were it not for the old frame the policy sits inside, which has a small, neat label reading:

Presented to the George Inn by the
Sun Life Assurance Society 23–4–1943.

The George is no museum though: it's a living, working pub. But it is still a monument, a lone survivor of past ages. There's more of course – much more – the former bedrooms upstairs, the old lofts, the long-gone other wings and internal courtyard. We got a glimpse of all that in 1737, and we'll be looking at them again later on.

While I want to give you a good look around the building, the story of the George Inn isn't just about that. Still, this setting, and this context, gives some big clues about why, if you decide that you'd like to write a history of one particular pub, this is a good one to choose.

There are arguably more celebrated pubs, such as the Cheshire Cheese in Fleet Street, which boasts a list of literary giants among its regulars that the George could never match, or Ye Olde Trip in Nottingham, which can prove its lineage several centuries further back. But if you're going to focus on the story of one pub, you've got to pick the one that lets you tell the best story. Its story is one that frequently wanders off the point in a tipsy fashion, before doggedly ignoring interruptions and getting back to what it was trying to say. If you've ever had a drunken conversation in a pub, you'll soon feel like you're on familiar ground. The mix of politics, glamour, theatre, sex, sin, commerce, architecture, nostalgia, celebrity and, er, road transport that congregates at the George Inn, Southwark, could keep us entertained by the taproom fireside for hours. Which is why, as we're about to see, I am by no means the first to attempt to tell that story.

CHAPTER TWO: CONCERNING DATES, NAMES, MUTYA, HEIDI &C.

History consists of a series of accumulated imaginative inventions.

(Voltaire)

As THE ROOM FILLED, the speaker consulting his (very copious) notes probably wished he were in a pub instead.

George R. Corner FSA, a Fellow of the Society of Antiquaries of London, was the special guest of the Surrey Archaeological Society, at their meeting on 12 May 1858 in a Southwark school hall. Why couldn't they have followed the example of Corner's own Society of Antiquaries? Back in 1707, its inaugural meeting had been at the Bear Tavern in the Strand. Later, it moved to the Young Devil Tavern. Even when the meetings were formalized ten years later, the first minutes show the society was incorporated at the Mitre Tavern in Fleet Street. Society meetings happened in pubs. That's what you did. So why the blazes was this talk in a school?

Especially given the topic of the speech.

But the central hall of St Olave's Grammar School, which taught without classrooms, was bigger than any room in a tavern or inn, and an awful lot of people were interested in what Mr Corner had to say. Victorian progress was starting to erase Old London, rewriting the city as if it were a blank page. The title of Mr Corner's talk – 'On Some Ancient Inns in Southwark' – had caught the collective imagination of those who were starting to realize that something they had cheerfully taken for granted might be worthy of deeper study and reflection.

Of course, within this seemingly obscure subject there were specific inns – one in particular – that everyone was most curious to hear about. The famous Tabard in the Borough High Street, a mere three hundred yards away from this school hall, simply had to be the first subject of Mr Corner's remarks. He prefaced these remarks with modesty, saying, 'So much has been written of this celebrated hostelry that the subject may be supposed to have been exhausted, and it may be considered presumptuous to attempt to tell anything not already known of the inn.' Pretty much everyone who could read knew that English literature had effectively been born in Southwark's (and arguably London's) most famous hostelry, when Geoffrey Chaucer chose it as the departure point for his Canterbury pilgrims. But Mr Corner was merely teasing his audience: he went on to talk at great length about references to the Tabard in various historical records over the previous 500 years. Perhaps because it was owned originally by men of the church, and was therefore far more likely to have details of its circumstances written down, there was far more to say about this most famous of Southwark's inns than any of its contemporaries.

Mr Corner then came to the White Hart, chosen by Jack Cade as his headquarters when he led the men of Kent in a rebellion against King Henry VI in 1450. The pub was specifically mentioned in Shakespeare's account of this rebellion in *The Second Part of King Henry VI*. And if that made it notorious, the man who Corner referred to in his lecture with remarkable understatement as 'a popular writer of the present day' had then immortalized the White Hart in the English-speaking world as the place where Mr Pickwick first made the acquaintance of Samuel Weller, a fictional character as popular in the late nineteenth and early twentieth centuries as any real-life celebrity in the age of electronic mass media a century later.

But between the Tabard and the White Hart, both still standing at this point, was the lesser-known George Inn. Mr Corner presented what he knew about it, which he admitted wasn't much in comparison to its illustrious neighbours. After one inn synonymous with Chaucer, and another immortalized by both Shakespeare and Dickens, the poor old George didn't stand much chance of making a strong impression.

Mr Corner stuck to the facts. There was no false modesty now: he seemed almost uninterested in his account, as if he had to force his way through this one for the sake of completeness, but it didn't contain anything that really engaged him.

As a history of a public building that has played host to countless people over several centuries, Corner's account read today seems sparse. And as a history of an inn – a place of entertainment, relaxation, excitement, controversy and bad behaviour – you would have to say it comes across as a little . . . dull. Whereas the previous two inns allowed Corner to quote Chaucer, Dickens and Shakespeare, here he spent fully half the words he nominally devoted to the George recounting instead the history of the Great Fire of Southwark of 1676. Yes, the George Inn burned to the ground in that fire – but so did every single one of the great inns of Southwark, as well as 500 houses. Talking about the Fire here, in so much detail, suggests Corner was trying to hide the paucity of information he had about the George itself.

And yet, Corner's account of the George, as first revealed to that packed Southwark school hall in 1858, was the first attempt to write any history of the inn whatsoever, the first to recognize that the George Inn, shadowed as it was by more celebrated neighbours, was a subject worthy of any kind of serious study at all.

Perhaps inevitably, the recorded history of the George

according to Corner begins with the Tabard. An account of Chaucer's Local from 1544, the thirty-fifth year of Henry VIII's reign, refers in passing to the 'St George' being 'situate on the north side of the Tabard', which it is. Or was. Like the many pubs that were known as the Pope's Head before the Reformation and the King's Head afterwards, the George lost its saintly status during Henry VIII's reign.

In 1598, the George is one of eight 'fair inns for the receipt of travellers' listed by John Stow in his groundbreaking *Survey of London*.

Throughout the first half of the seventeenth century, the only evidence of the continued existence of the George comprises two innkeeper's tokens. At a time when small change was scarce, tokens similar to coins were issued by merchants and innkeepers as an unofficial but commonly acceptable form of currency. There's a collection of them at the Guildhall, including the two referring to the George Inn, Southwark.

In 1656 there's a poem – hardly an endorsement – called 'Upon a Surfeit by Drinking Bad Sack at the George Tavern in Southwark'.

In 1670 the inn catches fire and burns to the ground. It's rebuilt, only for the same thing to happen again in the aforementioned Great Fire of 1676. After his copious digression into this fire and its causes, Mr Corner returns to his thread by giving some details of who owned the pub between 1739 and what was, for him, the present day.

And as far as the George is concerned, that was all he had to say.

Corner's lecture certainly attracted a great deal of local interest, and was reported by a variety of newspapers and magazines. But it would probably have been forgotten were it not for the admirable work of the venerable Dr William Rendle and his younger colleague Mr Phillip Norman (who was also a Fellow of the Society of Antiquaries of London) about thirty years later.

Born in 1811, Dr Rendle trained as a physician and practised medicine in Southwark for nearly fifty years. In 1889 the *South London Press* said of him, 'The clever, hard-working, plodding old Southwark doctor has done much good work in his day and generation. He was a sanitarian before sanitary science became fashionable, and when in practice in the Borough he killed fewer people, perhaps, than any other man in the profession in the same space of time.'

It's unfortunate, perhaps, that read from a modern perspective, the journalistic style of the 1880s makes this read like damning with faint praise ('plodding'!) before making a description of an excellent doctor sound like that of a lazy and inefficient serial killer. But you know what they were getting at.

This newspaper quote comes from a review of Dr Rendle's second book (his first and only collaboration with Mr Norman) titled *Inns of Old Southwark*, published late in 1888. Our reviewer quoted above describes it as 'one of the most interesting books which has fallen in my way for many years past', which is a view you may not necessarily agree with today, but you might have shared if you were living in Southwark in the late nineteenth century.

The book is out of copyright now, and you can download a PDF or Kindle version free from various bibliophile websites. But at a time when the publishing industry debates the future of the printed book, I wanted – if it were possible – to own an original, physical copy. It cost me £80. But seconds after opening the package, I realized it was money well spent. An e-book can never recreate the experience of holding in your hands a physical object that has existed since before your grandparents were born. The scuffed, rust-coloured binding is reminiscent of an old leather Chesterfield. The yellowed, liver-spotted pages are unevenly cut and rough to the touch. When you open those pages, the smell of old books – a melange of dust, incense, furniture polish and pipe tobacco –

fills the air between you and the desk, and you resolve not to open this precious thing too often, so as not to allow that perfume to dissipate to nothing.

Phillip Norman's illustrations weaken this resolve, however. They draw you back to the book long after you've supposedly finished with it. His own paintings and engravings, and those he has reproduced from elsewhere, evoke not just the appearance, but the multi-sensory experience of Southwark's old inn-yards, stables and taprooms, just as surely as if you had climbed into a TARDIS and popped back there for a pint of brandy and water.

And William Rendle's prose is that of the eccentric great-uncle you never had, played to perfection by Rex Harrison in the role that would have defined his career.

Rendle was well into his seventies by the time he wrote this book, and it's stream-of-consciousness stuff, wandering and digressive, not in a scatty-old-man way, but with the hungry, inquisitive energy of a much younger man, combined with the confidence of age that says 'I'm going over here now for a bit. If you want to come with me, that would be fabulous. If you don't, I'm not going to lose any sleep over it.' As the esteemed *South London Press* reviewer writes, 'he is an old man now, is the doctor ... and yet, in the book before me, he comes up smiling – fresh and youthful as ever!'

There's an urgency and immediacy in his need to tell you some of the new things he's just discovered. His previous book was a broader history of Southwark, and he tells us how the delighted reaction to that work has compelled him to follow it up with this one. You can see the places where, halfway through a chapter, he spontaneously decides to change direction. He'll mention Pickle Herring Stairs[1] in passing and

---

1. Where the Thames was embanked, watermen and other river workers would be based at sets of stairs that went down to the water. There were

then say something along the lines of 'Actually, you know what? I've found out loads of interesting new stuff about Pickle Herring Stairs, and pickling herrings in general, since I wrote my last book. I think I'd like to tell you all about it right now.' He starts one chapter with the intention of telling us all about the Anchor Brewery, and runs off down so many cul-de-sacs that he's halfway through before he remembers what he was supposed to be doing and drags himself back to the topic in hand, signalled by the oft-repeated phrase, 'But I must retrace my steps a little.'

I love Dr William Rendle. He's an inspiration to me. In fact, I'd go so far as to say he's become something of a spirit guide for this book. So if I ever wander so far down some blind alley that you, poor reader, find yourself thinking, 'Hang on, I thought I was reading a book about a pub. How did we get here?', blame Rendle.

Dr Rendle covers an awful lot of ground in his 400-plus pages. But even so, like Corner, what he has to say specifically about the George is naggingly brief and padded out with digression. He recounts Corner's lecture in great detail, and reveals various new discoveries of his own made during the intervening thirty years: he presents us with the earliest map of Southwark, a childlike drawing from 1542 which clearly shows the George located between the Tabard and the White Hart; he gives us some earlier details of the inn's ownership; a seventeenth-century timetable of waggons courtesy of John Taylor, the self-styled 'Water Poet' of the Thames; a similar but much busier coaching timetable from the 1820s; the heart-warming story of Edward, Sixth Baron Digby . . . and that's about it.

There are other chroniclers too – here and there you see a gentle accretion of additional detail, each writer adding an anecdote or two, or a contemporary account of their visit to

---

scores of them up and down the river, and they were often named after their primary trade.

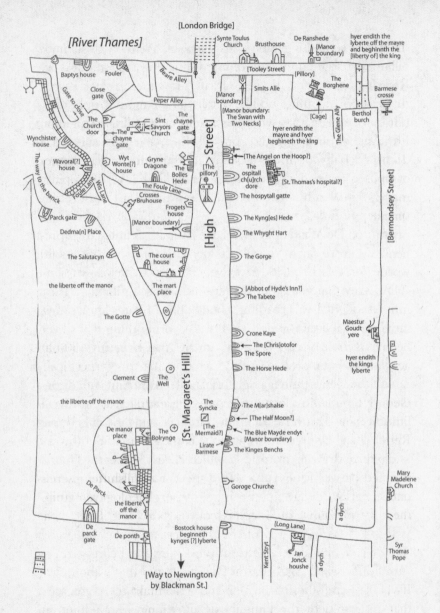

The earliest known map of Southwark, dating from some time between 1540 and 1542. It's a riot of inns and churches, with the George clearly marked between the Tabard and White Hart. (Helpfully annotated by Professor Martha Carlin, who can decipher badly scrawled Middle English.)

the inn. But these are mostly adornments added to the central pillar of the narrative sketched by Corner, and fleshed out by Rendle.

Contrary to how many people were taught it in school, history is more than a collection of known dates and names. I know this now, because over the past year, I've created a document on my laptop that originated with the bare bones of what Rendle and Corner discovered, but has grown, thanks mainly to digitized, searchable databases and archives rather than any newly discovered genius for historical research on my part, into what is undoubtedly the most detailed, comprehensive history of this building there has ever been. It's 25,000 words long.

And you know what? You really don't want to read it. Not in its original form. As a concentrated list of dates and names, in its raw state it is probably the most boring thing that's ever been written about the George Inn. And believe me, that accolade is not won easily.

What we need, therefore, if we are to truly understand the George, is not lists, but stories. And thankfully, if you dig a little deeper into the names and facts set out by Corner and Rendle there are plenty of those.

But whatever kind of historian you are or want to be, a storyteller or a list-maker, a trainspotter or a bullshitter, there's one thing you secretly crave, a kind of archaeological catnip, the elusive perfect academic fix:

The Earliest Date

If you're writing a history of anything, it makes sense to start that history with the date the damn thing was first built, invented, born or otherwise hurled into existence. The earliest date is the lottery win of historical research, because if you find an earlier date than anyone else has found, that makes you King Of All The History Researchers. Here we are on page 46 and we're only now getting to something you had every reason to expect on page 1, where it belongs.

So. Here's the question, the primary question, the most important question:

When was the George Inn built?

And here's the answer:

Well, there are two answers to choose from.

The short answer, after devoting a year of my life to researching the history of the George, after visiting every significant museum, public-records archive and collection that might retain any documents in which it is mentioned, and then compiling all this available information into what is, as I already averred, the most exhaustively detailed history of this pub that has ever been written, is this: I have absolutely no idea.

But since I'm sensing you're not entirely happy with that answer, I've got a long answer as well, if you want to hear it. This answer is a bit more complicated, and perhaps because drink hangs heavily over a book like this, it involves the philosophers of ancient Greece, a manufactured girl band, the sitcom *Only Fools and Horses*, and the metaphysics of the soul.

Here goes.

Post-Rendle, most of the repetitious accounts of the history of the George date it back to 1542, towards the end of Henry VIII's reign. What we mean by this is that 1542 is the earliest date we can prove that the George Inn stood where it stands today on Borough High Street. It's clearly labelled on the earliest known map of Southwark, as discovered by Rendle, a map that indicates no fewer than nineteen inns along the course of what was then known as 'Long Southwark', a broad thoroughfare leading south from the foot of London Bridge to St Margaret's Hill, which takes over after a few hundred yards. (Not that there's any scale to the map – it really does look like an 8-year-old's directions to a gang hut.) In the century-and-a-bit since Rendle, no one has found an earlier map. Believe me, I've asked around.

Obviously this doesn't mean the George was *built* in 1542. For it to be featured in this way, it was almost certainly an established concern by the time the map was drawn.

So we can *definitely* say the George extends back *at least* that far. We can say it *probably* goes back quite a bit further. But many historians don't like speculation, so you never see anyone citing an earlier date. If history is all about fact, 1542 is the earliest date for which we have factual evidence.

But in the ongoing pursuit of historical prizes, these 'first dates' get pushed back all the time as new discoveries are made. In the ten years I've been writing about beer, for example, archaeological evidence for the existence of brewing has moved back from 3000 BC to 7000 BC, and from ancient Mesopotamia to the Chinese interior, thanks mainly to advances in archaeological technology.

Similarly, things have moved on since Corner and Rendle each did their respective research. Archives have been logged and digitized. When they gave the earliest recorded mention of the George as 1544 (when it was known as the St George) and subsequently 1542, they had no way of knowing that in what is now the National Archives, there was a box of documents pertaining to various court cases, and that among these was the record of the case of Nicholas Dewe, son of Thomas Dewe, versus John Crall and William Phillip, 'feoffees' (trustees) to the estate of William Lettres and his wife Agnes, 'previously the wife of the said Thomas Dewe, and of two intermediate husbands'. Nicholas Dewe and the trustees acting for his mother, or more likely stepmother, were contesting ownership of the George Inn, Southwark.

And the case was heard sometime between 1475 and 1485. Yesssss! Thanks to the Internet and some determined

logging of data, I had moved the earliest record of the George
back in time between sixty-five and seventy-five years, without
breaking sweat.[2]

But this would prove to be the highlight of my new career
as self-appointed History Detective. After that, the trail went
cold again for quite a while.

This book was in its final stages when I came across the
work of Professor Martha Carlin. Carlin did her PhD thesis
on medieval Southwark, and published an abbreviated version of this in 1996 called, appropriately enough, *Medieval
Southwark*. A large chunk of her work is based on painstaking analysis of two surveys made of Southwark in 1555 and
1564–65. She used these to piece together a door-to-door
account of the whole of Borough High Street/Long Southwark. And on the plot where the George now stands was an
inn known at the time as both the 'George' and the 'Surcoat'.
A Surcoat was a type of heraldic tunic, similar to a Tabard
(the name of the pub next door). The Surcoat – also spelled
'Syrcot' or 'Syrcote' in these old accounts – was listed as
belonging to the heirs of one 'Comes', and Carlin managed to
find a reference to Thomas Combes, owner of 'tenements
called le Syrcote', in 1509. Then, because she's better at this

---

2. Flushed by my success, confident I was now a master historian, I took
my passport and a recent utility bill down to the National Archives in Kew,
obtained a readers card, and proudly took that box of legal archives out of
storage. I opened the box and carefully turned through piles of leafy, brittle
parchment with trembling, white-gloved hands . . . It's difficult to describe
the feeling of deflation that then occurred. Obviously, I hadn't thought it
through when I decided I was going to spend ten minutes reading and
copying out something that was written on a piece of paper at least 526
years previously. Even without the stains and the fading, the spidery
handwriting coupled with the evolution of the English language over the
last half-millennium meant that I admitted defeat after an hour, having
successfully copied the following: 'And of . . . [next line] . . . and of and . . .
[next line] the . . . Southwark.'

than me, she managed to push back even further. The churchwarden's accounts of St Margaret's, Southwark for 1452–53 mention a 'wyfe' (i.e. landlady or proprietress) at the 'Syrcote'. But beyond this, even Carlin's Herculean detective work has nothing more to add.

Nevertheless, this gives us a much better idea than we had before. There was an inn on the site of the George as early as 1450, possibly even earlier (there were a dozen or so inns on the street in 1381, as we'll see later). At that time, this inn was called the Syrcote. At some point, it changed its name to the George.

We know it was still being referred to as the Syrcote in 1509, but that it was also referred to as the George from 1475–85, and we know it was better known as the George or St George by 1542.[3] Edward III declared St George to be our patron saint and protector of the Royal Family in 1350, but the whole idea didn't really catch on until after the Battle of Agincourt in 1415. It's highly unlikely that there would have been many pubs called the George before this point, but at some point in the late fifteenth or early sixteenth century, it became a fashionable inn name, with examples cropping up all over the country in what seems to have been an industrious period of inn-building. This would have happened at almost exactly the same time as the syrcote disappeared from common use and became quite an obscure garment. So we know

---

3. It may seem a bit confusing that the inn was known by two names at the same time, but to an illiterate population, inns were known by their pictorial signs rather than words. The inn sign showed St George killing the dragon. In records, the name would have been changed simply to 'The George' pretty soon after the Reformation. But some would have continued to call it the St George, and it's likely the sign didn't alter. It was therefore probably known by both versions of the name for some years. Likewise, the change from the Surcoat to the George would have been a change of sign, and a generation of drinkers would probably have carried on calling it the Surcoat long after the sign had been changed.

why the Syrcote changed its name, and we know it did so sometime between the mid-fifteenth century and 1550. But we don't know any better than that, and we still have no idea when the original inn was built.

So what do historians do when the facts run out?

Some withdraw from the fray. If they cannot *prove* the existence of something before a given date, they refuse to say it *might* have existed, and leave it there, shrouded in temporal mystery, saying things like 'the George Inn only dates back to 1542 [or 1475–85]'.

But isn't that the same as saying it definitely *didn't* exist before that date? And – in the absence of proof – surely if it's wrong to say something did exist, isn't it just as wrong to declare that it didn't? If an inn falls down in Southwark and there is no one there with parchment and quill to hand, doesn't it still create an awful racket?

We know that by 1542, Borough High Street, or 'Long Southwark', was dense with inns, for reasons we'll go into in much more detail shortly. Nineteen inns don't just get built spontaneously in some kind of collective hostelry-based hysteria. Some go back further than others. We know that the White Hart, on the north side of the George, goes back as far as 1406, when it was known as 'le Herteshed'. There are records of the Bear-at-the-Bridgefoot in 1319, and the King's Arms goes back as far as 1379.

And of course we know the Tabard goes back at least to Chaucer's time. He began writing *The Canterbury Tales* in 1387, and as we'll see, both the Tabard and its innkeeper, Harry Bailly, really existed then. You could build a convincing case from what we do know that, in some form, the Tabard dates back as far as 1307. So what was to its immediate north when it was built? What prevented the Tabard from being built a few yards closer to the bridge, when that was presumably the more desirable spot?

This is where speculation grows a little wilder. We will

probably never know, but from what we do know, it's not completely unreasonable to suggest that there was already an inn on that spot. So on a sliding scale of certainty, I'd argue that it's highly likely the George Inn was standing before 1476, and fairly likely that, under a different name, it goes back at least to the 1380s.

Some people might leave it there. But you and me, we're made of sterner stuff. No, come on, we are. We need to press on with this date question still further.

Because even if you want to keep it in the realms of firm documentary evidence (and that evidence proves the George existed by name in 1542 and in body as early as 1452–53) how come many who refer to it – including the National Trust, who now own the place and are, after all, the *National Trust* and should know better than the rest of us about how this kind of thing works – how come they insist that the George only dates back to 1677?

In one sense, they and anyone else who puts this date forward are absolutely and undeniably correct. In another sense, they're completely missing the point and are entirely wrong.

The National Trust looks after buildings. That's what it's for. It preserves old and important buildings for the nation, and we must be eternally grateful for that. And if you think of the George simply as a building and nothing more – as the National Trust must – then it's simple: the building called the George Inn which stands today in Southwark was built in 1677, following the destruction of the previous building by the Great Fire of Southwark in 1676.

But are we right to think of the George Inn simply as a building?

The George Inn as an historic entity, and the collection of physical materials currently assembled as the George Inn, aren't quite the same thing. And this conundrum, this philosophical argument, has never been illustrated more clearly and effectively than in an episode of the sitcom *Only Fools and Horses*.

Trigger, who sweeps roads for a living, happens to mention to his superiors that he's been using the same broom for twenty years, and is subsequently awarded a medal for saving the council money.

Trigger's secret is that he *has* looked after his broom. He's maintained it. In those twenty years, he's replaced the head seventeen times, and the handle fourteen times. 'How the hell can it be the same bloody broom then?' asks someone. Trigger brandishes a photo of him with the broom twenty years before. What more proof does he need?

Google 'Trigger's Broom', and you'll probably also find a reference to fast-food girlpop band Sugababes on the same page. Just in case you're lucky enough not to know, Suga-babes is a pop group formed of three girls back in 1998 – Siobhan, Mutya and Keisha. In 2011, at the time of writing, Sugababes is still a three-girl pop group belting out the same kind of material to pretty much the same fan base. However, thanks to a seemingly endless succession of tabloid-friendly feuds and bitchy asides, they are now three entirely different girls – Heidi, Amelle and Jade. If you're reading this in 2170 as a dusty tome in the British Library or an e-book transmitted directly onto your eyelids, I'm sure you'll still be familiar with Sugababes, and that they will now consist of a sentient hologram, a tentacled beast from the other side of the Andromeda System called Grarg, and Kylie Minogue.

So are they still the same band in 2011 or 2170 as they were in 1998?

It seems the 2011 line-up[4] has never heard the Trigger's Broom comparison. When a *Guardian* journalist interviewed

---

4. I originally wrote 'the current line-up' here. And then realized there was no more effective way of making a book look out of date.

'Sugababes 4.0', at their (re)launch in spring 2010, his first question was 'Hi, Sugababes! If you buy a broom, then you replace the handle, then you replace the brush, is it the same broom?'

Unanimously, they answered with a resounding 'No!' – before going on to insist that they were, in fact, Sugababes.[5]

It's a conundrum that is thousands of years old, constantly re-expressed, with the oldest recorded version being the Paradox of Theseus' Ship – in which Plutarch mused over whether, if you replace the rotting planks of a ship, does it eventually become a different ship or remain the same one? The problem also vexed Heraclitus, Socrates and Plato, and Enlightenment thinkers such as John Locke (who framed it, endearingly, in the medium of darned socks) and Thomas Hobbes.[6] So once we accept that Trigger's Broom/Sugababes is a serious philosophical paradox rather than an annoying pub conversation (if you believe there is any difference between the two) we can see that it must also, inevitably, apply to buildings.

Being somewhat romantic and sentimental, I believe it's the same broom/ship/girl-band/building. But there are those who would disagree – the killjoys, the bricks-and-mortar

---

5. That's probably enough about Sugababes in the main text of this or any other book. But in the week I write this, there are rumours that the original Sugababes are thinking of reforming and are threatening to sue the new ones, leading one satirical news website to run the headline 'Original Sugababes to form Sugababes tribute band.'

6. Hobbes tried to go one step further by musing on what would happen if the original planks taken away from Theseus' ship, somehow preserved, were used to build a second, identical ship. Which would be the original? This makes me tearfully upset that Hobbes didn't live to see the latest Sugababes conundrum, as highlighted in the previous footnote. Twenty-first-century popular culture is playing out a hypothetical principle of Enlightenment philosophy in real time. Just as this book went to press, the three original Sugababes did, in fact, return – under a different name. This is the point at which this whole analogy became too difficult to navigate and entered quantum space.

hardliners. Well, the bad news for them is that Trigger's Broom trips them up either way.

If it's the *same* broom/ship/girl-band, the George goes back to at least the fifteenth century. Not 1677. End of.

However, if you insist that it's a *different* broom/boat/girl-band – well then, the George doesn't date back to 1677 at all.

Sure, some of it does – bits and pieces here and there. But if you're creating your yardstick from original materials, there aren't an awful lot of those left. The balustrades on the famous galleries are original, and most of the outer walls are, and there's a stone flag in the corner of the taproom that probably is.

But 75 per cent of what was built in 1677 was demolished in the late nineteenth century. The 125-foot-long south wing that remains is no more than a fifth of the building the George once was. Of that, the eastern third (now the nice bit with all the old pictures on the wall) was pretty much rebuilt in 1937 when it was found to be structurally unsound.

That leaves the main section, comprising the galleries above, and the taproom and restaurant below, and the upstairs restaurants, staff accommodation and empty lofts we haven't yet visited. In 2009, the National Trust carried out a 'non-intrusive survey' on this Grade One listed building, cataloguing every single facet of its physical construction in brain-juddering detail.[7] This report summarizes that there was substantial rebuilding and alteration in the mid-eighteenth century, again in the late eighteenth or early nineteenth century, and yet again in the early twentieth century. And

---

7. Don't get me wrong – I'm eternally grateful that the National Trust (*a*) completed such an extraordinarily thorough piece of work, and (*b*) allowed me access to it. But with sentences like 'Above the windows, the entire length is spanned by a late-eighteenth-century/early-nineteenth-century entablature with a simple reeded frieze surmounted by a projecting moulded cornice with a small paterae to the soffit (Plate 15)', it's not for the faint of heart.

since the report was published, we can add the significant refurbishment of summer 2011 to the list.

Around the back of the building, you can see the contrast between the red brick of the seventeenth century and the yellow brick of the twentieth. Looking at the front of the building from the courtyard, the quaint, small panelled windows are little more than a hundred years old. The taproom floor was replaced in 1947. There were howls of protest from Dickensian traditionalists in the 1940s when the wall in this room was demolished to turn the old taproom and kitchen into one bar, but the 2009 National Trust survey revealed that this wall had gone in long after the original building was erected – the removal of the wall therefore returned the room to its traditional layout. In what was the main bar, formerly the restaurant and before that the famous coffee room, the floor was replaced long after Dickens's death. The walls of the hall separating the taproom from the main bar were erected early in the nineteenth century, and the staircase up to the first floor from here was probably replaced at the same time. And we established a while ago the truth behind the 'traditional' roof beams.

In fact Les Capon, an archaeologist who took part in the 2011 examination of the George, believes the entire un-galleried main section of the inn was built later than the surviving galleried range. 'If you're going to have galleries, why not have them the whole way along?' he asks, quite reasonably, adding, 'If you look closely, there's a kink in the floor plan between the galleried and un-galleried sections. They don't quite match up.'[8]

---

8. I suggested to Les, of AOC Archaeology Group, that the truth might be revealed if you took samples of the wood and dated them, which no one has yet done. 'Maybe,' he replied, 'but how would you know if they were using new wood when it was built?' There are some secrets the George seems destined to keep.

So if Trigger's Broom was a *different* broom, the date the George was 'built' becomes essentially meaningless. Happily then, the consensus among thinkers who've spent far too much time contemplating this riddle is that, overall, it's the same broom after all.

Aristotle proposed that there are four different 'causes' or 'reasons' that describe a thing, only one of which is the 'material' cause: what the thing is physically made of, which could change if the thing were rebuilt. There's also the formal cause: how the thing is designed, what it actually is; the final cause: its intended purpose; and the efficient cause: how it was actually made.

When the George Inn burned to the ground in 1676, Mark Weyland, the landlord, rebuilt it to its original purpose, 'on the old plan' and old foundations, to the same design, using similar materials and techniques. So, according to Aristotle, it's 3–1 to the George. It's the same pub.

The George wasn't *built* in 1677; it was *rebuilt*. And it has been undergoing a continuous process of rebuilding since then, right up to the present day – just like Southwark outside, just like the rest of crane-bound London. It may be a new building, but it is still the same old pub. And if that's good enough for Aristotle – the first person to create a comprehensive system of Western philosophy, encompassing morality and aesthetics, logic and science, politics and metaphysics – it's good enough for me.

And beyond that, I think there's something more, something that I don't necessarily expect anyone to agree with me on, but which I believe all the same.

I think there is an intangible continuity in a public building such as the George. There's an atmosphere, a sense of place, a collection of memories that have accumulated in the space over the time it has been used for its unchanging purpose, over the centuries that people have laughed, drunk, argued, eaten, flirted, slept and done business there.

Would it be too much to call this continuity, this intangible presence, a soul? Probably. If you're being picky. But if so, why do we often describe places that possess none of what the George has as 'soulless'?

It's something you feel when you drink in the George, and it's something that, as we shall see, exerts a powerful influence on many who encounter the place, and bends them to its will, something mystical yet true that transcends mere bricks and mortar.

Maybe I'm being too romantic. But if you can't be romantic about an ancient coaching inn, well, then you've missed the point of what ancient coaching inns are all about.

CHAPTER THREE: BEING SOME REMARKS ON LONDON'S FIRST BRIDGE, AND HOW THIS BRIDGE GIVES OUR STORY ITS VERY SHAPE

✼

Sir ROGER obliged the Waterman to give us the History of his Right Leg, and hearing that he had left it [at the Battle of La Hogue] with many Particulars which passed in that glorious Action, the Knight in the Triumph of his Heart made several Reflections on the Greatness of the British Nation; as, that one English-man could beat three Frenchmen; that we could never be in danger of Popery so long as we took care of our Fleet; that the Thames was the noblest River in Europe; that London Bridge was a greater piece of Work, than any of the seven Wonders of the World; with many other honest Prejudices which naturally cleave to the Heart of a true Englishman.

(Joseph Addison, the *Spectator*, May 1712)

AT THE SOUTHEAST CORNER of London Bridge stands a building whose name reflects perfectly the creativity, imagin-ation and poetry of its architecture. Number One London Bridge is so bland, blocky and boring it looks like it was built out of Lego – though even that's an insult to the versatility a 3-year-old shows with the little plastic bricks.

Outside Number One London Bridge, marking the

southwest corner of the property, stands a curious spike hewn from Portland stone, three sided at the bottom and tapering to a very sharp point about fifty feet above. It stands on a big fat base built from the same material, which carries no explanatory plaque or sign, in fact no words at all apart from, at the time of writing, some graffiti reading 'piss flapps [*sic*]' and 'shitgoose', accompanied by a crude drawing of a bird that strongly resembles the comedy ostrich made famous by 1970s light entertainer Bernie Clifton.[1]

If you search around this curious monument, or even Google it, there's no clue as to what the spike represents, or why it's here. For years, coming over the Bridge to visit Borough Market, I would gaze at the spike and imagine what it would be like to fall out of a window of the Lego tower block and be skewered by it.

Visitors to the Borough today might see parallels between the unnamed London Bridge spike and the Shard, similar in shape but thrusting twenty times higher above the station. But in fact the spike commemorates a far more ancient local design feature, a grisly quirk long gone, but one that continues to exert its influence on Southwark's psyche and is, indirectly, fundamental to telling the story of the George Inn.

The George is not just a remarkable building – the building alone, outstanding survivor that it is, would be much less remarkable if it were in another part of the country. There are older inns and more beautiful inns that simply couldn't

---

1. Fans of my earlier books may be disappointed at the relative lack of swearing in this one. 'Shitgoose' is probably the best swearword in this book, because it's a prime example of what I consider to be 'postgraduate swearing', where you can give your favourite obscenities an extra lease of life by combining them with seemingly innocuous words to make something that is inexplicably more offensive and far more amusing. 'Bubble' is a good 'straight' word to use for this, but my favourite is 'wizard', which stands up to and enhances any potty-mouthed nastiness you want to throw at it.

support a book of this nature, despite their ghosts, galleries, reputed visits from Queen Elizabeth and legends of harbouring hunted kings. But the street on which the George stands is one of the most peculiar and important streets in British history – and the London Bridge spike provides our first clue to some of the extraordinary things the George, its staff and customers have witnessed over the years.

Picture the scene. The time: somewhere in the first half of the seventeenth century, let's say the early reign of James I – the age of pointy beards, pointy hats, and Guy Fawkes's Gunpowder Plot.[2] The place: the top end of Borough High Street, or 'Long Southwark', as it is still known. The street is, as I've previously hinted, a stressed-out buzz of competing purposes and opportunities. You've travelled up from Kent, or continental Europe maybe. You've come a long way, and you know the river is very close. The Bridge, and the promise of the City beyond it, are just around a slight dog-leg kink ahead of you. But even as you come around this shallow bend, you can see neither the river nor the City. The tall, gabled buildings of Long Southwark, three or four storeys high, run from south to north and when they reach the Bridge, they abut directly onto its huge, forbidding gatehouse, creating a cul-de-sac that obscures any view beyond, and gives no option of onward access apart from through the heavy gates.

These gates are almost as tall as the surrounding buildings. They're always guarded, and at night, they're closed altogether. Above them the tall, fortified gatehouse climbs up, punctuated by windows and arrow slits, to battlements high above.

Rather than giving access to the City, at the wrong time

---

2. Or more accurately, Robert Catesby's Gunpowder Plot. Fawkes was one of thirteen conspirators, but is famous as the one who was actually caught with all the gunpowder.

and to the wrong people, this Bridge presents a formidable barrier to it. You might think you've arrived in London, but the Bridge is telling you no, this doesn't quite count, not yet. This isn't *real* London; you're still outside, and the people who live and work around you are outsiders too. And if this stern architectural message needs any further reinforcement, just look up. Of course, you already are. You can't tear your eyes away. Because there, on top of the gatehouse battlements, what looked from a distance like a forest of giant porcupine quills reveals itself now to be a collection of tall pikes, each skewering a severed human head, each tip driven through the top of the skull, each head preserved in tar to allow it to remain up there for as long as possible.

For centuries, this was the welcome London extended to visitors coming up from the Channel ports and southern counties. More importantly, here at the focal point of the entire town of Southwark, the very reason for its existence, this is what the inhabitants saw every day of their lives.

Imagine living in this street, a street that was often an impassable dead end, with those dead heads staring down at you, reminding you who you are, where you are, and what the people in power on the other side of that Bridge think of you. How would this make you feel about yourself, about the place where you lived and worked? What would it do to your mind?[3]

So many famous heads found themselves on the ends of those pikes that London Bridge resembled a prototype Madame Tussauds designed by some medieval psychopath. The first

---

3. Surely the only way to find out today would be to create an effigy of a giant severed head, thirty feet high, and stick it on top of the Shard. We could run a competition to decide whose head it should be (I've got my choice down to two). Local schools could help make it, painting the popped eyeballs and lolling tongue, collecting bits of old rope for the tarred and matted hair. Come on, who's with me?

exhibit, in 1305, was William 'Braveheart' Wallace. When the English captured him after his revolt against Edward I, they decided to make an example of him. Wallace was partially hanged, cut down while still conscious, then opened up and eviscerated, his entrails burnt before his eyes. When merciful death finally came, he was decapitated and his body was cut into quarters, which were sent to Scotland and the north of England and put on display. And we wonder why the Scots will cheer any team, no matter who it is, playing England in any sport, no matter what it is. Wallace's head was boiled in tar, and stuck on London Bridge – not right here at the south end, but on top of the Drawbridge Gate at the north side.

Successive monarchs must have thought the rotting head made a really appealing design feature, or at least an effective deterrent. When Sir Thomas More refused to acknowledge Henry VIII as the supreme head of the Church of England, he was convicted of treason and ended up there. He joined Elizabeth Barton, a nun who had rather tactlessly prophesied that if Henry divorced Catherine of Aragon and married Anne Boleyn he would quickly die a horrible death. Cardinal John Fisher joined More later the same year, and five years after that the King's Chief Minister, Thomas Cromwell, met a similar fate.

In 1577 the Drawbridge Gate was demolished and the gruesome tourist attraction moved to the southern Bridge Gate, leaving dead traitors to gaze down on Southwark instead. Guy Fawkes himself gained a bird's-eye view of the Borough after the failure of the Gunpowder Plot in 1605.[4]

---

4. I don't know about you, but because of bonfire night tradition I'd got it in the back of my head that Guy Fawkes was killed by being burned alive. Not at all – he was sentenced to the same colourful death as Wallace, but jumped from the scaffold, breaking his neck, before they could partially hang him. He was still chopped into bits which were sent on tour, but he spared himself the agonizing end.

When Paul Hentzner, a German scholar, visited Southwark in 1598, he counted thirty heads on the iron spikes of the gatehouse. Surviving panoramas of London, such as the famous drawing by Claes van Visscher from 1616, typically show a dozen.

After the Restoration of the Monarchy with Charles II in 1660, many of those who had signed the death warrant of Charles I also found a final resting place on a spike. But shortly afterwards the practice of impaling people on London Bridge came to an end – not because of any sudden sense of remorse or worry that it might not be giving off the right image to tourists – it just became more fashionable to display severed heads at the Temple Bar gate to the City instead.

When excavations took place beneath the bridge a few years ago during the building of the 'London Bridge Experience', the practice was confirmed by the find of several skulls with holes in their crowns. This was perfect serendipity for the people doing the digging: the London Bridge Experience is a modern, interactive tourist attraction that, by its very nature, reveals the lasting mark the heads of London Bridge have left on Southwark's collective psyche. It's a new competitor to various other grisly attractions that many weekend drinkers in the George Inn probably visit before heading down for a pint. At the London Dungeon on Tooley Street, you can witness recreations of medieval surgery, torture and the Great Plague, or celebrate the achievements of Bloody Mary, Jack the Ripper and Sweeney Todd, the Demon Barber of Fleet Street. Alternatively, at the Clink Prison Museum just on the other side of the Bridge Foot, you can again experience torture and the Black Death as part of your school trip or corporate-entertainment package. And at the joint London Bridge Experience and London Tombs you can experience not just the routine severed heads and plague memorabilia, but also ghosts, chainsaw-wielding zombies and walls dripping with blood, all mingling with exhibits about Roman London and the Great Fire.

These three ghastly museums sit within little more than three hundred yards of each other at the southern foot of London Bridge. They have turned gore into a tourist attraction, sucking all the horror from the rest of London – Sweeney Todd, the Great Fire, Jack the Ripper – and giving it a home here.

The Borough has always had this grim, grisly streak running through its psychogeography. It's one lasting impact of the heads on spikes, and in that, it's also a consequence of the Borough's broader relationship with the City across the river. And perhaps it's also a manifestation of the land itself, the memory of what this place was like right back when it was first built upon.

And everything – all of it – relates back to the Bridge. The Bridge is the whole point of Southwark and, to some extent, the point of London itself. Understand the Bridge, and you understand Southwark. And only when you understand Southwark can you understand the George Inn and its neighbours – their purpose, their role, and the character that makes them unique. The inns were here because of the Bridge. And the people who drank in them, one way or another, were here because of it too.

Like many of the world's great cities, London is all about the river. The Thames once swept in a great curve through a broad alluvial flood plain, much broader, shallower and slower than it is today. Prehistoric peoples fished and worked its northern banks, which were high and probably wooded. The south bank, however, was a different matter. Much of it was lower than sea level, swampy and muddy, frequently flooded, a no-man's-land between ground and river with a few hillocks spending most of their time as low islands. But people still lived here, and eventually Southwark would be built upon this stinking swamp.

After Caesar came, saw and went home again in 54 BC, Claudius brought the Romans back to Britain in AD 43 and eventually made Londinium their capital, building a walled town that has effectively remained the City of London ever since.[5] London Bridge represents the point where seagoing ships could still find a deep enough draft to come upstream, but where the river was also narrow enough to build a bridge. It was a perfect meeting point: Watling Street came up from Dover, and Stane Street (now the A3) from another major Roman settlement, Noviomagus Ragnensium (or Chichester to you and me) was diverted to merge with Watling Street just south of the Bridge. Troops heading into the northern provinces came here. Goods from around the Roman Empire were traded here.[6] In many ways, then, the place where the Bridge crossed the river was the focal point of the whole of Roman Britain, and that's why they built Londinium where they did. London Bridge would remain arguably the most important river crossing in Britain for centuries to come.

The first London Bridge was built at pretty much the same time as the first settlement that would eventually become London. And despite its swampy nature, the southern bridge foot seems to have become quite a fashionable area, with evidence of comfortable villas built on piles or stilts to rise above the water, and featuring mod cons such as under-floor central heating – handy if you were accustomed to Mediterranean climes, especially here in the swamp. Borough High Street became the main thoroughfare through Southwark to the Bridge, but shallow boats were also used to ferry goods and people around the many creeks and rivers that criss-crossed the islets of the south bank. Southwark became London's first suburb.

---

5. The Anglo-Saxons left the city empty for several centuries and built a new settlement – Lundenwic – outside its walls, but it remained standing, and forms the site of the City today.

6. With French pottery, olives, olive oil and spices all being traded, parts of Roman Southwark resembled modern Borough Market much more closely than you might think.

Londinium was abandoned when the Romans left Britain in the fifth century AD. The wooden bridge fell away, and the Thames became a handy barrier between the hostile Saxon kingdoms of Mercia to the north and Wessex to the south. Those hostilities ended in the face of the much bigger threat of Viking incursions in the ninth century. Alfred the Great, King of Wessex, united various Anglo-Saxon tribes and became their king, taking control of large chunks of Mercia including London, which he re-occupied. At some point in the ninth or tenth century, a Saxon London Bridge was built, perhaps on the piles left by the Roman structure. Around the year 920 the southern bridge foot became known as 'Suthringa Geweorche', roughly translatable as 'the Surrey folk's defence work', and Southwark had its name.[7]

With this link between the walled city and the southern encampment, not to mention the physical barrier the bridge presented to ships, London managed to fight off several Viking incursions. But in 1016 a new invasion, led by Cnut, came up with a cunning plan that says a lot about the geography of Southwark. Cnut, remember, was the king who eventually united England, Denmark and Norway under the same crown, and then reputedly attempted to halt the incoming tide – and failed, obviously – in order to demonstrate to his subjects the limits of his power. But they must have thought he could do anything after the way he took London.

The walled city was well defended, and Viking ships coming upriver could be attacked from the Bridge, making it difficult to encircle the City and lay siege, which in turn allowed the Anglo-Saxon King Edmund to go between London and Wessex to raise more troops. So in an act of daring vision that must have left London's defenders thinking, 'Oh,

---

7. The name 'Borough' came later. It has various alternative origins, with a 'burgh' signifying a defensive work to protect the foot of the bridge being one possible explanation.

come on, that's just not *fair!*', Cnut had his men dig a canal through the swamps of the south bank, cutting from Rother-hithe (just across the river from what is now Canary Wharf) to Battersea, completely slicing underneath the big n-shaped loop on which Southwark sits, creating a channel around four kilometres long that was broad and deep enough to enable them to drag their ships around the bridge itself. London was besieged, the Saxons were outmanoeuvred, and Cnut became king. It wouldn't be the last time Southwark took a key role – actively or passively – in deciding the future of the kingdom.

Nevertheless, the Bridge had proved its strategic import-ance, and because of it Southwark still remained the key point of access to London from anywhere south. The trouble was, in a city built from wood and straw, the bridge was constantly catching fire (there were eight major blazes between 1077 and 1136 alone) and was battered by storms and by mighty ice floes whenever the Thames froze and subsequently thawed. London, growing inexorably in size and importance, needed a better bridge.

Work began on a new stone bridge in 1176. Over the next thirty-three years, 140 workers lost their lives as they attempted to span a distance of 1,000 feet with a bridge that was twenty-six feet wide and could withstand anything that man or nature threw at it. Begun under Henry II, by the time it was finished King John was on the throne, with construction having seen out the entire reign of Richard the Lionheart between the two.

But the result was a medieval bridge that would do its job for the next six hundred years. Or at least, it did *a* job for the next six hundred years – even if it ended up not quite fulfilling its main role as successfully as its designers had planned.

London is, more than anything else, a commercial city. If cities can speak (and they can) then while Paris says, 'Gaze upon me, and upon a history filled with pomp, majesty and romance', New York says, 'I don't care what anyone else has told you, this is where it happens, baby', and Rome says, 'Get out of my WAY!', London says 'Come on, three for a pahnd, that's the best I can do, I'm cuttin' me own throat 'ere.' For a good chunk of its life, London had virtual autonomy from the monarchy and was run by a powerful collection of professional Guilds, meaning money has always been the main thing on the city's collective mind.[8]

Once you build a bridge, someone needs to pay for its upkeep. The polite thing to do is charge a toll to users, but this was London, and London Bridge wasn't going to settle for that. King John decided it would be a much better idea to raise money by allowing people to build houses on the bridge instead. And as pretty much any house in London at the time was built above a shop, within a few years the most important river crossing in the country became an arcade full of glovers, goldsmiths, jewellers, fletchers, cutlers and tailors. Above the shop fronts the buildings projected outwards, each storey further than the last, until they pretty much met above the thoroughfare to create a tunnel arch over the road, while at the back the buildings extended over the river to create the constant fear of falling privy contents for any passing boats. This all made the Bridge something of a tourist attraction, and people came to browse and gawp, to linger and look, and to buy and consume. More than three centuries after it was built, the Elizabethan travel writer John Lyly was a huge fan:

> among all the strong and beautiful shows me thinketh
> there is none so notable as the Bridge which crosseth

---

8. It's useful to remember this in 2012, when London had a chance to show the world what it was made of. The entrance to the Olympic Park was framed not with scenic gardens, museums and public buildings, sports facilities for the underprivileged residents of the host borough, or some kind of exhibition or funfair, but with a shopping mall.

the Thames, which is in manner of a continual street, well replenished with large and stately houses on both sides. And situated upon twenty arches whereof each one is made of excellent free stone squared.

So London Bridge fulfilled its role as a money-spinning tourist attraction far better than it did its supposed primary function of facilitating passage across the Thames. Many important personages rode up Borough High Street at the heads of processions. Richard II, Henry V, Henry VI, Queen Margaret of Anjou, Charles II and William III all found the gates thrown open and the bridge traffic cleared as they returned or arrived for the first time from Europe. But for ordinary people, it wasn't quite as straightforward. The width for passing traffic shrank from twenty-six feet when built to a mere eight to twelve feet, and that was filled with gawkers, shoppers and sightseers. If you were pulling a cart across, or even just trying to walk it on foot, it would usually take you about an hour to cross from one side of the Thames to the other.

All of which begs one rather obvious question: if it became so obvious that this one bridge was so inefficient in its primary function of getting people from one side of the river to the other, why not just build another bloody bridge?

The cost (both human and financial) must have had something to do with it, but a shrewd Guild member would have been able to see beyond this to the financial benefits a second bridge would have brought to the City. And as London grew, the simple, practical need for a second bridge must soon have become achingly apparent. But London Bridge would remain the only bridge across the Thames within London until 1750, when Westminster Bridge opened.[9]

Why?

---

9. Putney Bridge was opened in 1729, but at this time London had not yet swallowed Putney within its rapidly spreading mass.

The answer is fundamental to understanding the George Inn, and the people who visited it.

The first reason was that sometimes, it suited London that access across the river was limited. As we saw when we looked at the gates and battlements, while the City needed the Bridge, it was often selective about who it wanted coming across it, and when. It was a bottleneck, sure, but that bottleneck was pretty useful if London ever came under attack.

As the last line of defence before the bridge, Southwark saw many more such attacks than you might think. William the Conqueror torched the place on his way into London in 1066, but he wasn't the last to come up Borough High Street at the head of an invading force.

The thing is, by fortifying the southern end of the Bridge so effectively, London was admitting that, should any invasion come, Southwark itself was expendable. Awkward. The City expected the Borough to sacrifice itself to save the rich people on the other side who stuck traitors' heads on spikes to stare down at them and wouldn't let them in after sundown. And unpopular monarchs found that the people of Southwark didn't really feel like laying down their lives to protect Londoners. Often, they welcomed invaders and rebels with open arms.

Louis, the Dauphin of France, found the Bridge open to him when he arrived to take the English throne at the invitation of nobles hostile to King John, though they changed their minds after John died in 1216, and persuaded Louis to return to France. John's son Henry III found the bridge of little use to him when London's residents simply opened it to rebel nobles under the command of Simon de Montfort in 1264.

In 1381, Wat Tyler led the Peasant's Revolt from Kent to march on London, protesting the new poll tax. He took Southwark, then found the bridge closed to him, but when he threatened to set fire to the southern end, the drawbridge was lowered and sympathetic Londoners welcomed him into the city. In 1450, Jack Cade again led the men of Kent in a revolt against a number of 'popular grievances' focusing around the creation of an excessively high tax burden on the poor to pay for the mistakes and corruption of those in high places. Again, he took Southwark, where he made his head-quarters in the White Hart Inn, next door to the George. He eventually negotiated a peaceful crossing of the bridge, pro-claimed himself Mayor of London, and forced the king to flee to Warwickshire. It was all going so well. But then his men began to ransack and loot the City. When they trooped across the bridge back to Southwark, tired and happy, the Bridge finally did its job: Londoners closed and barricaded it, raised the drawbridge, and the ensuing pitched battle upon the Bridge saw Cade's forces routed, with Cade himself quickly tracked down and executed.

These events provide an interesting parallel with more recent protests against similar issues: where once the people of Kent threatened to put London to flame for such indig-nities, today's equivalent ultimatum sees people pitch tents outside St Paul's Cathedral – let's see how they respond to *that*![10]

So there were times when London didn't actually want anyone coming across the river. But there was also another reason why London Bridge remained the only river crossing for five hundred years – the influence of a curious body of men who could often be found drinking in Southwark's inns and taverns, and who helped give the area its unique char-acter when they were both on and off duty.

It's a feature of great rivers that, as well as there being an awful lot of people wanting to go across them, they also do a brilliant trade in people wanting to go up and down them.

---

10. Although to be fair both Jack Cade and Wat Tyler ended up bodiless, tarred and gazing down on London for their sins.

The Thames, as well as being a barrier to the south, was also the main thoroughfare through London. Roads to places like Greenwich, Hampton Court or Richmond were poor and often dangerous. This, plus the nightmare of trying to get across the Bridge, meant that for almost as long as London has existed, the river has been full of bargees, lightermen and ferrymen. They plied their business from sets of ferrymen's stairs on the south bank of the river, taking people across who didn't fancy the hassle of the bridge, and taking goods out to the ships in the Pool of London, or across to the City on the other side.

Watermen were therefore crucial to making London work – and they knew it. In his 1598 *Survey of London*, John Stow estimated that there were 40,000 licensed watermen on the Thames, and by 1850 there were still seventy-five sets of watermen's stairs along the Thames as it ran through the City.

Navigating the river was a skilful and often dangerous affair, and the watermen obviously thought it fitting to run their businesses in a fashion that was in keeping with capricious currents and strong, unpredictable surges. Fares would be haggled, and sometimes even fought over between rivals. As a passenger it wasn't uncommon, having agreed your fare, to suddenly find yourself renegotiating it mid-river, where your bargaining position was significantly weaker than it had been on the bank minutes before. In 1193 the City Corporation began licensing riverboats, and in 1514 an Act was passed to attempt to regulate fares. But the river men were a powerful body, and in 1555 they came together to form the Company of Watermen. This raised standards on the river by instituting careful training that could take up to seven years to complete, but it also enabled organized opposition to any potential competition – such as a new bridge across the Thames, for example. These big men – frequent visitors to the inns of Southwark – were equally at ease with battling treacherous waters and intimidating disadvantaged customers, and formed a powerful lobby that successfully campaigned against initiatives to build new bridges for almost half a millennium.

The watermen added a great deal of colour to Southwark's social fabric. They were a close-knit community, and developed their own argot, seemingly based mainly on swearing and insults. Cesar de Saussure[11] was most intrigued by this when he visited London in 1725: 'Most bargemen are very skilful at this mode of warfare using singular and quite extraordinary terms, generally very coarse and dirty and I cannot possibly explain them to you.'

This rough, dirty reputation is one that stayed with the watermen throughout their history. Charles Dickens opens *Our Mutual Friend* with Lizzie Hexam in a boat with her father, Gaffer Hexam, who makes his living by robbing corpses that have found their way into the Thames at Bankside. But the watermen had no need of Dickens – centuries before he was born, they had their very own poet.

From Dr William Rendle onwards, every orthodox account of the history of the George Inn refers to the *Carrier's Cosmographie*, a work published in 1637 by John Taylor, the self-styled 'Water Poet', in which the George is mentioned. Every account I've read quotes the relevant lines about the inn from this work, and then moves on to the next historical reference without providing any elaboration.

But this sort of thing piques my curiosity. John Taylor was one of those minor historical figures whose life and works are recorded, but not widely known. That's because he leaves us a fully formed contemporary record of his times, without actually being all that good or successful in his chosen sphere. But he turns out to be one of the most eccentric and enter-

11. Cesar provided some brilliant period descriptions of eighteenth-century drinking habits in my first book, *Man Walks into a Pub*. It was nice to meet him again when researching the watermen.

taining people we're ever likely to meet, and in many ways his life and works touch on the main themes of our story.

Taylor was born in 1580 and undertook an apprenticeship as a Thames waterman. He joined the fleet of the Earl of Essex in the Anglo-Spanish war and in 1597 he was present at the sacking of Cadiz, one of the greatest English victories of the war after the defeat of the Armada itself. This battle also resulted in the plundering of a large quantity of Vino de Jerez. Sherry was already well known in England before then, but the sacking of Cadiz is credited with rapidly boosting its popularity and making it a common drink in taverns and inns such as the George.

After the war, Taylor returned to London and worked as a waterman on the Thames. It's hard to reconcile the rough picture of the watermen we've created in our collective minds' eye with someone as sensitive as a poet, and a surviving portrait of Taylor is no help, resembling as it does an unflattering caricature of a balding Richard Branson. But that didn't stop Taylor.

'The Water Poet' was a brilliant self-publicist who seemingly just wanted to be famous.[12] He pre-empted by three and a half centuries the recent trend for writing comedic books about accepting a bet to travel round Ireland with a fridge or cross the world meeting your namesakes when he rowed from London to the town of Queensborough on the Isle of Sheppey, Kent, in a boat made of paper with two stockfish (dried, unsalted cod) tied to canes for oars, to promote the virtues of hempseed. He also travelled from London to Edinburgh with no money, a journey recounted

---

12. Like the fictitious (but true) 'Animal' in chapter one, John Taylor's mates didn't call him The Water Poet: as most of them couldn't read or write, we have no idea what they called him. But given their reputation we can safely assume it was less flattering than what he, and he alone, chose to call himself during his lifetime.

in his catchily titled book, *The Pennylesse Pilgrimage; or, the Moneylesse Perambulation of John Taylor, alias the Kings Magesties Water-Poet; How He TRAVAILED on Foot from London to Edenborough in Scotland, Not Carrying any Money To or Fro, Neither Begging, Borrowing, or Asking Meate, Drinke, or Lodging*, published in 1618. He invented his own language (which he called 'Barmoodan', and which may or may not have had some relationship with the largely expletive-based 'language' of the watermen encountered by Saussure) and wrote a poem about Old Tom Parr, who allegedly lived to the age of 152 and is remembered – or perhaps not – by the various pubs across Britain named the Old Parr's Head.

Taylor was nothing if not prolific, which is perhaps the best we can say of his artistic merit. In total he published over one hundred and fifty works during his lifetime. He would publish them by subscription – proposing a book, asking for contributions, then writing it when he had raised enough money. (Over 1,600 people subscribed to the one about the trip to Edinburgh.) Anyone who pledged money and didn't cough up would then be roundly chastised in the foreword to his next work.[13]

Taylor joined the Guild of Watermen, and rose to become its clerk. While some people enjoyed his writing, he wasn't good enough to make a career from it (later critics would amend his chosen name to 'the literary bargee') and he remained on the river until, inevitably, he fell out with the Guild, as everyone seemingly did at some point. He chronicled the watermen's disputes with the players of Southwark (who we'll meet in chapter seven), the watermen's disputes with the Borough's butchers (chapter eight), the watermen's disputes with the coaching trade (chapter nine), their disputes with the general population of London

---

13. Just wait till you see what he had to say about those who reneged on their pledge to finance the *Carrier's Cosmographie*.

(I had to cut that bit for lack of space) and the watermen's disputes among themselves (you get the idea). What he lacked in poetic talent he made up for not only with his work rate, but also his keen observational skills and genuine interest in the world around him. And best of all, he's very good value to poke fun at, which we'll be doing more of later on.

So Taylor reveals to us how powerful the watermen were, and helps explain why London Bridge remained the only London Thames crossing until 1750. Southwark came into existence as the southern end of London Bridge. And the Bridge's monopoly, retained for so long, defined Southwark physically, economically, politically, strategically and psychologically, making it one of the most curious and infamous districts of London or any other city. With a place as odd and important as this, you'd obviously need to have clear and effective government to make sure it didn't descend into complete and utter chaos.

Ah.

London owned the bit of Southwark where the Bridge landed, around which the earliest settlement grew. But the rest of the area was divided into manors owned by rich landowners including various bishops and the king himself. Southwark was close enough to the City to be handy if you had business there, but was conveniently separated from it by the river. In the twelfth century it became a fashionable place for important men to build a second residence. These manors came with certain perks, such as being excluded from the jurisdiction of London's sheriffs, and they became known as 'liberties'. As the town of Southwark bled out from the foot of the bridge and into these various liberties, it therefore became a place of competing jurisdictions over which London had little, if any, control. On top of that, the various parishes in Southwark – which exercised quite a degree of control over the daily life of their citizens – corresponded only vaguely with the division of the liberties. The fact that the area has always been known by two names – Southwark and Borough, which are often used interchangeably – just scratches the surface in terms of describing how complicated legal and civic life south of the river became.[14]

It was obvious what would happen. Anyone who didn't want to conform to the rigid rules of the City's Guilds – or was denied access to them – came here to set up business instead. Tradesmen who couldn't wait to get across the Bridge would often just do business here instead. Criminals on the run from the City, if they could make it here, could legally claim sanctuary, and if they could abide by the laws of their chosen Liberty for a year and a day were permitted to leave as free people. And if they didn't feel like abiding by those laws, the dark woods and murky swamps that fringed the Liberties made perfect hiding places. Southwark therefore became a haven for all the City's lowlife. A Charter from Edward III in 1327, the year the City took control of the Guildable Manor at the foot of the Bridge, says of the 'town and borough of Southwark':

> [the] parliament at Westminster have given us to understand that felons, thieves, and divers other male-factors and disturbers of the peace, who, in the aforesaid city and elsewhere, have committed manslaughters, robberies and divers other felonies, secretly withdraw-ing from the same city after having committed such felonies, flee to the town of Southwark, where they cannot be attached by the ministers of the said city, and there are openly received; and so for default of

---

14. There's no easy way of explaining the difference between Southwark and Borough. Essentially, what we think of as Southwark consists of the Bankside – as the name suggests, the strip of land along the bank of the river itself – and Borough, which has come to refer to the streets inland, with Borough High Street, often simply referred to as 'the Borough' itself, as the main thoroughfare.

due punishment are emboldened to commit more
such felonies.

There were reports of gangs of up to one or two hundred
rowing across the Thames from Bankside to rob Westminster
and the City en masse. No wonder the sheriffs over in the
City referred to the Liberties as 'bastard sanctuaries'.

London's response was to treat Southwark as a dumping
ground for anything that might look unsightly in the City
itself. Stick it over the river and it was close enough if you
needed it, but not too close that it was in your way, spoiling
the view. Southwark became a black mirror to London's sins
and desires and their consequences. Anything dark, seedy
and undesirable ended up here, and then London criticized
the place for being dark, seedy and undesirable.

This is where London built most of its prisons – for much
of its history, Southwark had far more prison places per
square foot than any other part of London. It's also where
London tried to dump most of its sick and homeless people,
in the hospitals that were run by monks and nuns to care for
the sick, but also provided broader, more general care for
the poor and less able in society.[15] And where better to stick

15. St Thomas's Hospital, named after Thomas Becket, was at the top of
Borough High Street and was originally run by Augustinian monks and
nuns to provide shelter and treatment for the poor, sick and homeless. In
1721 Sir Thomas Guy, a governor of St Thomas's Hospital, founded Guy's
Hospital close by as a place for 'incurables' discharged from St Thomas's,
with some maps of Southwark cheerfully indicating the presence of a
'Lunatic House' in the grounds. Guy's Hospital has grown steadily over the
centuries, and plays a key role in the story of the George later on. Apart
from its role in this story, Guy's is probably more famous as the place
where pathologist Thomas Hodgkin discovered the disease that bears his
name, and William Gull, physician to the Prince of Wales and notable
suspect for Jack the Ripper, first used the term 'anorexia nervosa'. Alex-
ander Fleming, who discovered penicillin, Sir Frederick Gowland Hopkins,
who discovered vitamins, and even the poet John Keats all worked here.

all your lepers? London's leper colony was situated on Kent Street, on the southern outskirts of Borough, and lepers were prohibited from crossing the Bridge. Finally, if there was an industry that caused pollution, that went here too. Noxious practices such as lime burning and soap making were invariably centred on Southwark, thickening its already foetid atmosphere. And as for the inns, being free of the strict regulations inside the city walls meant they quickly became an important and colourful part of the Southwark landscape.

From the Middle Ages, then, Southwark was more like we might imagine a North African seaport to be than a London suburb, full of strange, shady characters, people who were reluctant to be identified and authorities who struggled to appear in control.

It was full of so much that the City wanted to keep out, we could almost forget that the primary purpose of London Bridge was to let goods and people in, which it wasn't very good at. Even when the mighty gates were open, large waggons and, later, stagecoaches were not allowed on it at all.

So on top of the lepers, lunatics, criminals and workmen, Southwark became the transport terminus for anyone and anything arriving in London from all points south. Arrive here late at night and the gates would be closed – you could go no further.

All Southwark's teeming masses of merchants, criminals, undesirables, sailors, refugees, nonconformists and fortune seekers needed somewhere to eat and drink – especially drink – and often, a place to stay. And that's why, by the fourteenth century, the street leading to London's only bridge became an unbroken run of inns offering refreshment, beds, stabling and storage, fringed by countless alehouses, taverns and places of more dubious entertainment. It's why this street of inns was in many ways the centre of the world. And it's why the denizens of these inns – an exotic, seething jumble of races and religions, and hopes, fears and desires – between them helped shape the social history not only of London, but the entire nation.

The George Inn is the last survivor of these places. If only its walls could talk, they'd tell us stories that could make this book explode. While they remain silent, we have to look further afield to build the picture of what the inn was like in its colourful, turbulent youth.

CHAPTER FOUR: ON INNS, TAVERNS, ALEHOUSES, PUBS AND BOOZERS. BUT MAINLY INNS, AND THE DISTINCTIVE NATURE THEREOF.

Being spiritual people, we were ready for any paranormal activity we might encounter! Orbs were caught on video, in the Prince of Wales suite, and the King's suite. Our room no 210 was to be the highlight of our night! As it wasn't until we watched the footage the next day, that we saw orbs all around us, the room was clean and comfortable, and the food was excellent! The staff were friendly and professional. Will def stay there again and would HIGHLY recommend a stay here!!!

(Google review of the Best Western
Angel and Royal Hotel, posted November 2011)

HERE'S A SENTENCE I never thought I would write: I really want to go to Grantham.

I'm not saying there's anything particularly awful about Grantham, apart from it giving Margaret Thatcher to the world, obviously. I come from Barnsley (and we gave Arthur Scargill to the world) so if we're going to start taking the piss out of provincial towns, I'm on shaky ground. It's just that, until very recently, Grantham's role as Thatcher's birthplace was the only thing I knew about it.[1]

---

1. I just Googled it: Grantham has a population of about 45,000, and is notable for having the first female police officers in the UK in 1914,

My reason for wanting to visit Grantham so desperately is the latest example of how, when I write a book, it makes profound changes to my life. My first book got me seriously into beer and prompted me to leave a successful career to attempt to become a full-time writer. My second saw a self-confessed 'crap traveller' embark on a 45,000-mile trip around the world, and develop a serious appreciation of the vast array of global beer styles. My third had me on a three-month sea voyage to India, narrowly avoiding pirates and prostitutes and going into therapy on my return. Dramatic stuff, every time.

This book has made me start planning trips around the UK with my wife, visiting surviving examples of medieval coaching inns.

OK, not quite so dramatic.

Maybe it's a sign of incumbent middle age, but I dismiss any accusations of becoming more boring. If you love pubs, and you stumble across details of some of these old inns, of course you're going to want to visit them. And one of the oldest and most impressive surviving medieval inns is the Angel at Grantham, now better known as the Best Western Angel and Royal Hotel, the one visited by our friendly spiritualists at the start of this chapter. I don't want to visit the Angel for its lovely orbs though. I want to visit it because it can trace its history back to 1203, and the current building is over six hundred years old. I want to visit it because in the research for this book, I find people raving over it in books published in 1927, and 1850, and 1710, and 1544, and that – in the grand sweep of talking about pubs – is pretty mind-blowing.

---

producing the first running diesel engine in 1892, and the UK's first tractor in 1896. Norbert Dentressangle, the Woodland Trust, McCain's frozen chips and the firm that makes the Corby Trouser Press are all based there. It has one of only three branches of the Melton Mowbray Building Society. And there's a really big Morrison's. At the time of writing, Grantham Town Football Club play in the Evo-Stick League Division One South.

The Angel is probably the inn mentioned most often and most fondly in historical accounts, but when you track down the other surviving medieval inns, your map of the country changes: as well as Grantham, places like Gloucester, Bletchingley and the tiny Somerset village of Norton St Philip take on a sexy allure. Implausible maybe, but true. The George Inn at Norton St Philip, for example, makes my heart race. It's an incredible survivor from the Middle Ages and a perfect example of medieval architecture generally, with galleries that look prehistoric next to those of the George, a stone façade weathered and softened by the centuries, tiny doors and windows and a labyrinth of nooks and secret dens. It was built in a seemingly sleepy location by the local Carthusian priory, and prospered because the village was an important venue for the sale of cloth and cattle, and held two fairs annually. Today, with its open fires and cool stone, it's the kind of place you want to head for as winter sets in, and hibernate.

Norton St Philip and Grantham are a long way from Southwark. But I went there because while we know that the George Inn stretches back at least to the late fifteenth century, we have absolutely no record of what it looked like or how big it was before it was rebuilt after burning down in 1676. We know from written records that there were inns in Southwark by the Middle Ages, but because London has been perpetually rebuilt ever since, we have no idea what they were like. To figure this out, we need to extend our search and look elsewhere, probing the history of inns more generally and applying what we discover back to the George.

We can only take an educated guess as to when Britain first had inns as we know them. The Anglo-Saxon word 'inne' literally meant a 'dwelling or abiding place'. The kind of inn we're talking about was defined as 'a publick house for the entertainment of travellers'. But other large buildings such as public lodgings for students – what we'd now call halls of residence – were also referred to as inns, which is why we still have 'Inns of Court' in Central London that don't serve beer and food or offer accommodation to travellers. At a stretch, an ordinary private dwelling could be referred to as an inn, and some larger ones were. In fact the earliest recorded inn in Southwark, the Green Dragon Inn, first mentioned in 1309, was the home of the Cobham family at the time.[2]

To add to the confusion, while 'inn' was a term for a broad range of large-scale dwellings, it wasn't the only word used for such dwellings. In an evolving language, with elements of French, Anglo-Saxon and Norse all having moved in together quite recently, an inn could just as easily be referred to as a 'messuage' or 'tenement'. Not all inns were referred to as messuages or tenements, and not all messuages and tenements were inns, and the terms were often used interchangeably – it was common while researching this book to find documents from as late as the sixteenth century referring to 'a messuage called the George Inn'.

This ambiguity muddies a search that wasn't that straight-forward to begin with. Writing in 1877, archaeologist Thomas Hudson Turner argued that inns didn't exist before the mid-fourteenth century, on the basis that there was no archaeolog-ical evidence for them. But that's because inns were built from wood in populous places that have been demolished and rebuilt many times over the centuries. While the inn trade certainly took off in the mid-fourteenth century, we do have written evidence of them long before then. And anyway, where was Jesus was born?

People have always travelled – mankind used to live a

---

2. It also managed to up the stakes of confusion quite perfectly by later changing its use to become an inn as we think of inns. The Green Dragon Inn in Foul Lane was centuries later still referred to as the Cobham Inn long after it had ceased to be the private residence of the Cobham family. Meanwhile, Foul Lane was renamed Green Dragon Lane, which still runs through Borough Market today.

nomadic existence. When we built settled communities, some people travelled between them. Not many – most people would spend their entire lives without venturing more than a few miles from home. But some did, and when they were away, they needed places to stay. The inn at Bethlehem obviously wasn't called an inn until the Bible was translated into English, but there have always been places of some description that provided refreshment, lodging and stabling.

The religious connection is not entirely fatuous. Before commercial inns, pilgrims could stay at monasteries, which had an obligation to provide food and shelter for any traveller who came asking. Churches and universities provide the first records we have of bodies branching out and custom-building commercial inns, which stands to reason – a building big enough to provide stabling, chambers and refreshments to a number of people would require substantial investment, which only moneyed organizations or wealthy families would have been able to afford. Many of the earliest recorded inns in Britain fit this bill: the New Inn at Gloucester was built by Gloucester Abbey, the Golden Cross at Oxford by New College, the New Inn at Sherbourne by Sherbourne Abbey, and so on. If these places weren't built for student accommodation (several Oxford colleges still own pubs today) they were built at pilgrimage destinations, or on the way to them.

The earliest known reference to the 'host' of an 'inne' dates back to 1254, but people who received guests for profit were more commonly known as 'hostelers' or 'herbergours' well before then. The earliest surviving mentions of these professions are 1184 and 1204 respectively, so inns as we know them existed from at least the late twelfth century, even if they were rare.

The problem for our story is that none of these early mentions relate to London. Inns came a little later to the capital than elsewhere because senior clergymen and nobles coming to London 'to councils and assemblies, or drawn thither by their own affairs', were so wealthy they could afford to build their own private places in or near the City.

The liberties of Southwark were fairly typical of this arrangement. After the Norman Conquest, land was parcelled up and given to favoured nobles. Swathes of Southwark went to William the Conqueror's half-brother, Bishop Odo of Bayeux. In 1090 he passed these lands to the Abbot of the Priory of Bermondsey, who in turn granted a stretch of land along the Bankside to the Bishop of Winchester in 1107. This became the Manor of the Bishop of Winchester, later known as the Liberty of the Clink – in many ways the most notorious part of Southwark, as we shall soon see. By the early fourteenth century, nine prelates (within the Church, a Bishop or higher) from Surrey, Hampshire and Kent had town houses in Southwark. Some of which, remember, were called inns, even if they were private residences. The Bishop of Rochester's inn stood within the grounds of Winchester Palace on the Bankside, for example. But as the capital grew, so did the number and variety of people visiting, and inns as we understand them – establishments offering board and lodging to the travelling public – were common in London by the late thirteenth century.

To get a picture of what the earliest inns were like, we have to piece together what we can from the few surviving medieval inns scattered around the country, and mix in some more general principles of medieval architecture. This is exactly what Oxford historian William Pantin did in 1961. There weren't many surviving medieval inns in England by then, but there were more than there are now, and Pantin's analysis of them remains unmatched fifty years later.

Whether they arose from big houses like the Cobhams' or were built from scratch by the Church, the design of the earliest inns probably evolved from large private dwellings. You might think design features such as courtyards and galleries would be a bit extravagant even for the richest clergy and nobles, but courtyards were actually fairly common in large manor houses from Roman times onwards. Medieval town houses such as Arundel House in London and the Strangers' Hall in Norwich were often built along or around a courtyard, set back and screened from the main street by a fringe of houses and shops.

Pantin describes how two main types of inn design emerged from this basic idea: the 'Blockhouse' and the 'Courtyard'. The Blockhouse had an imposing street-front presence, with the most important buildings at the front, and was often built from stone. There would usually be a proud archway leading under the centre of the building into a courtyard at the back, which would have been a little rougher and readier. The George Inn at Norton St Philip and the Angel in Grantham remain stunning examples of this type of inn.

The second type – the courtyard inn – was closer in design to those courtyarded private houses like Arundel and Strangers' Hall. There would be little if any street-front presence apart from a gate leading back from the street, and all the main buildings – often built from wood rather than stone – would be focused around the courtyard. Most of Southwark's inns, including the George, followed this example, meaning that while inn-yards stretched back from the street, one abutting the other, on the street-front itself there was room for shops between them.

The floor plan for the George Inn in its prime – between the seventeenth and nineteenth centuries – shows two courtyards, the main one and the stable yard to the rear, and Southwark's other great inns followed a similar pattern. But these buildings only date back to the stagecoach era, specifically from the seventeenth century. Pantin's analysis of medieval inns, plus plans he discovered for inns that were long vanished, or never even built, show that the earlier George would have been much smaller, with one yard being sufficient at a time when people only travelled on horseback rather than by waggon or coach, and there weren't as many people on the roads at any one time.

Apart from the layout, how the rooms were arranged and what they actually did was pretty similar across both courtyard and blockhouse inns. All Pantin's inns are slightly different, but they share a common theme: they're usually two-storeyed, with bedchambers on the upper floor. The ground floor would have a large hall and parlour nearest the entrance, with kitchens and stabling towards the back. Breweries were common, and most had a buttery. This perplexed me for hours as I tried to figure out the huge demand for butter at old inns (surely you'd have had a bakery first?) until I learned that the word had nothing to do with dairy comestibles, but was in fact a place where you kept barrels – or butts – of beer.

The chambers upstairs invariably had access to external galleries overlooking the courtyard. Galleries were common in monastic architecture before the first inns were built, so it's surely no coincidence that this particular design feature was carried across. They weren't just used to allow light to rooms and access to the yard, they also occasionally also used to connect different buildings across a courtyard at ground level, suggesting their presence may have had something to do with England's lousy weather too. It wasn't until much later that they became ornate design features.

The functional side evolved steadily. Bill Bryson's book *At Home: A Short History of Private Life* explains how the hall – the place where we now wipe our feet and hang our coats – was once the most important room in the house. In fact for many, it *was* the house: one big hall in which families and their servants (if they had any) would eat and sleep together. Likewise, because inns developed from large houses, the earliest inns were all about the main hall, where everyone ate together. Upstairs, it was then common to have a single dormitory where everyone slept together. The floors were bare earth or stone, covered with rushes that weren't always changed as often as you'd like. Guests slept on straw, fashioning beds as best they could from cloaks and anything else they had with them. Fleas were a constant complaint.

In private homes the innovation of a split-level mezzanine or upstairs floor allowed wealthier families to retreat from the big hall to more secluded quarters, but this only became common in the fifteenth century. It happened much earlier in inns, where you were otherwise bedding down next to complete strangers. Commercial travellers wanted privacy and a lockable room where they could secure valuables, stock or samples. The inns of the Borough, like those in provincial market towns, would therefore have had such private chambers much earlier than most.

Even when private chambers became commonplace though, privacy was a relative concept. As well as tables and chairs for dining, bedrooms contained two, three or four beds. Even as late as the eighteenth century, guests at an inn often found themselves sharing not just their rooms with total strangers, but their beds too. When John Cannon stayed at the Hart Inn, Stocksbridge, Hampshire, in 1726:

> [I] had for my bedfellow one William Phippen of East Pennard, who in his sleep grasp'd me & cry'd out, Ah my dear Peggy, thinking he had been in bed with his wife, but I soon made him sensible of ye mistake by awaking him.

Bed chambers were historically the first rooms to be sectioned off from the great halls in which Saxons lived. In private homes the hall was eventually divided up into sitting rooms, dining rooms and drawing rooms, and inns followed a similar pattern, with classier parlours being split off from the main hall for more discerning guests. Even the large rooms that remained would then be further subdivided with partitions to create small snugs and compartments. An inventory of the King's Head Tavern in Leadenhall Street from 1627 describes six 'drinking rooms' with partitions each containing benches, some with tables, where small groups could drink with a measure of privacy, and the Tabard in Southwark also had 'drynkynge bowers' in the yard for the same purpose.

This trend towards subdividing large spaces into smaller rooms and snugs was a steady constant right up to the late twentieth century, when it was typical to have separate bars for separate classes of customer, and within them there would be screened snugs, or banquettes that created a barrier between your party and the one next to you. And then, something weird happened.

Collectively, we seem to have decided in the last thirty years or so that we now have enough privacy, thanks. Our homes are luxuriously furnished and we spend more time in them than at any stage in our history, and as families we are now further isolated and subdivided within them, each staring at a different screen in our own rooms. Conversely, the snugs have been ripped out of our pubs, and often even the separate rooms are knocked through, so that pretty much any modern conversion from a traditional pub is now one big open space again. There are economic benefits to the pub owners that drive them to do this, but punters seem to love it when they do. And so, modern, fashionable bars and eateries have, in some fairly fundamental ways, become more similar in design and atmosphere to the great hall of the medieval inn than any pub in the intervening centuries.

So we can infer from all this general stuff a great deal about what London and Southwark's inns looked like in their earliest guises. There are no surviving examples of them, but there are records of how they spread, and why.

As London grew, so did the number of people coming to visit. By the late thirteenth century the capital was home to the royal court, the law courts, parliament, an international port and the country's main marketplace, and was soon playing host not just to nobles and clergymen who could afford to build their own residences, but to place-seekers and petitioners, lawyers and litigants, shoppers and sightseers, drovers and shippers, all visiting on a regular basis.

But the City wasn't happy about all these inns, because the petitioners, lawyers and so on were not the only guests they harboured. The authorities were paranoid that inns were full of criminals and wrongdoers, in an age when anyone travelling was referred to as a 'foreigner' and treated with suspicion. In 1285 Edward I charged that foreign-born 'brokers, hostelers and innkeepers' were responsible for all London's burglaries and robberies.

The City was therefore quick to regulate its commercial inns. Hostelers had to be freemen (that is, not a vassal of a feudal lord) or else able to produce good character references and guarantees. They had to register with the alderman of their ward, and had to take personal responsibility for their guests, and disarm them while they were on the premises. They had to promise to lodge no evildoers, and to report any suspicious persons upon their arrival. And they had to keep strict hours. They also had to sell provisions and horses at fixed rates that could not be exceeded, and bill after bill was passed to combat, as one fourteenth-century example put it, the 'great and outrageous cost of victuals kept up in all the realm by innkeepers to the great detriment of the people travelling across the realm'.

In 1384 new regulations insisted that no inn could lodge a guest for more than a day and a night unless the hosteler would vouch for them personally, and these regulations were strengthened again by the 'hosting statute' of 1446. This last piece of legislation prompted the formation of the 'Misterie of the Hostillars of the City', which still survives today as the City Company of Innholders, an ancient and august organization that doesn't respond to emails from writers researching the history of inns. In 1473 they successfully petitioned to be recognized as 'innholders' rather than 'hostelers' or 'vintners', to distinguish the fact that they were far richer and more important than the people who worked for them.[3]

Behind the paranoia and the red tape, the basic truth was that the City of London was a delicate balance of commercial interests, with the various Guilds existing in a loose partnership that ensured none got too much more powerful than the rest. And the trouble with innkeepers was that their basic business set-up potentially allowed them to become very powerful indeed. By offering stabling, accommodation, food, drink, animal feed, safekeeping for valuables, horses for hire, entertainment and more, inns were central to the entire economy of the City. They had to be kept in check somehow, or so the Guilds believed. So they did their best to tie innkeepers up in so much red tape, they wouldn't be able to flex their economic muscle.

So if you were a London innkeeper who felt like you couldn't be bothered with it all, there were two options in particular that were open to you.

The first is that you could give up on an inn, and just run an alehouse or tavern instead.[4] By 1309 the City of London had 354 taverns and an estimated 1,334 brewhouses or alehouses. They mostly brewed their own beer, which was an activity normally done by women. Alehouses were often run by widows – it was one of the few professions women could turn to if they had to make a living on their own, especially if they wanted to keep their clothes on while working. Later,

---

3. Over the next couple of centuries, 'Hosteler' lost its 'h' and one of its 'e's and 'ostler' became a term for someone who just looked after the horses rather than ran the place. And everyone tacitly agreed just to drop 'herbergour' because it looked ugly and no one really knew how to spell or say it.

4. Though for the last four hundred years we've used the words 'inn', 'tavern' and 'alehouse' interchangeably, this wasn't the case in the fifteenth century. Then, alehouses and taverns didn't provide accommodation, only drink, and as such weren't subject to the same legislation as the inns.

some of the most formidable hosts in the history of the George were actually hostesses.

But if you really wanted to run an inn rather than an alehouse or tavern, and you didn't really have the time or patience to dash to the nearest alderman to report a bloke who'd just checked in with a squint and a funny accent, you could simply build your inn outside the City walls instead. In 1384, of 197 innkeepers registered in London, 95 were just outside the walls in Farringdon ward, along Holborn, Smithfield and Fleet Street – within spitting distance of the City, but outside its suffocating laws.

And of course, the same thing went for Southwark too. The earliest definite reference to inn-keeping in Southwark dates to 1338, when an unnamed 'tenement herbergerie and brewhouse' on the site of the later Cross Keys inn (now long gone, but formerly fifty yards down the High Street from the Green Dragon) was leased at the high annual rent of nine marks (£6). There were no tiresome regulations down Borough High Street, within the mess of competing and sometimes conflicting regimes of the various liberties and parishes. And on top of that, over here where it was less busy and there was no imposing Roman wall hemming you in on all sides, there was abundant pasture behind the street, providing ample facilities to keep 'hackney' horses for hiring. Yet more reasons then, why this bottleneck into the City, this 'highway to the continent', proliferated in inns from the fourteenth century onwards, until it became a wall-to-wall, unbroken run of them.

And this is where we have to thank the people who dreamed up the 1381 poll tax against which Wat Tyler staged his rebellion. Never mind the gross injustice of it, it was brilliant for future historians because when it was collected, the name and occupation of each payee in Southwark was carefully noted.

These records show that the Borough had more tailors

than anything else, with quite a few cobblers, and many unskilled labourers. But after that, the most popular occupations were innkeeper/hosteler, and brewer/brewhouse keeper. Add in the servants (a typical innkeeper would have two or three, and there are thirty-one servants recorded in total), the carters and 'hackneymen' (who hired out horses), and the brewing and selling of beer, with optional accommodation and stabling, was the biggest industry in Southwark. Of the twenty-two innkeepers in Borough, twelve were located on the High Street, along with ten or eleven brewers, a tapster and a vintner, making a total of around twenty-five inns and drinking houses down one street about half a mile long.

By 1550, this number had grown to over thirty down the east side of the High Street alone, with another twenty across the road. And somewhere within this rapid growth, sometime between the big stone London Bridge being built and the reign of Henry VI, the hostelry that is now the George Inn opened its doors for the first time. It opened without fanfare, without leaving any surviving record of its early years, just one of scores of inns in a crowded, seedy dumping ground of criminals, travellers, conmen, outcasts, fugitives, refugees, non-conformists and eccentrics – and the highest concentration of drinking places known to man. Life at the George was never going to be boring.

There were inns, and then there were great inns. By the reign of Elizabeth I the big hitters in Southwark had grown substantially larger than the small but beautiful medieval hostelries we visited a few pages back, and in 1598 they were immortalized by John Stow – another crucial link in pulling this story together. A tailor's son, Stow was born in London in 1525, when Henry VIII was in his prime, and lived through the entire reign of Elizabeth I and into that of James I. He had a passion for learning, especially history, and at the age of 36 wrote *A Summarie of English Chronicles*, basically his attempt to put the history of the nation into some kind of order. The book was so successful it became a standard text in Elizabethan schools, but in an age before copyright and bookshops, writers made little or no money from book sales, depending instead on subscriptions, like John Taylor, or patronage from wealthy individuals.

Stow was particularly unlucky on that score. He had never got on well with authority figures,[5] and was regarded with suspicion by the authorities. He had a voracious mind and gathered books around him, which was, in the reign of Elizabeth, clearly the behaviour of some kind of pervert – or worse, a Catholic. He was reported to the Queen's Council as 'a suspicious person with many dangerous and superstitious books in his possession', and had to fight to convince the authorities that he was no Papist.

Despite the lack of support, at the age of 40 Stow gave up the day job to research and write his histories full-time, knowing he was committing himself to a life of poverty once his modest savings were spent. He travelled widely, always on foot, in search of old records. A friend described him as tall, lean, with clear eyes and a pleasant, kind face, 'very sober, mild and courteous to any who required his instructions'.

The period of Stow's life saw London grow and change beyond recognition or imagination, and in his late seventies Stow decided to write the first definitive history and description of the capital. It's hardly been out of print since, and is one of the first references anyone researching London reaches for, thanks to its detail and thoroughness, and clear, gentle style. Stow first published the work in 1598. Five years later, he was granted a thank-you of sorts – a licence to beg legally in the City. He died the following year.

---

5. Possibly because when Stow was 6 or 7, Sir Thomas Cromwell, Henry VIII's chief minister, moved into the next street to young Stow's family, and promptly stole half their garden without offering any compensation. Because he could.

After dealing with the history, Stow walks the whole of London on foot describing everything that grabs his attention, from the bakers of Stratford-atte-Bowe bringing their 'divers long carts loaded with bread', to the skaters on the frozen fens to the north of the City. Coming up Borough High Street from the south, Stow pauses at the Marshalsea Prison to tell us how it was, among other riots and rebellions, 'broken down' by Wat Tyler's poll-tax rebels in 1381. At this time, the Marshalsea was on the east side of the High Street, and Stow takes us from there, noting: 'Towards London bridge on the same side, be many fair inns for the receipt of travellers; by these signs: the Spurre, Christopher, Bull, Queen's Head, Tabard, George, Hart, King's Head.'

By 1598 then, this roll call of great inns, one after the other, was the most notable feature of Borough High Street. The George wasn't the first of them to be built, and it wasn't the last. It was neither the biggest nor the smallest. And it certainly wasn't the most famous. That accolade went to the inn next door, the next plot down the High Street. And in the absence of many records of the George at this early point, we must examine this neighbour in detail to build up the next pieces of our story. It's a story which reminds us that, as well as being the place where everyone arrived in London, Southwark was also the place where people left the City – especially those who were on their way to enjoy medieval England's most popular excursion.

CHAPTER FIVE: THE POET'S TALE, OR, HOW ENGLISH LITERATURE WAS BORN IN A SOUTHWARK INN

Befell that, in that season, on a day
In Southwark, at the Tabard, as I lay
Ready to start upon my pilgrimage
To Canterbury, full of devout homage,
There came at nightfall to that hostelry
Some nine and twenty in a company
Of sundry persons who had chanced to fall
In fellowship, and pilgrims were they all
That toward Canterbury town would ride.
The rooms and stables spacious were and wide,
And well we there were eased, and of the best.

(From a translation from the Middle English of
The Canterbury Tales, Geoffrey Chaucer, 1387–1400)

AMONG THE MANY EVENTS I now take part in, in an attempt to shore up my meagre income from writing, I'm often asked to run pub quizzes. Mine is a 'pub quiz squared': it's a quiz that takes place in a pub, with its usual rituals such as team names like 'Quiz-team-a Aguilera' and arguments about how it's not fair because they've got, like ten students in that team and there's only three of us, so on a per-capita basis we've won, actually, and anyway they were using their iPhones. But it's also a quiz *about* pubs.

One of the problems with spending as much time skulking

around the subject as I do is that you lose all sense of where the base level of general knowledge is. I forget that something which seems like everyday knowledge to me is obscure to others. I keep making the mistake of thinking that everyone in the country knows that the UK's most popular pub name is ... anyone? ... yes! The Red Lion. (And for a bonus point, how many pubs are there with that name?[1]) I assume that just because newspapers are regularly scaring us with the 'epidemic' of '24-hour drinking', the truth about the percentage of pubs, clubs and bars that actually hold 24-hour licences will be on the tip of your tongue.[2]

But one common gap in general pub knowledge does genuinely surprise me: 'What's the name of the pub from which Geoffrey Chaucer set off on his pilgrimage to Canterbury?' I thought everyone knew that.[3]

This is not just because of my aforementioned loss of perspective. And it probably doesn't have much to do with my studying *The Canterbury Tales* for English Literature A level, given that I've been trying to suppress the memories of doing so ever since. No, the main reason I forget that not many people know about Chaucer and the Tabard is because, for a long time, it seems everyone did – although the only reason I even know that is because of what I've read while researching this book.

Back in the nineteenth century the Tabard was the most famous pub in London, if not the country, if not the world. Everyone who could read had read Chaucer, or at least knew the gist of his most famous work, and where it fitted into the literary canon. It was simply acknowledged that the Tabard

---

1. 729. But you knew that, didn't you?

2. Two per cent. Some epidemic, eh?

3. I think 13 out of 50 is a perfectly fine score and the sign of an enjoyably taxing evening. I've never been invited back anywhere to do my 'pub quiz squared' a second time. Even though I've made it multiple choice now.

in Southwark was a pub with huge historic, literary significance. It was so famous that Charles Eamer Kempe was commissioned to render the scene of the pilgrims leaving the Tabard in a stained glass window for Southwark Cathedral. Kempe, devoutly religious himself, initially objected to portraying a public house in stained glass. The rector, Canon Thompson, replied that as Jesus had been born in an inn, he couldn't see a problem. Kempe's atmospheric work remains above the old Norman entrance to the Cathedral cloisters today.

I suppose we have to bear in mind that an education and subsequent interest in literature was much more straight-forward in the Victorian era than it is now. Back then, there simply wasn't as much stuff around. Anyone interested in reading still had a relatively small pool to choose from, so if you were lucky enough to have received an education, you'd know Chaucer, Shakespeare, the ancient Greeks, and you'd be devouring Dickens and Austen for pleasure. It's compar-able to when I was a kid and there were only three TV channels: if you saw a half-decent TV programme, or a funny advert, you could be reasonably sure all your mates had seen it too. Now the audience has fragmented in the face of overwhelming choice, the most popular programmes on TV are lucky to reach half the audience levels broadcasters would have taken for granted twenty years ago. Similarly, when statistics in the US suggest that less than half the population have read a work of fiction in the previous year, and 'heavy readers' manage an average of sixteen books a year, and more statistics in the UK reveal only around half the population has bought a book of any kind in the last twelve months, at a time when there are over 200,000 new books published in the UK every year, I'm pretty sure it means the chances of anyone having read anything at all equate to approximately zilch.[4]

---

4. I am also available for motivational speeches, especially to writing classes.

So at the risk of patronizing anyone lucky enough to have parents who paid for a better education than mine, let me give a brief precis of *The Canterbury Tales* and its literary significance, before eventually dragging the narrative kicking and screaming back to the main point of Southwark and its inns and, eventually, the George Inn in particular.

Geoffrey Chaucer was born in London sometime around 1340–43 into a family of vintners. He was a successful author, poet, astronomer and alchemist, and still found time to be a bureaucrat, courtier and diplomat. Because of his public service, there are more documentary records of his life than we should expect from the fourteenth century – certainly far more than for any of his contemporaries.

The Canterbury Tales is a long-form poem (very long, if you've ever had to try to read it in the original Middle English) and Chaucer's masterpiece. It was one of the first works of literature written in the vernacular, the Middle English most people actually spoke, rather than Latin or French, the accepted literary languages of the time. Chaucer wasn't the first writer to do this, but he was certainly the most successful, which is why he's credited as being the Father of English Literature. As it was written half a century or so before Johannes Gutenberg invented the printing press, copies had to be made by hand. The fact that eighty-three such handwritten copies still survive, six centuries later, is testament to the huge popularity of the work. It is of course fictional, but as well as giving historians a real flavour of fourteenth-century life in general and providing priceless information on the evolution of the English language, the reason we're so interested in it here is that its fame, and the 500 years of scholarship that have followed it, give us vital clues to what the earliest inns were like, especially in Southwark, at a time when we have no records about the George itself.

The central device of the *Tales* is the medieval equivalent of the Easyjet city break – a pilgrimage on horseback from

London to the shrine of Thomas Becket in Canterbury Cathedral.

Pilgrimage became a popular religious pursuit, not to mention a social one, and Becket was a very popular saint. At a time when roads were poor and the only ways of travelling were by horseback or on foot, it made sense to proceed as a party, not just for safety against robbers and bandits along the route, but also because it was a great way to meet people.

That was presumably the attraction for Chaucer. If he did indeed undertake the pilgrimage himself, the date for him doing so is often given as 1383, and he is believed to have worked on the poem from 1387 to his death in 1400. This is when the popularity of the pilgrimage was at its height. Rather than the pilgrimage itself (he tells us next to nothing about the route or happenings along the way) he used the journey as a device to write about the interesting collection of characters in the party, whom he assembled to represent a cross-section of late-fourteenth-century English society, and which includes the brave knight, a veteran of the crusades; the fraudulent pardoner selling fake religious relics; the boozy, outspoken miller; the monk who would rather hunt and feast than devote himself to religious contemplation; and the amorous, worldly, five-times-married Wife of Bath, with whom I had a traumatic, sado-masochistic affair at the tender age of 16.

All these characters – twenty-nine in all – gather at the Tabard on Borough High Street, right next door to the building that would later become the George Inn, the night before they set off for Canterbury. The inn's landlord, Harry Bailly, serves them a hearty supper with strong wine, and then declares that he hasn't seen a company 'fitter for sport' than the one before him now. He suggests an entertainment for the journey: that each member of the pilgrimage tells stories to pass the time, two on the way there, two more on the return leg. In a modern translation from Middle English:

And well I know, as you go on your way,
You'll tell good tales and shape yourselves to play;
For truly there's no mirth nor comfort, none,
Riding the roads as dumb as is a stone;
And therefore will I furnish you a sport,
As I just said, to give you some comfort.

He announces his intention to join the party, and declares that the person with the best yarn will receive a slap-up feast back at the Tabard, on the house.

The Tabard itself is far more than simply the place where they happen to meet at the start of the story; it's instrumental in bringing them together. In choosing the Tabard – an inn that really existed at the time of the pilgrimage – Chaucer wasn't just picking a pub name at random; he was telling us a great deal about how both travel and polite society functioned at the time. We don't know if the inn was in any way renowned when Chaucer selected it, but the fact that he did so has made it world-famous ever since. That fame means records of it have been particularly well preserved, with mentions being pieced together from all kinds of accounts down the centuries.

There were obvious practical reasons for starting the pilgrimage in Southwark. The southern end of London Bridge stood about fifty-six miles away from Canterbury, linked directly by old Roman Watling Street. There was a shrine to Becket standing halfway across London Bridge itself, so after paying devotions there while negotiating the slow, tedious passage across the Bridge, a night in Southwark provided a good head start for the first day's travelling. Because of the closure of the gates on London Bridge at night, Southwark's burgeoning inns served not only those who arrived from the south late in the evening, but also those wishing to set off from London early in the morning, before the Bridge gates opened and the congestion instantly began.

But why the Tabard in particular, when the Borough had a variety of inns to choose from? One likely reason is that it had some pretty strong religious connections, which go back to Southwark's weird legal status. One of the biggest 'liberties' on the south bank of the Thames belonged to the Bishop of Winchester, who had a massive palace there. Southwark, as well as being a London suburb, was in its own right the largest town in the old diocese of Winchester, and as Winchester was the old Saxon capital, its Bishop was a powerful man. South-wark allowed him to be on his own turf and close to the centre of London at the same time. One member of the Bishop's retinue, the Abbot of Hyde, acquired a plot of land on Borough High Street sometime between 1304 and 1306, and built an 'inn' for himself and his colleagues, which became known as the Tabard. By the 1380s it was one of the dozen or so inns lining Borough High Street, and its links with the church made it an appropriate place from which to start a pilgrimage.

At this time, inns, taverns and alehouses were known by their painted signboards rather than any name, as most of the population was illiterate. Buildings were numbered from at least the sixteenth century, but even then, you had to be able to count, and the gaps between buildings and the open fields surrounding them made it confusing even if you could. So places of public entertainment of all kinds relied on signs that not only identified them, but also provided navigation around them. A Tabard was easily recognizable in the Middle Ages, and among a street of Bulls, Bells, Swans and Harts, would have looked quite noble and important. Stow tells us what a tabard was, and what the inn sign depicted:

> A jacket or sleeveless coat, whole before, open on both sides, with a square collar, winged at the shoulders; a stately garment of old time, commonly worn of noble-men and others, both at home and abroad in the wars, but then (to wit in the wars) their arms embroidered, or

Chaucer's pilgrims leave the Tabard Inn for Canterbury, as imagined by the illustrator of Urry's seventeenth-century edition of The Canterbury Tales. *Could that be the George – or its predecessor – just out of view to the left?*

otherwise depict upon them, that every man by his coat of arms might be known from others; but now these tabards are only worn by the heralds.

Having said that, this description sounds very similar to a Surcoat, so the inn next door to the Tabard, which would later become the George, would have had a very similar sign. William Rendle believed the Surcoat was in fact the Tabard, with the George emerging mysteriously sometime later, though this theory has now been disproved by Martha Carlin's later research.

So did the George/Surcoat host pilgrims too? If there was no room at the inn, did people go next door instead? I can't prove it, but I'd argue that it's very likely, especially at peak times such as early May, when Chaucer travelled and the roads were more passable than they had been through the winter.

So Chaucer had many clear reasons for choosing the Tabard as his starting point: geographically, it made perfect sense. It was owned by the Church. It provided stabling and beds. So far, so practical. But *The Canterbury Tales* wasn't a practical work mundanely describing the pilgrimage; it was a literary, symbolic work, a broader comment on society at the time. Professor Steven Earnshaw of Sheffield Hallam University believes that Chaucer's choice of an inn is as symbolic as anything else in *The Canterbury Tales*. In his book *The Pub in Literature* (which you should track down immediately if you enjoy this chapter) he compares *The Canterbury Tales* with the only other work from that period that's still as well known and important: *Piers Plowman* by William Langland.

Langland lived and worked around the same time as Chaucer, and *Piers* is another social satire as long-form poem, this one in alliterative verse. But whereas Chaucer's work is convivial, with each character tasked to entertain the rest of the company (and us) with their tales, *Piers* is much more serious, laying down a moral and religious message with a trowel and a sledgehammer. Piers the Plowman himself is a Christ-like figure attempting to lead humanity away from the dungeon of hell and the seven deadly sins (which are represented in the work as living characters) to gain admission to the tower of heaven.

Earnshaw points out how the two works draw a sharp line between the very different concepts of the inn and the ale-house. Chaucer's tale begins with the characters in the Tabard enjoying wine over a meal. Langland's begins with a warning against drunkenness. Chaucer delights in the 'gentile hostelrye' where 'we were eased, and of the best'. His characters, while supposedly a diverse mix representing society as a whole, feature no whores, beggars or thieves (making the Tabard possibly the only building in Southwark in 1381 that was free from such types). Meanwhile Langland has Glutton lured into an alehouse full of people of the worst description: pick-pockets, prostitutes, a tinker and his mates, a hangman, a street sweeper, a rat catcher and a ditch digger. They all get riotously hammered, and Glutton disgraces himself in some style. From a modern translation:

> Glutton had put down more than a gallon of ale, and his guts were beginning to rumble like a couple of greedy sows. Then, before you had time to say the Our Father, he had pissed a couple of quarts, and blown such a blast on the round horn of his rump, that all who heard it had to hold their noses, and wished to God he would plug it with a bunch of gorse . . . And after all this dissipation, he fell into a stupor, and slept throughout Saturday and Sunday. Then at sunset on Sunday he woke up, and as he wiped his bleary eyes, the first words he uttered were, 'Who's had the tankard?'

'As a story, *Piers Plowman* loves to have its cake and eat it,' Professor Earnshaw told me when I met him in the Fat Cat (a Sheffield alehouse) to discuss the English literary canon over several pints. 'It paints all these wonderfully vivid and entertaining pictures, which is why people enjoyed reading it, and then says, "Nah, you can't have that – that's wrong. You should be disgusted by this, not entertained." '

Even within *The Canterbury Tales* itself, there's a clear association between the type of drinking place and the kind of tale you'd expect to hear within it. Before the Pardoner begins his tale, he suggests the party go to an alehouse. Immediately there's a protest from everyone else, saying they don't want to hear something lewd, but would rather hear a moral tale.

The earliest examples of English literature therefore give us a clear insight into the differences between classes of drinking establishment that would later blur into one another. Inns and innkeepers were a class above the tavern and, especially, the alehouse.

Even if the distinction between inn and alehouse has disappeared today, the establishment disapproval of the alehouse has not. 'It's an attitude that still holds fast,' continued Prof. Earnshaw as we greeted our second pints. 'The pub isn't considered a "proper" subject for the study of English literature. My book was greeted with a great deal of scepticism and many academics considered the idea of it to be a bit of a joke. Any literary consideration of pubs is class-based, and pubs – specifically alehouses – are places for the lower classes. This is a moral judgement that's replayed constantly in literary representations of pubs down through the ages.'

And this happens despite the central driver in the primary work of English fiction being an innkeeper. Earnshaw suggests that it's not just the Tabard that plays a deeply symbolic role, but Harry Bailly himself. By setting the pilgrims their challenge, Bailly is 'not unlike the connoisseur of literature, eager to find the best story there is, told in the best way possible. But he is also like the author, the overseer and organizer of the material at his disposal.'

So it's wonderful to discover that not only was the Tabard a real pub; delightfully, Henry 'Harry' Bailly was its real landlord at the time of the pilgrimage. 'Henri Bayliff' is listed as an 'ostyler' in the Southwark Subsidy Rolls (tax records) from 1380–81. He represented Southwark in the 1376 parliament at Westminster, and again in 1378. He was also, somewhat awkwardly, one of the collectors for that infamous 1381 poll tax. He was therefore clearly a successful and influential person in Southwark. But given that Chaucer supposedly met him in 1383, a mere two years after the Peasant's Revolt against that tax, it's surprising in some ways he was even still there.

Then again, Bailly seems to have had the character to weather any temporary hostility that being the collector of a massively unpopular tax may have earned him. Chaucer describes him as the ideal host:

> He was a large man, with protruding eyes,
> As fine a burgher as in Cheapside lies;
> Bold in his speech, and wise, and right well taught,
> And as to manhood, lacking there in naught.
> Also, he was a very merry man

Effectively, he was the prototype pub landlord, a character type that has remained consistent in both the myth and reality of the good pub ever since. In the 1920s Thomas Burke said that Bailly was 'with minor emendations, good for all efficient hosts, and a fair portrait of the Englishman'.

The Canterbury Tales also gives us a few practical hints about what staying in an inn was like. The night before their journey the pilgrims all sleep together in one large dormitory. The 'Pilgrims Room' was a celebrated feature of the Tabard as late as the eighteenth century, even though by this time the inn had burned to the ground and been rebuilt, with historians and enthusiasts arguing over how much, if any, of the original wooden building had survived, right up to the point it was finally demolished in 1875. At the other end of the journey, the Chequers, or 'Chequer on the Hoop', was an inn built at Canterbury to receive pilgrims, with a dormitory boasting 100 beds.

While shared dormitories were still the norm, it had become common by this time for the innkeeper to ask guests if they would prefer to take their meals in the main hall or in the privacy of their own chambers. The available fare would often be simple – bread, meat and cheese – with ale the drink of choice (especially in Southwark), although wine was also common. Langland has a good moan about this practice in *Piers Plowman*, attacking the rich for leaving the main hall to the poor:

> Woe is in the hall each day in the week.
> There the lord and lady like not to sit.
> Now every rich man eats by himself
> In a private parlor to be rid of poor men,
> Or in a chamber with a chimney
> And leaves the great hall.

That's right – the selfish rich bastards preferred their own room with a Fancy-Dan chimney and everything. *A chimney!* They'd be wanting private yachts and Lear jets next.

The pilgrims enjoy a pleasant night's sleep at the Tabard, and set off early the next day. They head away from London through Deptford and Greenwich, and follow Watling Street through Rochester, Sittingbourne, Ospring, Boughton-under-Blean and Harbledown. They never do quite reach Canterbury though – at least, not in the published work. They get as far as the White Horse in Boughton, which is still in business today and well worth a visit, but the road runs out shortly afterwards. From its original premise of four tales each – two there and two back – our twenty-nine pilgrims should in theory give us a total of 116 tales. But Chaucer only completed twenty, with two incomplete and two intentionally cut short – a bit of a shame for the canon of English literature, but a blessed relief to generations of teenage students thereof.

An anonymous fifteenth-century writer decided to remedy this premature end, and continued the adventures of the pilgrims in the *Tale of Beryn*. Here, the party finally reach the Chequers in Canterbury, and we get another insight into the conditions of the medieval inn. Harry Bailly calls for dinner to be served, and afterwards most of the party go to visit the cathedral. But not the good old Wife of Bath and her friend the Prioress – they're too tired. Instead, they buy each other rounds of wine, and walk though the inn's garden, admiring its neatly raked alleys and beds of sage and hyssop, before coming to a quiet 'drykynge bower', a secluded place where they can sit and gossip.

The fashion for pilgrimages was brought to an abrupt end by the religious Reformation instituted by Henry VIII in the 1530s. To make sure absolutely no one misunderstood his intention, Henry – who wasn't without his own 'turbulent priests' – ordered Becket's shrine demolished, the martyr's bones destroyed, and mention of him erased.

But the Tabard survived. At the dissolution of the monasteries it was sold to John and Thomas Master. The deeds for that sale describe it as 'The Tabard of the Monastery of Hyde, and the Abbot's place, with the stables, and the garden thereunto belonging.' The Tabard would of course continue to trade on its literary fame, with Chaucer's work surviving even when it was really unfashionable to talk about saints and pilgrimages. From 1676, a sign hung from the gate on a great beam that stretched out into the high street, reading:

> This is the inne where Sir Jeffry
> Chaucer, and the nine and
> twenty pilgrims lay in their
> journey to Canterbury, anno 1383.

It hung there proudly until 1763, when it was removed because it was a hindrance to traffic.

But for all its fame, the Tabard was not the only one of Southwark's inns to be immortalized in poetry. The George too had its moment, even if this is not remembered quite as fondly as *The Canterbury Tales*.

In the 'let's just list all the mentions of the place' approach to the history of the George pioneered by George Corner in 1858, one of the many checkpoints duly ticked off is a poem from 1656 entitled 'Upon a Surfeit caught by drinking bad Sack, at the George Tavern in Southwark'. Corner doesn't even give us this title, he simply tells us the poem comes from a collection called *Muses Recreations* and quotes the following lines:

> Oh would I might turne Poet for an houre,
> To Satyrize with a vindictive power
> Against the Drawer: or I could desire
> Old Johnsons head had scalded in this fire;
> How would he rage, and bring Apollo down
> To scold with Bacchus, and depose the Clown,
> For his ill government, and so confute
> Our Poet Apes, that doe so much impute
> Unto the grapes inspirement!

Subsequent chroniclers add only that the collection was published with its title in Latin, *Musarum Deliciae*, and that it was written by Sir John Mennis and Dr James Smith. The twentieth-century historian William Kent – who I'll introduce you to properly later – has the temerity to criticize the poem for not being very good, in a comment I'll paraphrase as 'Ha! He says he wishes he could turn into a poet for an hour – well he *failed*!' But as we'll soon see, this is fairly typical of William Kent and his anger-management issues. That aside, no other writer on the George has looked any further into this poem, or the collection of which it was part. Which is a shame, because for the idly curious in search of childish giggles – and I hold up my hands on that score – it's immensely rewarding.

By 1656 the George was a large and (mostly) reputable inn. England was under the rule of Lord Protector Cromwell and at war with Spain, with whom the future Charles II was scheming and signing deals in an attempt to regain the throne. You might think this would mean Sir John Mennis, a senior naval officer, would have too much on his plate to go getting drunk and then writing poems about it. But Mennis was a royalist who would be appointed Comptroller of the Royal Navy upon the King's restoration, and he seems to have spent much of Cromwell's rule trading poems with his friends rather than doggedly pursuing the Lord Protector's interests at sea.

Mennis would have known the George well – his naval duties meant he spent a lot of time in Southwark. *Musarum Delicae* is a collection of poems sent back and forth between him and his friend Smith, and 'Upon a Surfeit . . .' is one of his.

He begins with an ocean-going metaphor, boarding the George for a journey to Spain:

> Who thought that such a storm, Ned, when our Souls,
> From the Calme Harbour of Domestick Bowles,
> Would needs abord the George, t'embark our brain,
> To the Cantabrian Calenture of Spain?

But soon the sack (sherry) was rising back up his throat. It wasn't his fault for drinking too much of course – it was the old 'must have been a dodgy pint' excuse:

> A bawdy-house would scorne it, 'twas too poor
> For those that play at Noddy on the score.
> Felt-makers had refus'd it; Nay, I think
> The Devill would abhorre such posset-drink,
> Bacchus, I'm sure detests it, 'tis too bad

> For Hereticks, a Friar would be mad
> To blesse such vile unconsecrable stuffe

If only he'd realized it was so bad before he drank so much of it.

There may be some justification in Mennis's defence, however: William Rendle tells us that in 1364, a city taverner who had sold bad wine was forced to drink some of it, and had the rest poured over his head – surely a penalty which is in urgent need of reinstatement in city taverns today. Either way, Mennis promises himself 'never again' – from now he's sticking to beer:

> while there's a Cup
> Of Beer or Ale, I do forswear to sup
> Of wicked Sack: Thus Solemn I come from it,
> No dog would e're return to such a vomit.

One of the consolations of persevering with mediocre seventeenth-century comic poetry is the enormous pleasure in the discovery that the comedy value of bodily functions is as old as those bodily functions themselves. It may be impossible to keep up with the unrecognizable and incomprehensible fads and trends your kids are into, as they were for our parents when we were kids, but I promise you unreservedly kids think farts, willies, bums and poo are hysterically funny. Of course we're supposed to grow up, to 'grow out of' finding such things hilarious. But the continued success and excellence of *Viz* magazine proves there are many of us who don't.

That includes Sir John Mennis and Dr James Smith. Because I wanted to examine 'Upon a Surfeit...' in its entirety, I tracked down a full version of *Musarum Delicae* online. As I scrolled through searching for the familiar title, I discovered three poems written by these eminent gentlemen about farts, and one about having a shit.

'Upon a Fart unluckily let' begins as a decidedly ungentle-
manly response to a lady passing wind:

> Well Madame well, the fart you put upon me
> Hath in this kingdom almost quite undone me
> Many a boystrous storm, & bitter gust
> Have I endur'd, by Sea, and more I must:
> But of all storms by Land, to me 'tis true,
> This is the foulest blast that ever blew.

Although the author then admits he did it:

> Mine Arse doth sing so merrily to day

and faces a lifetime of social exclusion as a result.

Then there's 'The Fart censured in the Parliament House',
a 166-line epic which is possibly (hopefully) satirical. Oh, and
'The Fart's Epitaph' is a short piece, heavy on ancient Roman
imagery, written from the point of view of a fart:

> Reader, I was borne and cryed,
> Crackt so, smelt so, and so dyed.

None of this, however, prepares the reader for 'Mr Smith's
taking a Purge', which takes eighty-six lines to describe a poo
in far more detail than anyone apart from 'Doctor' Gillian
McKeith really needs, and reveals that words like 'shit' (there's
a clever bit of wordplay about 'city' and 'shitty'), 'turd' and
'bum' have a longer and more distinguished history than you
might think.

Samuel Pepys was a friend of Mennis, whom he referred
to as 'a fine gentleman and a very good scholar'. He tells us
Mennis had a deep love of Chaucer, but confesses to Lord
Sandwich that in comparison to the Father of English Literature, the esteem in which Mennis is held 'is nothing but for a
jester or a ballad maker; at which my lord laughs, and asks
me whether I believe he could ever do that well'.

I can't believe that previous historians of the George, such as William Rendle and George Corner, had any idea what the *Musarum Deliciae* was like when they duly quoted the relevant lines from 'Upon a Surfeit . . .' in their accounts. They must have looked at the fancy Latin title, perhaps seen it was written by an eminent physician and a knight of the realm – Comptroller of the Royal Navy no less – and imagined they were quoting from something quite respectable.

If only it was. It just doesn't seem fair when you think about it: the Tabard gets Geoffrey Chaucer and the birth of English literature, while next door the George Inn gets potty-mouthed Sir John Mennis, an amateur poet who wishes he was as good as a jester or ballad maker, but isn't. The Tabard is immortalized for its legendary Southwark ale, the George for some dodgy wine. The Tabard welcomes the Wife of Bath, the Knight and the Miller – still iconic and much-loved characters 600 years later – while the George shares space with a talking fart.

But this is all quite fitting, isn't it? Chaucer chose to assemble his cast of characters in an inn because it was a place where all society – above a certain level at any rate – could plausibly be expected to meet as equals. And that is a wonderful thing.

Three centuries later, the social distinctions so carefully outlined by Chaucer in his 'gentile hostelrye' and Langland's depiction of Gluttony farting, pissing and vomiting in the alehouse, have been erased. We have men of far higher social standing than any of Chaucer's pilgrims sitting next door in the George – a reputable inn – getting drunk, vomiting, and giggling about farts.

Such is the enduring magic of the traditional English pub.

CHAPTER SIX: IN WHICH WE MEET THE INHABITANTS OF SINFUL SOUTHWARK, AND THE PATRONS OF ITS DIVERS INNS, TAVERNS AND ALEHOUSES

> The slaughter houses, the shambles, the blockhouses of the Devil, wherein he butchers Christian men's souls infinite ways.
>
> (Puritan pamphleteer Philip Stubbes, fondly describing taverns in his *Anatomie of Abuses*, 1583)

IF THE HEADS ON SPIKES weren't bad enough, the whole place stank.

It wasn't just the brewers, the lime-burners, the soap boilers, dyers, leatherworkers and blacksmiths and their collective industrial fug; Southwark could never quite escape the swamp. By the sixteenth century the streets and alleyways separating squalid, damp houses were criss-crossed with drainage ditches and other works, all reduced to open sewers by the poor, overcrowded populace. Disease was a constant feature, the Plague a frequent visitor.

Sometimes it seemed like everything about the place was configured to make it cartoonishly nasty. Even the street names – Axe Yard, Deadman's Place, Foul Lane, Dirty Lane – sounded like they were from a Disney theme-park-ride pirate film. In 1594 the Lord Mayor, Sir John Spencer, described the settlements on the south bank as 'very nurseries and breeding places of the begging poor', and demanded that beggars be prevented from crossing the Bridge into London.

As well as the criminals in its prisons, languishing in its liberties and hiding in the forests that fringed it, by the sixteenth century Southwark was home to prostitutes, beggars, bear pits, bull fights, bare-knuckle prize fights and disreputable alehouses, as well as somewhat more reputable inns, and a market where you could buy pretty much anything or anyone if you knew where to look and who to ask.

And like an abscess you keep pressing your tongue into, the City couldn't leave it alone. Traffic across the bridge went both ways, and for those who wanted to get across the Thames a bit quicker, the small, nimble wherries of the surly watermen constantly criss-crossed the river during the hours of daylight. The gentlefolk of London wanted Southwark at arm's length – just out of reach, but easily accessible should they wish to reach that little bit further. A contemporary Londoner's reaction could be summarized as, 'Oh God, Southwark is really horrible. It's disgusting. Look, come and look again at how revolting it is. See? It's worse than last time. I can't believe how bad it is. I'm going to have to come back soon just to check it really was this bad.'

On the face of it, a swampy, low-lying riverbank, liable to flooding and on the wrong side of the river, may not sound like the ideal location for a successful business. But there's a perverse optimism in the heart of the shrewdest entrepreneur, an ability to see the potential for profit in any situation. If your property was on Bankside, the one thing you did have going for you was that if you could make your business eye-catching, all the people with money on the other side of the river had a clear, uninterrupted view of it, giving you potential advertising opportunities unmatched by any signage within the narrow, crowded streets of the City itself.

That's why, from around the twelfth century to the six-teenth, if you stood on the north bank of the Thames and gazed across, you'd see a line of alehouses that put any others to shame. Not for these houses the trifling adornment of the painted sign swinging above the door – not when they could paint the whole riverside wall white, then paint their signs on them so large they were clearly visible from across the river.

There they stood, recorded in 1547 as an unbroken row of animals, flowers and various random objects: the Castle-on-the-Hoop, the Gun, the Antelope, the Swan, the Bull's Head, the Crane, the Hart, the Elephant, the Horseshoe, the Hart-shorn, the Boar, the Little Rose, the Rose, the Barge, the Bell, the Cock,[1] the Unicorn, the Fleur-de-Lys, the Boar's Head, the Cross Keys and the Cardinal's Hat, each enticing you with promises of a good time. The Bridge may have been difficult to cross, but all you had to do was step down to the shore and pay a waterman, and he would row you to a set of stairs beneath those walls within minutes.

There was only one small problem with this arrangement: if you were heading directly towards a very easily identifiable alehouse in a small boat, anyone watching you could see exactly where you were going. And while it wasn't the worst thing in the world to be spotted visiting an alehouse – unless your mates were all Puritans – the issue was that although these establishments looked like alehouses, and were named like alehouses, and often claimed to be alehouses, it was an open secret that many of them were in fact brothels, or 'stews'.

Their presence was hardly secret. The line between stews and alehouses was a hazy one, and regulations were at best

---

1. I'm really sorry about this. It should be beneath me to point this out. But William Rendle tells us that the Cock was very popular with sailors from coastal vessels coming into Southwark's wharves. I can't help it – the Cock was often full of seamen. Rendle tells us that if missing crewmembers were enquired after, the reply would invariably be 'Oh he is at the Cock with his jolly companions'. And he usually was.

only half-enforced. This is hardly surprising: in the 1370s both the Bishop of Winchester and William Walworth, Lord Mayor of London, owned several stews. Centuries later Edward Alleyn, the actor and contemporary of Shakespeare, made so much money from the Bankside stews he owned that he was able to found Dulwich College.

Officially, the stews were finally closed down in 1546 by Henry VIII,[2] and many of the buildings with the white walls and painted signs were demolished. Some buildings continued as ordinary alehouses, but others were replaced by something altogether different. Between the 1570s and early 1600s, several new fine inns appeared on Bankside, built around courtyards with arches big enough for coaches to pass through them. In the classic inn style, halls, parlours and dining rooms were arrayed around the courtyards, with chambers upstairs. There was one interesting quirk about these Bankside inns though: some of the serving staff would wear white aprons, while others did not. A keen observer might have spotted that the ones wearing aprons were younger and prettier than those without, and that they could often be seen disappearing to the upstairs chambers, soon followed by one of the inn's patrons. Effectively, little had changed.

Elizabeth I banned them again, but at the same time her cousin and Lord Chamberlain, Lord Hundson, owned at least one. Even when regulations were enforced, stewholders left open back doors and windows for quick getaways, built trapdoors leading to hiding places, and bribed the beadles and watchmen who were supposedly enforcing the regulations, in money or in kind.

But after the English Civil War of 1642–46, the Puritans finally seized political power. It would be wildly inappropriate to say 'had a field day' or 'went to town' or anything else suggestive of pleasure, but they certainly indulged their enthu-

---

2. Ironically himself in the final stages of syphilis.

siasms to suppress anything that might bring a smile to one's face. In 1650 Parliament passed an Act making adultery a felony punishable by death. Even a bit of harmless fornication was deemed a crime for which the offender might serve three months in prison. And this was on top of the dreaded pox, which was obviously God's own punishment on fornicators. If a man were caught visiting a prostitute, he would be imprisoned and fined. The prostitute, meanwhile, in a revealing detail about seventeenth-century attitudes to the equality of the sexes, would be publicly stripped naked and flogged. Professional killjoy Philip Stubbes felt this was too soft, and that convicted whores should be killed. Or if he couldn't have that, he'd settle for them being branded on the cheek and forehead, 'to the end [that] honest and chaste Christians might be discerned from the adulterous Children of Satan.' The little poppet.

And yet, just over a decade later (by which time, admittedly, the decidedly more fun-loving Charles II was on the throne and the Puritans were back out in the cold), Samuel Pepys was visiting Mrs Palmer's south of the river, 'thinking, because I had heard that she is a woman of that sort, that I might there have light upon some lady of pleasure (for which God forgive me)'. Pepys simply couldn't stay away from the Bankside brothels, and he wasn't the only one. Southwark, separated from the City by the permeable barrier of the river, was not only a dumping ground for what London didn't want, but also for what it did want, but didn't want to acknowledge wanting.

So did prostitutes ever use the George? That's a difficult one to answer. Any place that was known as a venue for them would have quickly acquired a bad reputation, and the George never did. There are records of them working up and down the High Street that never mention the great coaching inns. But there was a great social range among prostitutes, from the desperate whores in the alleyways to the very expensive ladies of the infamous Holland's Leaguer.[3] Travelling businessmen away from home have always been a key target market for such women, and they gathered in great numbers at the inns. It's not outlandish to suggest that higher-class prostitutes would have worked at the George. There may be no record of this, but it's hardly the kind of thing that would have been routinely documented or proudly boasted of by anyone keen to record the inn's comings and goings.

Over the course of the sixteenth and seventeenth centuries, London became the largest city in Europe. The flow of people into and out of the city soared, and Southwark's appalling, seductive chaos intensified. In 1550 the Crown sold the Southwark manors it owned to the City of London, and the portion of Southwark immediately around the bridgefoot became the Bridge Ward Without, finally absorbed into the City as its twenty-sixth Ward. So while Borough was now officially (though not very effectively) within City control, Bankside was still wholly outside it. This distinction would shape the development of the two areas over the next century or two.

As ever, Southwark gave refuge to non-conformists of all kinds; not just beer-swilling, whoring thieves. The Puritan movement that gathered strength during Elizabeth's reign was initially mocked by a more fun-loving establishment, and struggled to be taken seriously in the City. So Puritans also found haven south of the river, where their numbers were swelled by an influx of Protestant refugees from the Low Countries fleeing religious persecution, as well as a more general population of hardworking middle-class craftsmen and tradesmen.

---

3. The 'Holland's Leaguer' was an infamous brothel in Paris Garden, Bankside. A large, fortified house, it even had its own moat and drawbridge, and was run by Bess Holland, a 'woman of ill repute' who gave the house its name. It served fine dinners to gentelmen who would sometimes pay just for the privilege of dining with the madam, but could often be tempted to a sinful *digestif* afterwards.

Southwark therefore became the setting for a long-running battle between the highest concentration of hedonists in the country, and a movement whose adherents believed that if you tapped your foot to music, you might as well just go the whole hog, rename yourself Beelzebub and have sexual intercourse with the corpse of a recently sacrificed goat. Being sober in every possible sense, the Puritans were highly industrious and took most of the various positions of authority within the Borough.

The Puritans saw Southwark as hell on earth, with its drinking places at the heart of the problem. Christopher Hudson described them in 1631 as 'nests of Satan where the owls of impiety lurk and where all evil is hatched, and the bellows of intemperance and incontinence blow up'.[4]

To be fair to the Puritans – and this is the first of only two occasions when I will be – many Southwark drinking dens looked like the nests of something that, if not exactly Satanic, certainly hadn't been to Sunday School for an awfully long time.

And there were so many of them. In 1622 it was estimated that there was one drinking establishment for every fourteen householders in the Borough. More than one Southwark historian has observed that Thomas Dekker's 1632 claim that in some suburbs 'a whole street is in some places but a continuous ale-house, not a shop to be seen between red-lattice and red-lattice' wasn't much of an exaggeration here.[5]

Inevitably, given the nature of Southwark's population and

---

4. I'm hugely curious as to what image the author had in his head when he came up with the metaphor 'the owls of impiety'. Of all the animals on earth, I would never have thought of owls as looking particularly impious – if anything they look quite serious and reverential. What would a disrespectful owl look like? How would it look different from a pious owl? I'm fascinated. On the other hand, I have absolutely no desire to conjure up any mental images linking incontinence and a set of bellows.

5. Red-painted lattices were one common indication of an alehouse.

the proliferation of boozers, the link between drinking places and crime was a strong one. In 1605, Southwark constables complained, 'there are 350 alehouses, in which there is much disorder'. Around the same time, Robert Harris said of alehouses in general that 'too many of them are even the nurseries of all riot, excess and idleness', while another Puritan pamphleteer claimed they were the lairs of 'sheep stealers, robbers, quarrellers and the like'. And it got worse: pubs were also the fomenting grounds of revolutionary thinking and dissent against Church and State. Another commentater, John Downame, obviously knew a lot about this, in the way people who don't often go to pubs do, claiming, 'When the drunkard is seated upon the ale-bench and has got himself between the cup and the wall he presently becomes a reprover of magistrates, a controller of the state, a murmurer and repiner against the best established government.' The writer William Vaughan made the same argument with alarmist alliteration, declaring that alehouses 'breed conspiracies, combinations, common conjurations, detractions, defamations'.

We do have to entertain the possibility that all this danger, disorder and dastardly deed-doing was exaggerated and used as a scare tactic by Puritan propagandists. After all, the pub was a secular rival to the Church in what was, for many people, its primary role: meeting your neighbours. Historian Jeremy Boulton describes pubs as 'informal binding institutions', standing in opposition to the Church's more formal mode. Tudor and Stuart artisans often worked from home, so the primary appeal of the Church was as a place to gather and socialize. You could do the same in a pub without the weekly guilt trip. It was probably warmer, and the songs were better too.

So when we read of Puritans demonizing pubs, we might, while not denying that they could be dens of iniquity, be a little sceptical about the true extent of the problem. And the evidence suggests we'd be right: studies of seventeenth-century crime show that most of it was opportunistic and small-scale. While sellers of drink were often in the courts, this was invariably for infringements such as selling short measures or selling without a licence. There's no historical evidence at all of pubs being centres of widespread or organized crime.

Alehouses did have their problems though. There were frequent public-disorder offences arising from drunkenness, which in itself was a problem when it became excessive. In 1552, the first Licensing Act was passed. Its opening words were:

> For as much as intolerable hurts and troubles to the Commonwealth of this Realm doth daily grow and increase through such abuses and disorders as are had and used in common alehouses and tippling houses.

Possibly the most notorious troublemakers in the Borough at this time were the apprentices to its trades, young hotheads whose high jinks often spilled over into violence and nastiness. At the cry of 'Clubs!' they were programmed to run riot. Large-scale street brawls and attacks on foreigners were common, and many inns were fined for serving them. Though you have to wonder if it was as difficult to keep a straight face then as it is now when reading about how, in 1582, the Borough alderman was called upon to examine 'certain lewd persons who the last night did very disorderly disguise themselves and went up & down the street in the borough of Southwark almost stark naked, with their swords drawn in their hands, making great noises, shootings and cryings to the great disquieting of the inhabitants there, being then most of them at rest.'

Within the spectrum of drinking places, the alehouses and 'tippling houses' (essentially another description of alehouses) were singled out as the main problem. They catered to the lowest strata of the population and gave them a taste of freedom and enjoyment, so obviously they had to be strictly controlled. After the Licensing Act, they could only be legally operated with a licence from local magistrates. The law was soon extended to cover such new regulations as banning the sale of meat on fish days (Fridays and Saturdays), playing unlawful games, drinking during the times of Church service, buying and selling stolen and pawned goods, selling tobacco, and harbouring rogues, beggars or 'masterless men'.

For the first time, alehouses across the kingdom were covered by the same regulations. The Act was soon extended to cover inns and taverns, and after this point some of those old distinctions between the different establishments began to blur. By the 1650s and the time of Sir John Mennis's creative peak, taverns, inns and alehouses all sold beer and wine, for example, and status-conscious diarists such as Samuel Pepys and John Evelyn would invariably refer to any drinking house as a 'tavern'. The tavern and the inn tended to get a better press than the alehouse because everyone likes a drink, and taverns and inns tended to set their prices higher than alehouses to keep out undesirables.[6] John Earle, in *Microcosmographie*, said, 'A tavern is . . . the busy man's recreation, the idle man's business, the melancholy man's sanctuary, the stranger's welcome, the Inns of Court man's entertainment, the scholar's kindness, and the citizen's courtesy.' The strange thing is, when read in context, it seems he thinks he's being critical.

But true taverns were rare in Southwark, because the wine was expensive and the area wasn't affluent. If you had money you could drink wine at an inn, which was even better. For centuries, the only real tavern was the Bear-at-the-Bridgefoot. First mentioned as a 'wine tavern' in 1359, by the seventeenth century it was one of Southwark's oldest drinking holes and one of Pepys's locals. When he came over by boat he would alight here and often have his waterman wait for him. Just because the clientele at the Bear was more upmarket, it

---

6. A practice echoed today by many high-street pubs that find themselves standing opposite a Wetherspoon's.

doesn't follow that their behaviour was any more decorous. The drink of the house at the Bear was Canary, a sweet Spanish wine named after the islands it came from. To get the party started, ladies would reputedly remove their drawers, and their beaus would drink Canary filtered through their pants.

A few quite wonderful distinctions between inns, taverns and alehouses did remain. For example, that ban on 'unlawful games' stipulated that an innkeeper was permitted to have a bowling green, skittle alley or quoit ground, but alehouses and taverns were not. Behind any seemingly random sixteenth-to-eighteenth-century regulation such as this, the same answer usually lurks: show your average Tudor or Stuart alehouse-goer any leisure activity, and what they'd see was a brilliant opportunity for gambling.

People would bet on anything, so anything people liked to bet on would be banned. Dice and tables (backgammon) were common, as were card games, and all were summarily banned on pain of heavy fines for both the players and the inn-, tavern- or alehouse-keeper who permitted them. In Southwark in the 1630s the fines imposed by the Court Leet of the Great Liberty went from 13s 4d for a first offence to £2 13s 4d for persistent offenders – about fifty days' wages for an average craftsman. If you've ever met a gambler, you'll realize the utter futility of such a course of action – it's like trying to ban breathing. Even if you forced them to sit together in a featureless, windowless room, they'd bet on how long they could stay there before someone farted, or went insane. But as lawmakers have always done and continue to do today, licensing regulations attempted to legislate against the symptoms rather than the causes.

It was hard to legislate effectively against alehouses simply because there were so many of them, and they weren't often easy to pin down. Even when occupations were recorded, such as in the 1381 poll tax, they weren't always reliable because people had more than one job and often switched between them. A tailor or rope-maker might open his house as an alehouse with his wife doing the brewing and serving to make a little extra money, and this might not be listed officially. Things became a little clearer after the Licensing Act of 1552, but it was still a tricky area – some alehouses were nameless, and could just be part of an ordinary house, shop or cellar.

And because this was Southwark, every licensing initiative seemed to create new problems to replace the ones it solved. For most of the seventeenth century, the City and the County of Surrey were at loggerheads with each other over who had control over the licences of the Borough's inns, taverns and alehouses, and any attempts at effective governance were left to the manorial courts of the liberties, and the ecclesiastical courts of the parishes – two separate, overlapping systems.

The manorial courts held the assizes of bread and ale, which penalized those who served short measures. It tended to be those lower down the pecking order who were done for this: pretty much every victualler (sellers of food and drink including beer) in the Borough was presented to the manorial courts for this offence between 1620 and 1624, while inns were mentioned far less frequently.

But when it came to the ecclesiastical courts, every type of drinking den fell foul.

In the sixteenth century, St Saviour's church had a pretty clever way of ensuring attendance, which was effectively compulsory in Southwark under Puritan control. They would go to each household and sell a token – which you had no choice about buying. Then, at church on Sunday, you would hand the token back in. The church kept careful records of tokens sold and received back, and could tell from them who was staying home on Sundays. The churchwardens would then visit the premises of absentees. When they checked up on inns, anyone found serving customers during the hours of church service was breaking the law. Going for a pint after church has been an honourable English tradition for centuries, one even clergymen are fond of. Going for a pint instead of going to church? That wouldn't do at all. Culprits were presented at the twice-yearly visitation of the Bishop of Winchester, where they were convicted and fined.[7]

Between 1632 and 1640 at least eighty-eight victuallers, vintners and innkeepers were presented for 209 offences connected with receiving guests during the hours of divine service. One Sunday in July 1634, the Churchwardens of St Saviour's launched a sting on the local hostelries. In this single action alone, thirty victuallers and innkeepers, including those from the George, White Hart, King's Head and Queen's Head, were duly presented by the wardens at the Bishop's visitation.

Despite their authority, the churchwardens were often denied entry by innkeepers or even received with open hostility. Nicolas Jarvis at the Peters Head in Pepper Alley was 'suspected because he stood at the door within and would not speak nor open his door'. Elizabeth Lawes of the Ship is noted for using evil language to the churchwardens and refusing to open her doors to them, and worse even than that, 'for not living with her husband for seven or eight years'. John Jennings at the King's Arms tavern was presented no fewer than ten times between 1633 and 1635, 'having been divers times formerly presented'. Still, the fact that he was able to remain in business long enough to offend so persistently, coupled with the openly hostile attitude of the innkeepers, suggests the penalties for offending couldn't have been too harsh.

7. Given the type of people living and working in Southwark at the time, seventeenth-century churchwardens were obviously able to look after themselves pretty well.

The George may have been one of John Stow's eight fair inns, but it was far from immune. Thanks in part to the churchwardens, the Elizabethan and early-Stuart era is when we first start to get some detailed records about the George itself. Henry Blunden, sometimes called Blundell, took over as innkeeper in 1626, running it on behalf of the owner, Thomas Combes. In 1634, Henry Blundell, 'innkeeper at ye George', was up before the archdeacon for 'having 2 or 3 persons drinking in his house at the time of divine services on Sunday 13th July last'.

And the wardens were clever. Six weeks later, they launched a follow-up raid to see if Southwark's innkeepers had learned their lesson. Whoops. Blundell was presented once again, this time for 'denying to open his doors in time of divine service Sunday 24th August last when we suspecting him to be entertaining'. Blundell's language and behaviour on that occasion was deplorable – he was accused of 'making a scoff at the churchwardens'.

Try to picture the scene. Having already been caught red-handed, Blundell decides to try to brazen his way out of a second charge.

'Mr Blundell, open up. It's the churchwardens.'

Sounds of giggling and shushing come from behind the locked door of the George. Then, footsteps approach the door, which remains shut. From inside a voice says, 'What? Who is it?'

'Churchwardens, Mr Blundell, come on, we know thou art in there.'

'Oh, not today, thanks. I already gave at ye coffee morning.'

'Now Mr Blundell, as you well know, this being 1634, we're not that kind of churchwarden. We're tooled up and we demand entry.'

'No. You can't come in. (I said shush!)'

'Why not?'

'I, erm, I'm washing the cat. And she's agoraphobic.'

'You've got people drinking in there again, haven't you, Mr Blundell?'

'Haven't.'

'Mr Blundell, or Blunden, I can hear them eating crisps.'

'Scoffing. That's "scoffing" crisps. Now bugger ye hence, you're not coming in.'

Of course, I can't prove the incident happened exactly like this. But you can't prove it didn't. Agonisingly, the results of the hearing are not recorded. Though I imagine it ended in a fine that Blundell was comfortably able to pay. Because by this time, the great Southwark inns had already become large, sprawling affairs.

Inns tended to be bigger (and cheaper) in Southwark than in London, and we can deduce that despite all the problems with the authorities, they thrived and grew throughout this period. In 1629 the old Abbot's lodging at the Tabard (now renamed the Talbot as the tabard, along with the surcoat, became semi-forgotten heraldic terms) was converted into a brewhouse. Six years later the inn itself was rebuilt, 'a newe building of brick' erected on the old foundations. The George had also been rebuilt: while they were busy stinging the innkeepers, the churchwardens also found time to make a return of new buildings in the Borough in 1634. They describe the George as '2 seu'all buildinges part Timber and parte brick worth £6 per Annum', built on 'old foundacons aboute 12 yeares past'.

These rebuilds were not about fire damage – the usual reason for rebuilding inns – but about expansion. The waggoning trade was thriving by now, having grown to compete with the alternative trains of packhorses common in Chaucer's time. Inns that had been designed simply to have stabling for horses now needed sheds for waggons too, and their archways needed to be able to accommodate these tall, bulky vehicles. It's therefore likely that this is when the George was expanded to include the stable yard at the back, as well as more accommodation including private tenements. We know from early records referring to the George and other tenements or 'messauges' that the inn sat on a larger plot of land with other buildings on it. As its importance grew, the inn expanded to incorporate the rest of the property within it.

Historical accounts of inns differ in tone quite markedly from those we've seen of alehouses, and even taverns. A petition in Borough from 1618 says that 'the innkeepers and tradesmen (which live by the help of one another) are the ablest persons in the place.' This is because their functions went well beyond those of mere drinking shops, and made the innkeeper a far more respected person in society. The City Guilds may not have liked this, but everyone else seems to have done.

Historian Alan Everitt outlined three basic functions of the urban inn that really grew in importance between the sixteenth and eighteenth centuries. Obviously, there was the social function, and this was driven by the rise of the gentry, a leisured class who had made enough money for themselves and their families to spend time at play, but didn't want to be seen frequenting the common alehouse.

Secondly there were the administrative and political functions. From Elizabeth's reign onwards, inns became the centres of local administration, county business and local politics. Until the 1832 Reform Act they played a crucial role in parliamentary elections, and were regular meeting places for political clubs and seats of county administration. In Southwark, they were places where people met to conduct all kinds of business. Edward Alleyn chose inns and taverns as places to arbitrate in local disputes – in 1621 he wrote in his diary, '14 September, spent at the Bull Head at the arbitration with Jacob, 5s.'

But their most important function was trading, especially in Southwark. From 1575 onwards, inland trade within

Britain grew rapidly. As movement of goods became easier, manufacturers began to sell their goods wholesale, and this resulted in travelling factors and merchants touring the country, doing deals on sample with goods shipped afterwards. Much of this happened in inn yards, particularly with the hop trade. Inns even played a banking role: it could be dangerous for these merchants to carry large sums of money on the open roads, so if they trusted the innkeeper and returned often, they would leave cash in his keeping. Innkeepers also brought buyers and sellers together, opening up important channels of trade between them. Across the country, wholesale trade gradually shifted from open markets to inn yards.

Yet again, this caused some headaches in the Borough. Fruit and vegetable markets on Borough High Street stretch in some form right back to the Romans. Around the time of the creation of the Bridge Ward Without, during the reign of the young, frail Edward VI, the Borough Market began in earnest. During Stuart times it ran in the High Street every Monday, Wednesday, Friday and Saturday, from the Bridge Foot to the Counter prison, clogging up an already-congested street. The street market was abolished by George II and land was purchased from the Bishop of Rochester in 1756 to establish a permanent market space, which remains today as a famous foodie mecca. But during the sixteenth century the market was in the thick of the street's bustle.

This overcrowding in the Borough accelerated the general trend towards trading in inn yards. A petition of 1618 remarked that 'tradesmen in the Borough and upon London Bridge . . . have their greatest utterance of their wares . . . by such as lodge and guest in the common inns.' But such trade was technically illegal. It counted as 'forestalling the market' – preventing goods from coming to the open market and thereby driving up the price of those that did. The most common articles sold illegally in Southwark's inn-yards were dairy products and poultry. In 1541 five innkeepers were fined for selling these to forestallers, and many landlords were fined for forestalling themselves.

In 1624 the Guildable Manor of Southwark ordered that 'no persons buy any provisions in any inn or private warehouse but in the open market'. But that very same year, the neighbouring King's Manor ordered that inns 'kept beams and scales in their yards that they have their measures sealed by the clerk of the market and chained with a chain, that ever traveller may have the full measure of their cattle [goods]'. So here we have one Southwark Manor saying the practice must not happen, and the one next door to it saying it must happen properly. In the rapidly growing, massively congested high street, most people knew trading in inn-yards made sense.

The inns' ventures into capitalism even included coining their own money, after a fashion. From the reign of Elizabeth I through the best part of the seventeenth century, small change was scarce. Made from copper, lead and sometimes even leather, 'trade tokens' were officially just advertisements for a business. They would have a symbol representing the business on one side, and probably details of its location on the other. Large numbers were printed particularly from the 1640s, and so many pubs made use of them they were commonly known as 'tavern tokens'. They changed hands quickly, and by mutual consent became a form of currency, standing in for absent farthings and half-farthings. Several were issued by the George, and still survive in a collection held at London's Guildhall. One bears the name of Anthony Blake, tapster at 'Ye George Inn, Southwarke', and shows four tankards and three pipes on the reverse – possibly suggesting the recipe for a perfect evening. A farthing token made for John Gunter may also have been produced for the George because it showed St George and the Dragon on the reverse, and a third surviving coin for John Cole shows that he resided 'next the 3 Cups' and 'against the George Inn

Southwark'. In 1672 a new supply of Royal farthings was issued, and the use of trade tokens was abolished under pain of being 'chastised with exemplary severity', but they were still being used sneakily as late as the nineteenth century.

Apart from trading in them, holding political meetings in them and settling civic disputes in them, it wasn't unknown for people to simply go and drink in Southwark's inns too. From the seventeenth century onwards there were still penalties for inns which served anyone who was not a gentleman or bona fide traveller, but these were indifferently enforced and eventually disappeared altogether. Inns may have catered for a higher class of customer generally, but there was always room for the locals in the taproom, out of sight of the coffee room or restaurant.

For a long time there wasn't a bar as such – orders would be given to a tapster or potboy who would go down to the cellar or into the buttery where the barrels were kept. If you were particularly impatient, some cellars were even fitted with seats, tables and latticework partitions, so beer could be served direct from the barrel.

The term 'bar' dates to around 1596. The earliest example was simply a serving hatch in the door to the buttery – a buttery bar – and was purely for serving drinks rather than providing somewhere to stand and consume them. This eventually evolved into a sort of bay window affair that sounds remarkably similar to the curious little shop/post-office-style bar we saw when we went round the George in chapter one. This strange little area therefore reveals itself to be an authentic preservation from the very earliest bars. It's probably been rebuilt over the centuries, but is the same in form and function as it would have been in the seventeenth century – remarkable when you consider that it remained the main serving area in the pub until the 1970s.

Thanks to the tireless work of the churchwardens, we can draw up a pretty good idea of exactly who drank in the

George at this time, apart from the carriers and commercial travellers staying at the inn. Sitting up there at God's right hand (on a spike, if *Blackadder II* is to be believed) it must give the Puritans endless comfort to know that their careful logging of who was and wasn't going to church, and who was drinking in Satan's Lair instead, has been preserved for four hundred years and now plays a vital role in helping us celebrate the history of the pub and all its works.

Like the 1381 poll-tax records, the churchwardens' token books (the tokens relating to church attendance, not the tokens used as small change) kept careful records of the occupations of each head of household they visited. In the Middle Ages a huge proportion of houses were occupied by wealthy churchmen and aristocrats, but by the sixteenth century most of these had been sold off as the rich gravitated towards Westminster, London's newer, more fashionable suburb. Southwark became cheaper and poorer, home to craftsmen, tradesmen and the wandering poor. They lived in subdivided tenements within larger buildings, including inns such as the Christopher and the Bell, which were eventually converted entirely into long-term housing. Those who couldn't afford a tenement might lease a room or even a cellar from someone who had leased a tenement from an entrepreneur, who had leased it in turn from the owner.

Most people either worked from home or very close to home, and they used inns, taverns and alehouses to meet and socialize with their neighbours. So if we know what kind of people lived in these crowded, subdivided tenements down the High Street, we can deduce who drank in the George and its neighbours.

Another heroic historian, Jeremy Boulton, did a painstaking analysis of the token books from 1622. This reveals that taken together, victualling and inn-keeping tied with shoe-making as the most common employment along Borough High Street, with tailors following a close third. There were forty-five victuallers and seven innkeepers (these terms were pretty much interchangeable by this point). Throw in the ten brewers, twelve brewers' servants and ten coopers (barrel makers) and the brewing and selling of beer employed a sizeable chunk of the Borough. In addition, many of the eight carmen (carters) and thirty-three porters – a classification that also included ostlers, tapsters and draymen – plus a few of the eleven blacksmiths, also relied on the inns for their work. Making shoes, hats and clothes was also popular, and then came bakers, grocers, cheesemongers and butchers – overall, the provision of food and drink employed a third of all people living in the Borough. There were also rope makers, chandlers and soap boilers, as well as one falconer and a mousetrap seller.

The George focused its custom on travellers of course, and while London Bridge remained the only Thames crossing it played host to a diverse clientele. The taproom was full of waggoners and, later, the coachmen who had delivered the passengers eating and drinking next door, the inn having by now subdivided so it could segregate classes and give those with money the privacy they now wanted. The George would have been more expensive than the neighbouring alehouses, but the taproom of the George would still have been a jolly mix of waggoners, tailors, cobblers, cheesemakers, victuallers, brewers and butchers – a sort of Stuart-era mash-up of *Saturday Kitchen* and *What Not to Wear*. One of the laws of the time stipulated that innkeepers were barred from sourcing their own meat, and with so many inns in such a small place, the butchers of Borough, in particular, did great business.

As with innkeepers and watermen, butchers were often able to transcend the confines of social class. One of the many butcher's shops was run by a man called Robert Harvard, who also owned an inn or tavern (brilliantly getting around those troublesome laws). We can guess how profitable these occupations were from the fact that Robert's son John was educated at Cambridge. But the Plague reduced the large Harvard family to just John, his brother, Thomas, and his mother, Katherine, and after Katherine died she left the lease to the Queen's Head, another of Stow's eight fair inns a few yards down the road from the George, to John.

But John favoured a career in the church. Rather than run the Queen's Head, he emigrated to Massachusetts, a move that Reverend S. Benson in his account of Southwark's history suggests was motivated by anti-Puritan religious persecution, saying the respectable Harvards were 'men of independent tone, and some of them were not of the sort which would stay in a country to the loss of liberty of conscience and freedom of religious worship'. By all accounts, Harvard did quite well for himself over there, and ended up having a relatively well-known university named after him. Not bad for a butcher's son.

By now the occupational make-up of Bankside was very different from that of Borough High Street and its immediate environs, or 'Boroughside' as it was sometimes known for convenience. It may have only taken a few minutes to walk from the George to the heart of the Bankside, but thanks in part to the split jurisdiction from 1550, these two main constituent parts of Southwark developed very differently. Food and drink only employed 13 per cent of people along the river, but this is where all the watermen lived, as close as possible to the Thames and the sets of stairs down to it, and close to the brothels, bear gardens and theatres that gave them so much of their custom. Just as it is today, in Stuart times the Borough was all about work, and Bankside all about play. Bankside may not have given the George much of its day-to-day custom, but it did give Southwark its notoriety and fame, which in turn had a profound indirect effect on the George's clientele. But most importantly, it gave us the somewhat tenuous claim which is the title of this book. It's now probably time I 'fessed up and analysed that claim in detail.

CHAPTER SEVEN: CONCERNING BULLS, BEARS, ACTORS AND OTHER BEASTS, AND THEIR VARIOUS 'ENTERTAINMENTS', INCLUDING THE SAD TALE OF A MONKEY ON A HORSE

William Shakespeare walks into a pub. He goes up to the bar and says, 'Pint of Stella, please mate.'

The barman replies, 'I'm not serving you; you're Bard.'

(Anon)

WILLIAM KENT MAY NOT have been the most pioneering historian of the George Inn, but he was certainly the most persistent. Between 1932 and 1970, he self-published ten editions of his little pamphlet, called, simply, *The George Inn Southwark*. It's heavily derivative of previous works, adding little to what people like George Corner and Dr William Rendle had discovered, but it was clearly popular enough to earn repeated publication.

Although, perhaps there were other reasons to bring out new editions.

The copy I tracked down is the seventh edition, from August 1954. When I subsequently found a previous edition in the John Harvard Library in Southwark, I checked to see if anything was different. Content-wise, it was identical – even in later editions published a quarter of a century after the first one, by which time all manner of things had happened to the George, Kent's history still stops in 1930. But there was one change: my edition had a new foreword by the author.

In this newly penned preface, Kent mentions that William Shakespeare must have known the George from the time he spent living in Southwark . . . *or he would have done if he was real! Which he wasn't!!*

Yes, Kent was a Shakespeare denier, and it quickly turns out that the only reason he brought out the seventh edition of his book on the George was so that he could bang on about his colourful theories.

'To me he is Edward de Vere, seventeenth Earl of Oxford', Kent writes, before becoming increasingly hysterical and attacking the many people he clearly regards as idiots for believing that Shakespeare was, in fact, Shakespeare. He claims a number of professors support his view, by which he means, they *share* his view, having first proposed it long before he did. The first person to make the claim about de Vere – surely to the delight of the pro-Shakespeare or 'Stratfordian' camp – was someone called J. Thomas Looney, thirty-four years before Kent's rant.

Why did Kent go to all the trouble of launching a new edition of his pamphlet on the George just so he could mount this blistering attack? He would have us believe he had no choice. He's tried to take on the Stratfordian authorities about this, and they're running scared. He asked them to debate him on the matter at Oxford University . . . *and they never even replied!* Neither the Chief Librarian of Birmingham nor the Vice-Chancellor of Birmingham University could find an exponent of the 'myth' to face him in battle, 'so neither the so-called "birthplace" and [sic] the largest city in "Shakespeare's county" can provide a defender!' he howls in triumph, like a hoodlum silverback gorilla. If he were still around, we might suggest to him that there was another possibility regarding this wall of silence, and that when he writes that they couldn't find anyone, he's missed out the words 'be bothered to' from the middle of the sentence.

Like most Shakespeare conspiracy theorists, Kent dismisses centuries of scholarship as myth without supplying a single shred of evidence to support his own theory.[1] Still, Kent's increasingly unhinged rant – which remained in place right through to the tenth and final edition in 1970 – is by far the most entertaining part of his pamphlet on the George.

But for the purposes of this book, I'm going to side with centuries of scholarship and what still stands as the most obvious, likely sounding version of history, and assume that William Shakespeare of Stratford-upon-Avon wrote most or all of the work attributed to him.[2] Although maybe you guessed that, given the title of this book.

Now, about that title . . .

If you bought this book in the hope of finding lots of detailed accounts of what the Bard got up to with the lads on a Friday night, with details of his favourite pints, salty snacks and cheesy chat-up lines, approaching the halfway point I have to confess that there are no such stories. That's because there are no records at all of what pubs Shakespeare went to, or what he did while he was there. And that, obviously, means there are no records of Shakespeare ever having visited the George Inn.

Sorry.

But before you angrily put your foot through your Kindle screen and send me the bill, or march back into the bookshop

---

1. For a brilliantly level-headed and typically amusing rebuttal to the Looney point of view, among others, see Bill Bryson's *Shakespeare*.

2. Apart from being true, it's a position worthy of support purely on the grounds that many who support the de Vere theory find it impossible to believe that 'a commoner' could have written so well. Surely only a nobleman could have been this clever. Seriously, this is one of the main planks of their argument.

and demand a refund, Shakespeare is still central to the story of the George. And more importantly, the George and other inns like it are central to the story not only of Shakespeare, but the very development of theatre as we know it.

In the sixteenth and seventeenth centuries, strolling singers, acrobats, musicians, actors, clowns, fencers and puppeteers were all hugely popular around England – and pretty much all of them were banned from London by its restrictive Guilds, and the City authorities. As ever, Southwark proved their haven. And during the rapid population growth of this period, these descendants of the medieval wandering minstrel, who often faced the risk of being arrested for vagrancy, realized they could now make a pretty good living by staying in one place.

Plays were sometimes commissioned for private houses, and noble patronage was fundamental to the survival of more respectable troupes, as evidenced by Shakespeare's company being called the Lord Chamberlain's Men (thanks to their support from Lord Hundson, Queen Elizabeth's brothel-loving cousin) and, later, during the reign of James I, the King's Men. But even then there was a constant conflict between the Lord Chamberlain, who found players a handy source of entertainment for the Royal Court, and the city authorities, who disapproved of public performances.

The Puritans of course regarded such lewd entertainment as sinful, no better than the bear baiting and dog fights that were widespread. In 1632, William Prynne, a famous polemicist, claimed that, during a performance of Marlowe's *Doctor Faustus* at the Bel Savage Inn, Satan himself was summoned up to the stage, resulting in several audience members losing their sanity. The make-up and props guys must have been torn between congratulating themselves on their art and shaking their heads in despair.

But even more practical-minded authority figures worried that the gathering together of so many people in such a small space created a hotbed for crime, disease, social disorder and probably any other kind of trouble they could imagine. In 1574 the Corporation of London expelled actors from the City on the pretext that plays were a breeding ground for the Plague.

For most itinerant players, the obvious place to show up and say 'Hey, let's put on a show!' was the inn-yard. And one of the best places to do this was Southwark. Inns were increasingly competing with each other by offering entertainment to their guests as well as food, drink and accommodation. William Rendle tells us the host would ask if the gentleman guests would like music – 'minstrells, musicians and chawntors' were all to be had, and players were always moving between inns, striking agreements with those who had the best facilities to give 'a taste of their quality, dramatic and musical, shows and entertainments of all sorts'.

The inn-yard was perfect for larger performances in that it offered a ready-made amphitheatre, and many inns became well known for their plays. The Bel Savage Inn on Ludgate Hill was arguably the most famous of these, and various other inns dotted on the fringes of the City, just inside or outside its walls, were also known for their theatrical performances. John Strype, who updated Stow's work in 1720, reckoned five or so eventually became small theatres rather than continuing as inns, and in the late eighteenth century Matthew Concanen and Aaron Morgan claimed in their *History and Antiquities of the Parish of St Saviour, Southwark* that you could still see the remains of permanent stages in the yards of the Cross-keys in Gracechurch Street and the Bull in Bishopsgate Street.

They went on to claim that 'the form of these temporary playhouses seems to be preserved in our modern theatres', and there certainly are some striking similarities between, say, the reconstructed Globe Theatre and the model of the Rose Theatre in the Museum of London, and inn-yards like that of the George. Inn-yard galleries were ranged around three sides of the building, just as balconies are in theatres now. And while in theatres these balconies eventually became deep enough to seat various rows, the Elizabethan examples were much shallower, with wooden balustrades just like those of the inns. The stage would be erected just inside the gate to the inn-yard, facing the galleries. Admission could therefore be charged at the gate, with money being kept in a box that would eventually give us the 'box office'. The ground or 'pit', after the cockfighting and dogfighting that sometimes went on, was where commoners paid their penny and stood, while another penny bought you access to the better views from the galleries.

Ben Jonson gives us an indication of what the inn-yard stage was like in *The Poetaster*, his 1601 meditation on 'the poet's moral duties in society', and a satire on poor poets (the title is a term for someone who writes insignificant or shoddy poetry). In Act III, Scene iv, Captain Tucca advises Histrio, an actor, to ingratiate himself with Pantalabus, an actor, poet and plagiarist, thought by some to be a critical portrayal of Jonson's friend, Shakespeare:

> If he pen for thee once, thou shalt not need to travel
> with thy pumps full of gravel any more, after a blind
> jade and a hamper, and stalk upon boards and barrel
> heads to an old cracked trumpet.

The stage made of 'boards and barrel heads' and the 'cracked trumpet' belong to the inn-yard, whereas the pretentious, 'lofty, new stalking style' of the poet will see the actor on the stage of a more reputable theatre.

Did inn-yard theatre happen in the George? In historical accounts of Elizabethan theatre it's never mentioned alongside the Bel Savage, the Bell in Gracechurch Street or the Saracen's Head in Islington as one of the famous venues. But then, neither are any of Southwark's great coaching inns, and we have evidence of plays being performed in at least some of them. We know plays were being performed somewhere in Southwark as early as 1547, decades before the first permanent theatre was built, because Bishop Stephen Gardiner announced a solemn remembrance of the deceased Henry VIII, but complained that the players of Southwark were proposing a competing event, 'a solemn play to try who shall have most resort, they in game, or I in earnest'. The George had a bigger inn-yard than some of its rivals, and was arranged in a neat square, whereas some twisted and wound around jutting-out stables and warehouses. Obviously the George was busy in its day job as an inn for the receipt of travellers, and therefore wouldn't have had a permanent stage as some inns did, but from its location and layout, it's almost certain that it hosted plays at some point.

But for ambitious theatre companies hanging around London's walls, inn-yard theatre was less than ideal: as drama's reputation grew, so did the desire for a permanent home, where both the performance and its finances could be better controlled. The biggest inn-yard could hold about 500 people, whereas the theatres would soon host up to 3,000. Added to this, the theatres took away the need to travel, and the need to give a cut to the innkeeper.

The first public theatre was called, simply, the Theatre, built in Shoreditch by James Burbage in 1576. Burbage enlisted the help of Dr John Dee, royal courtier, magician and alchemist, to come up with a design that could be cheaply built, but was impressive. The aim was to maximize the number of people who could attend, and therefore the profitability of performances.

When the lease on the Theatre's land ran out in 1598, Burbage's sons (he had died the previous year) Richard and Cuthbert came up with an ingenious plan. They hired Peter Street, a carpenter, to secretly take the Theatre apart timber by timber. On the night of 28 December 1598, they transported the materials from Shoreditch across the frozen Thames, and began reassembling it on a plot newly leased by Cuthbert Burbage on Bankside – just beyond the City's reach, but easily accessible via the watermen who ran their businesses from there. This new theatre, called the Globe, opened in 1599.

William Shakespeare moved to London sometime in the mid to late 1580s, and his work was well known by 1592, when he was accused by bitter, university-educated rivals of being an unruly common upstart. At some point between 1596 and 1599 he moved from Bishopsgate to Southwark, to a house whose foundations are now covered by Blackfriars Bridge. He would live there until 1604, when he returned north of the river. It's here in Southwark that he is thought to have written much of his best work, including *Hamlet*, *Othello*, *Macbeth* and *King Lear*.

Shakespeare was a shareholder in Burbage's company and part-owner of the Globe, and definitely saw his plays performed there, acting in at least some of them. But he also had them performed at other playhouses by other companies, and he acted in other people's productions, including several plays by Ben Johnson. By the end of the nineties, his activities as playwright, poet, impresario and actor had made him a wealthy man.

While Elizabethan theatres took many design cues from inn-yard entertainments, they improved the basic shape. In *Henry V* (which Shakespeare wrote specifically for the Globe and may well have been the first play performed there) the theatre is referred to as 'this wooden O', but it's more likely that the theatres were many-sided polygons, approximating a circle as closely as possible without bending the wood from which they were built (although the Fortune theatre, built by Philip Henslowe in 1600, was square). In this, they followed the design of the nearby bear pits and bullrings that were established on Bankside in Henry VIII's reign and soared in popularity under Elizabeth I's patronage. The use of pits, balconies and raised stages retained a link to the inn-yards, while the evolution of the design aimed to evoke classical Roman amphitheatres, raising the reputation of the players and their works by drawing comparisons with classical Greek theatre – at the same time as implicitly promising thrills on a par with Southwark's somewhat lower-brow entertainments.

By the time the Globe was built on Bankside, some of the Lord Chamberlain's Men's competitors had already had the same idea. Their great rivals were the Admiral's Men under Philip Henslowe and, later, his lead actor and son-in-law, Edward Alleyn – considered to be the finest actor of his generation. Henslowe built the Rose on Bankside twelve years before the Globe arrived. And that was followed by the biggest of all, the Swan, opened by Francis Langley in 1595. The following year Johannes de Witt, a Dutch traveller, wrote about four great amphitheatres in London, each performing a different play every day. But he found the Swan, with its 3,000 capacity, the most impressive:

> It is built out of flint stones stacked on top of each other (of which there is great store in Britain), supported by wooden pillars which, by their painted marble colour, can deceive even the most acute observers. As its form seems to bear the appearance of a Roman work, I have made a drawing of it.

This drawing shows a large raised stage with a balcony above it, a roof over the stage, a trumpeter announcing the performance, and three tiers of galleries surrounding the pit and stage, which look distinctly reminiscent of an old inn.

Using the same pictoral language as inn signs, each theatre would fly a flag showing its emblem when a play was being performed, and actors would take to the streets foisting handbills on the populace, urging them in. If the play wasn't very good, the audience would hurl oranges at the stage along with torrents of abuse and gobs of phlegm. If it was alright, they'd simply treat it as background noise, playing cards or dice, munching apples and cracking nuts, buying ale from the vendors wandering through the crowd.

At the end of a play, the actors would literally beg for the approval of the audience – something you can see written into the closing lines of plays such as *The Tempest*. Sometimes the company would go further, and it was common for even great tragedies to be capped off with the cast rising from where they had been slain and dancing a little jig in a desperate attempt to make the punters leave with smiles on their faces.

But even if people disliked the play itself, the pastime of going to the theatre became riotously popular for all classes in society, and a huge source of income for Southwark. John Taylor describes how the watermen would bring three or four thousand punters a day across the river to places like Paris Garden stairs.

By trying to stamp them out, the killjoy authorities had inadvertently helped the players go from scrounging slots in inn-yards to entertaining thousands in purpose-built venues. And the killjoys were not happy. Sir Walter Besant went to one play and complained that 'There was dancing in it, music, mockery, merriment, satire, low comedy; all these things the misguided flock enjoyed and the shepherd deplored.' And true to form, Philip Stubbes, in an essay in his famous *Anatomie of Abuses* titled 'Stage-playes, Enterludes and their Wickedness', moaned:

> All Stage-plays, Enterludes and Comedies are either of divine or profane matter: If they be of divine matter, then they are most intolerable, or rather Sacrilegious, for that the blessed word of GOD is to be handled reverently, gravely and sagely, with veneration to the glorious Majestie of God – and not scoffingly, flout-ingly, and iybingly,[3] as it is upon Stages and Playes and Enterludes.

---

3. I'm probably showing my ignorance here, but I think Stubbes just made this word up, because after slagging off just about everything – including

You just couldn't win with Philip Stubbes. Here he was declaring that if a play had holy themes it was sacrilegious, because it dared to act out depictions of God's love. Whereas on the other hand, if it didn't have holy themes it was dishonouring God, because it wasn't about God, which was even worse. Such filth was so bad it could only have been 'sucked from the Devil's teats'. Clearly then, going to see any play at all, no matter what it was about, was 'to worship devils and betray Christ Jesus'. Stubbes's rhetoric was attacked and ridiculed by Thomas Nashe in his *Anatomie of Absurdity*, but Stubbes was hugely popular at the time, a proto-*Daily Mail* columnist in cloak and breeches.

Not everyone thought that everything on stage was sucked from the Devil's teats. What really worried saner authority figures was not the stage itself, but the crowd gathered in front of it. Bad things happened when the people gathered in large numbers – you could guarantee it. Even before purpose-built theatres, play-going crowds gathering in inn-yards had to be treated with suspicion. In 1574, while petitioning for the licensing of plays and playing-places, the Common Council asserted that:

> sundry great disorders and inconveniences have been found to ensue to this city by the inordinate haunting of great multitudes of people, specially youth, to plays, interludes, and shows, namely occasion of frays and quarrels, evil practices of incontinency in great inns having chambers and secret places adjoining to their open stages and galleries.

And this was Southwark, remember, 'frequented by libertines of the lowest cast'. Philip Henslowe's diary reveals that the

---

football, drinking, inns, barbers, contemporary fashion, church festivals, prisons and astrology – he'd simply run out of critical words. I can't find 'iybingly' in any dictionary, and if you type it into Google the only hits you get are scanned-in copies of this one passage.

Bankside theatres attracted 'lewd disposed persons' such as thieves and con men. Thomas Dekker, who was obviously familiar with the more expensive seats, said, 'Pay thy twopence to a player, and in his gallery mayest thou sit by a harlot.' The poet John Dryden agreed, commenting that 'the play-house is their place of traffic, where Nightly they sit to sell their rotten ware.'

But despite these manifold attractions, the Bankside theatres faced tough competition for both the custom of curious Londoners and the disgust of the Puritans. In the search for new thrills, one question was asked of a range of acts – a question whose answer contained as much creativity, variety, comedy and tragedy as the complete works of Shakespeare himself. And that question was:

'How do you think it would do against a pack of angry dogs?'

Claes Van Visscher's famous 1616 panorama of London from the south bank gives us one of our main indications of what theatres looked like from the outside: a tall, polygonal building is clearly labelled 'The Globe'. But only yards away from it stands another structure, almost identical in size and shape, and this one is labelled 'The Bear Garden'. John Stow described the scene in 1598:

> There be the two Beare-gardens, the old and the new places, wherein be kept Beares, Bulles, and other beasts, to be bayted. As also Mastives in several kennels are there nourished to bait them. These Beares . . . are . . . baited in plottes of grounde, scaffolded about for the beholders to stand safe.

The 'sport' of chaining a bear to a wall and setting a pack of mastiffs against it was popular in England from the reign of Henry II (1154–89). In 1526, the Earl of Northumberland visited Paris Gardens to enjoy the bear baiting which was surging in popularity under macho Henry VIII's reign, even

Detail of Claes Visscher's London panorama from 1616,
showing London Bridge with Southwark in the foreground.
The heads on spikes are a lovely touch.

though he would attempt to ban it not long before his death, on the grounds that people were gathering there to plot against him. That ban failed, and in 1550 the poet Crowley wrote:

> Every Sunday they will spend
> One penny or two, the bearward's living to mend.
> At Paris Gardens each Sunday, a man shall not fail
> To find two or three hundred for the bearward's vale.

Originally these sports too happened in inn-yards, but moved to purpose-built stadia as the size of the crowds soared in the mid-sixteenth century. Southwark's bear garden and bullring stood in two adjoining fields, separated by a small strip of land and a large pond, and there was a further bullring in the High Street. They were circular and open-roofed, like theatres, in imitation of Roman amphitheatres. It cost a third of a penny to stand on the ground, or a penny to sit in the raised seats that would be familiar in arrangement to any modern theatre or concertgoer.

Huge amounts changed hands in bets, and Edward Alleyn said the profits were 'immense'. Bears were valuable and hard to get hold of. They would be baited by dogs until they were tired, and then taken away. Bulls, on the other hand, were usually baited to death. Johannes de Witt's account of theatres refers to bears, bulls, and dogs of stupendous size which tore each other apart to provide 'a most pleasant spectacle to the people'.

Most of us can probably side with the Puritans on this one. In 1583 they celebrated – sorry, wrong word again – experienced a sense of grim, joyless satisfaction when the seating at the bear baiting in Paris Garden collapsed as if 'heaven-directed', and eight people died with many more injured. Even though they conceded that the wood was probably rotten and that might have had something to do with it, Puritan commentators said this tragedy was a clear sign that the Almighty wanted the bear gardens closed down. Oh yes, and the theatres. And all the inns, alehouses and taverns.

Yet again, the Puritan screams of protest fell on deaf ears, which is hardly surprising when you learn that posts such as 'Master of the Queen's Game in Paris Garden' and 'Master, Guider and Ruler of our Beares and Apes' were official court offices.

In 1596 Paul Hentzner, a German lawyer who travelled through England, visited a theatre where bulls and bears 'are fastened behind, and then worried by the great English bulldogs'. Five or six men would then whip a chained, blind bear without mercy, and the bear 'defends himself with all his force and skill, throwing down all who come within his reach, and are not active enough to get out of it; on which occasions he frequently tears the whips out of their hands, and breaks them . . .' Having built his tale to this peak of righteous disgust, he then goes on to describe how the crowd were constantly smoking tobacco, and gives us a rundown of the fruits, nuts, ale and wine that were on sale.

Torturing animals was also a long-standing inn-yard tradition, remembered today in pub names like the Dog and Duck, the Fox and Hounds and the Fighting Cock, with a depiction of the latter also forming the logo of Courage Beers. There was a Dog and Duck in Lambeth Road in Southwark, an alehouse of ill repute, which stood next to an area of open ground with several ponds. The pub got its name from the main entertainment offered: sending out packs of hounds to attack the ducks on the pond.

Samuel Pepys talks of going to the bear garden to see a prizefight, and finding the house full. So instead, he goes to an alehouse 'into the pit, where the beares are baited' to see a different fight.

It was also common for such events to happen in the theatres themselves. In 1613 Henslowe built the Hope theatre on the site of one of the old Bear Gardens. The contract for the building of the Hope, which still survives, calls for a 'Playhouse fit and convenient in all things, both for players to play in and for the game of Bears and Bulls to be baited in the same.' The Globe was notable for being the only theatre devoted purely to plays.

And when people got bored of bears or bulls – or perhaps when these proved too expensive to get – the pit fights became ever more fantastical. When Shakespeare took his plays to theatres like the Rose, which he frequently did, programming meetings presented some difficult choices:

'OK, so we need to draw up the schedule for the next couple of weeks. What have we got?'

'My bear might have recovered by then. I mean, now he's had his other eye torn out he might get shorter odds, but . . .'

'Boring. What else?'

'Um, I've written a new play.'

'Have you, Will? That's great! The last one went down really well. I reckon you might have a knack for this, you know. What's the new one about?'

'It's basically boy meets girl, and—'

'Boring! This audience doesn't want RomCom! It wants blood, guts and gore!'

'Yes, I know that, which is why this is boy meets girl – with a twist. It starts with a massive fight, then boy meets girl, then there are a couple more fights, a bit of sex, and then both boy and girl die horribly at the end.'

'Interesting. Go on.'

'The twist is, boy and girl belong to two rival, feuding families, so no one on either side wants them to get together. But then, when they die, the tragedy prompts the two families to bury the hatchet. So it's kind of like an action play, but it's got a message about how true love is greater even than death. I'm calling it *Romeo and Juliet*. I'm actually quite pleased with it.'

'I love it!'

'Me too!'

'Yeah, it sounds good. We could get it on by next week. Or . . .'

'Or what?'

'Or, I'm just thinking. Go with me on this one, right? You know how last Wednesday we had that monkey torn apart by a pack of hunting dogs, and everyone took bets on how long the monkey would last?'

'Did you see his little face when his arm got ripped off? That was brilliant!'

'Yes, on that occasion he certainly had just cause to exclaim "ooh-ooh, ah-ah!"'

'Well what if, right – I'm blue-skying, here, just trying to push ye envelope, yeah? What if . . . we made things a little more interesting?'

'How?'

'What if we tie a monkey to a horse's back, and *then* see how long it lasts against a pack of dogs?'

'Gadzooks, Ned, that's a brilliant idea! Sorry Will, old friend, I mean, you're pretty good, but you can't argue with genius like that. Maybe next month, eh? Or when we've run out of monkeys. This is the kind of thing that will have Bankside theatre remembered for years to come, you mark my words.'

This programming meeting is of course my invention. But I'm sorry to tell you the monkey on the horse's back isn't. One handbill from the time read:

> Tomorrow being Thursday shall be seen at the Bear-garden on the Bankside a great match played by the gamesters of Essex who hath challenged all comers whatsoever to play five dogs at the single bear for £5 and also to weary a bull dead at the stake; and for your better content shall have pleasant sport with the horse and ape and whipping of the blind bear.

The fierceness of the rivalry between these various 'entertainments' is also true. In 1591, Elizabeth's Privy Council issued an order forbidding plays to be acted on a Thursday, because this day was reserved for 'bear baiting and such pastimes'. The Lord Mayor then publicly complained that 'in some places the players do use to recite their plays to the great destruction of the game of bear-baiting and other such like pastimes, which are maintained for her Majesty's pleasure.'

And in this case 'her Majesty's pleasure' was no euphemism: on 26 May 1599, Queen Elizabeth treated the French ambassador to a day's bull- and bear-baiting at Paris Gardens, clearly enjoying the 'favourite holiday pastime of her London subjects'.

Seventy years later bull and bear baiting were still going strong. Samuel Pepys thought it 'a very rude and nasty pleasure', but it was one he frequently attended, sometimes taking his wife along. But there was a growing disquiet about the sport, which John Evelyn captured when he visited Bankside in 1670:

> to the bear garden, where there was cock-fighting, dog-fighting, bear and bull-baiting, all these butcherly sports, or barbarous cruelties. The bulls did exceedingly well, but the Irish wolfe-dog exceeded, which was a tall grey hound, a stately creature indeed, who beat a cruel mastiff. One of the bulls tossed a dog full into a lady's lap, as she sat in one of the boxes at a considerable height from the arena. Two poor dogs were killed, and so all ended with the ape on horseback, and I, most weary of the rude and dirty pastime, which I had not seen, I think, in twenty year before.

The fashion for bear- and bull-baiting was on the wane, and the final bear pit was pulled down a few years later – although the 'pleasant pastime' wouldn't actually be banned until 1835.

But none of these rival entertainments would go on to be as widely celebrated as the players of Bankside. So the 64,000-groat question is, obviously, did Shakespeare ever visit the George? If we dare to allow ourselves to speculate further – did he perform there?

There's no documentary evidence that he did, but that's hardly surprising given that there are scarcely any written records of Shakespeare's life at all, and those that do exist tend to be dry legal documents – court cases being pretty much the only things that were carefully noted down. But if we want to make hunches about Shakespeare and Southwark inns, the plays are a good place to start.

As is so often the case, the White Hart gets all the kudos with Shakespeare. *The Second Part of King Henry VI* gives a

dramatization of Jack Cade's Kentish revolt of 1450, in which
Shakespeare demonizes Cade, the rebel against the establishment (with the Lord Chamberlain's patronage, Shakespeare
was part of that establishment). We know the White Hart was
built by this time, and Shakespeare decided to use it as Cade's
base of operations when he mounts his invasion of London
via the Bridge. In Act IV, Scene viii, Cade is directing his
assault from the inn when he is visited by the Duke of
Buckingham and Lord Clifford. These representatives of the
King come to parley and offer pardon to any rebels who will
put down their arms and return home. Cade urges his men to
pay no heed:

> What, Buckingham and Clifford, are ye so brave? And
> you, base peasants, do ye believe him? will you needs
> be hanged with your pardons about your necks? Hath
> my sword therefore broke through London Gates, that
> you should leave me at the White Hart in Southwark?

His men change their minds with this speech – and then
change them again with every speech that follows ('Was ever
feather so lightly blown to and fro as this multitude?' wonders
Cade), before finally agreeing to disperse, after which Cade
flees the inn.

Shakespeare does mention another inn called the 'Saint
George' in *King John*, which is set before the Reformation,
when our George Inn would still have been canonized. The
tricky bit is that the play is also set before St George was
officially declared England's patron saint, but we can put that
down to Shakespeare's prioritizing of poetic licence over hard
fact for his Elizabethan audience. In the play, Philip the
Bastard, John's older brother's illegitimate son, is at the King's
side when both he and the King of France appeal to the
citizens of Angiers to swear loyalty to them. The citizens say
they are loyal to the true King of England – whichever one of
the two speech-making monarchs at the gates that happens to

be. Philip builds himself up into a patriotic fervour, during which he says:

> Saint George, that swing'd the dragon, and e'er since
> Sits on his horse back at mine hostess' door,
> Teach us some fence!

This has been interpreted by many as a reference to an inn – 'mine hostess' – and an inn sign, a device that allows for a play of words on 'swing'. Of course, there were scores of inns called the George or St George in England at the time the play was written. But Shakespeare wrote this play at some point in the mid-1590s – when he was probably living in Southwark. It's therefore highly likely that he was at least thinking of our George Inn when he wrote the lines.

Beyond this fleeting association, in the absence of any written record we can make certain assumptions. For example, even though we have no record of him doing so, it is a fact that William Shakespeare ate, drank, pissed, shat, farted, laughed, joked, flirted, had sex, felt happy, felt sad, did something irresponsible, got upset and cried, albeit probably not all in the same day. We know this to be true because all human beings do these things, and we know that Shakespeare was a human being (some of the wilder conspiracy theories aside).

Obviously, the more specific we become, the less certain we can be. Did Shakespeare eat fish, for example? Well, we know he was in London towards the end of Elizabeth's reign, and we know people at that time ate fish on Fridays and Saturdays. So barring a piscine allergy, we can be pretty certain that Shakespeare ate fish on a Friday.

Did he drink beer? I'd stake my life on it. Pretty much everyone drank beer at the time because it was safer to drink than water. We have mentions of him visiting taverns with friends such as Edward Alleyn and Ben Jonson. Beer, inns and taverns feature all through his work. It would therefore be far harder to argue the case that he didn't drink beer than that he did. The Anchor in Bankside makes a strong claim to be the place where Shakespeare rested between performances at the Globe, which was very close by. Circumstantially it has a very strong case, but there's no more evidence than there is for the George.

So what about the George Inn?

Well, Shakespeare lived in Southwark when John Stow listed the George as one of his famous 'eight fair inns for the receipt of travellers', so he certainly knew it. Beyond this, it becomes more speculative. Maybe he preferred a different tavern, but there's a very high probability that he drank there at least occasionally. I can't prove that he did – no one can, just as no one can prove he did not. On this point, I can't better what H.E. Popham wrote in 1927, when he was considering exactly the same question in relation to the claim that Shakespeare drank in the Anchor: 'When Shakespeare in person was at the Globe Theatre hard by in Park Street, he probably came here. He should have come here. He must have come here. Let us say, definitely and finally, that he did.'

But did Shakespeare perform plays at the George? Much as it pains me to say so, probably not. Many writers have invoked the same spirit as Popham over the years and simply asserted that he did – Oh, come on, he *must* have! For the sake of the story, surely he did! But Shakespeare's Company, the Lord Chamberlain's Men, are on record as having used the Cross Keys Inn in Gracechurch Street for a while. From 1576 they had the theatre in Shoreditch, and would have been located there when Shakespeare first moved to London. We have record of him acting in Southwark theatres, some of which were established when he moved across the river, and from 1599 he had the Globe. If he ever did perform inn-yard theatre in Southwark, it certainly wouldn't have been a regular occurrence.

Happily though, one thing we can say with absolute certainty is that Shakespeare's plays have been performed in the George Inn yard, even if the Bard himself was long gone by the time they were. In the 1920s, local theatrical groups began performing plays in the old inn-yard tradition every Shakespeare Day (23 April) in what was, by then, London's last remaining galleried inn. These productions were so celebrated they were covered every year with large picture stories in national newspapers including *The Times* and the *Daily Telegraph*, where large photographs – still rare at the time – would sit in the pictorial section alongside images from the FA Cup Final. These performances carried on through the war before eventually petering out sometime in the 1970s, by which time plans were afoot to rebuild the Globe.

These inn-yard performances played a vital role in keeping alive the memories of Bankside's theatrical tradition. Almost three hundred years after giving birth to theatre as we know it, the old coaching inn came to the Bard's rescue once again.

CHAPTER EIGHT: FURTHER UNSAVOURY ACTIVITIES IN INNS AND ALEHOUSES, AND HOW THESE PLACES WERE BURN'D BY ALMIGHTY GOD'S FURY (IF YOU BELIEVE IN THAT SORT OF THING)

Sir W. Batten not knowing how to remove his wine, did dig a pit in the garden, and laid it in there; and I took the opportunity of laying all the papers of my office that I could not otherwise dispose of. And in the evening Sir W. Pen and I did dig another, and put our wine in it; and my Parmazan cheese, as well as my wine and some other things.

(Samuel Pepys gets his priorities right during the Great Fire of London, 1666)

IT'S QUITE AMAZING, given how wonderfully intelligent human beings are, and considering their indomitable strength of will and unquenchable drive for survival, that for centuries millions of them chose to live together in streets of densely packed wooden buildings that stretched out over the streets, almost meeting on their upper storeys, topped with thatched roofs, and lit and heated by candles and open fires. You'd think that after the first few times an entire city burned to the ground someone might have rethought this principle, but no. Even the Romans had had a fire brigade in Southwark, and there is evidence of many a conflagration throughout the centuries. Fire had destroyed London Bridge and much of Borough High Street in 1212 or 1213. It had destroyed the Globe in 1613. And in the late seventeenth century, fire would change the shape of London, and the George, for ever.

The portent was the Great Fire of London in 1666. It started not far from the northern end of London Bridge, and consumed most of the City over several days. That time, Southwark was only spared by a gap in the buildings on the Bridge itself, created, ironically, by an earlier fire. Samuel Pepys watched the climax of the Great Fire from the safety of an alehouse on Bankside[1]:

> When we could endure no more upon the water; we to a little ale-house on the Bankside, over against the Three Cranes, and there staid till it was dark almost, and saw the fire grow; and, as it grew darker, appeared more and more, and in corners and upon steeples, and between churches and houses, as far as we could see up the hill of the City, in a most horrid malicious bloody flame, not like the fine flame of an ordinary fire . . . The churches, houses, and all on fire and flaming at once; and a horrid noise the flames made, and the cracking of houses at their ruins.

Southwark's turn came ten years later.

In an ancient equivalent of those movie trailers that give the whole plot away so you needn't bother going to see the film itself, a pamphlet titled *A True Narrative of the Great and*

---

1. Today the Anchor on Bankside claims to be that alehouse, even though Pepys makes no mention of it by name and there were countless alehouses on Bankside at that time. It also claims to have been much favoured by Christopher Marlowe, Dr Johnson and Charles Dickens. Today it's a tourist trap with its own fish-and-chip shop inside and an unspeakably ugly Premier Inn growing out of its backside, for which it acts as the restaurant. If ever you're looking for an example of how not to keep an historic inn, there's nowhere better.

Terrible Fire in Southwark, 1676, wherein those eminent innes the Queens Head, the Talbot, the George, the White Hart, the King's Head and the Green Dragon, together with the prison of the counter, the meal-market and about Five hundred Dwelling-Houses (as moderately computed) were burn'd down, blown up, and wholly destroyed tells us most of what we need to know about the Great Southwark Fire of 1676. It's only seven pages long, and this title takes up one whole page.

As we've seen, because the inns stretched back and broadened out from the street, they could be adjacent along the length of their main inn-yards while still having shops between them on the street front. Between the George and the Tabard (which was known by now as the Talbot) stood an oil shop owned by a Mr Welsh. In the early morning of Friday 26 May, Welsh and his family were away, leaving just one son and a servant maid at home. Some passers-by noticed a flickering light in a cellar window, looked in and saw that, 'through simple carelessness', a fire had started. If they had been able to either get into the house or rouse the people within it, they were sure they could have put it out without a problem. But when they could do neither, the fire reached 'a great store of Oil and combustible matter' and the building went up. Several fire engines were called – water pumps basically – but as the fire was fuelled by oil it 'became rather the more raging for those petty sprinklings which did but increase, instead of mitigating its fury'. The flames raged across the street, 'and now the Fiery Torrent like an invading Conqueror spread its flaming Colours through the Air on both sides of the way, and carried ruin and desolation along with it at its pleasure.'

The fire burned from 4 a.m. until 7 p.m., destroying all the buildings so concisely listed in the pamphlet's title. Charles II, who seemed to have an obsessive interest in fire fighting, turned up to personally oversee the battle against the blaze. He and the other fire fighters had learned hard lessons from the Great Fire of London ten years before, when a reluctance to blow up buildings to create a break had allowed the fire to spread where it wanted. They weren't about to make that mistake again. The problem this time was that they were so enthusiastic about blowing things up, twenty people were killed by various explosions before they had a chance to get out of the way. The fire was less damaging to property than the Great Fire of London – but that fire had, to the best of anyone's knowledge, only killed five people.

Conspiracy theories soon abounded. Catholic-bashing remained a popular sport in England, and the flames had hardly been damped down before the Reverend John Ward was claiming 'Grover and his Irish ruffians burnt Southwark, and had 1,000 pounds for their pains ... Gifford, a Jesuit, had the management of the fire.' But our conscientious chronicler above dismissed such speculation, 'all grounded in no knowledge or proof, but the mere results of their active and suspicious Imaginations'.

Either way the George Inn, along with most of the High Street and the rest of Stow's fair inns, was razed to the ground. Southwark, and the George, had to be rebuilt from the ground up, and the great Inns of Chaucer's time were lost forever.

This was particularly bad luck for the George, which had already been rebuilt after a fire six years earlier. In 1670, an eyewitness account claims that a Frenchman had entered the George Inn and asked for 'six cans' of beer. When the tapster disappeared to the cellar to draw these beers, the man disappeared down the inn-yard towards the rope and hop sheds. He returned and quickly drank his beer with his companions, but by the time he was making to leave, the inn was in flames. The fire was, like the bigger one six years later, asserted to be arson caused by the French (who were, of course, Catholics) and this theory was allowed to grow by the fact that none of the mysterious Frenchmen (if indeed they were – Frenchmen were very rare in London at the time) were ever apprehended.

As the current landlord, it was Mark Weyland's responsibility to rebuild the inn after the fire. He did so in 1670, and as compensation for his efforts he was granted a forty-year extension to his lease and a reduction in the rent from £150 to £80 a year.

In 1676 Weyland faced an even greater task. Legally, once again he was responsible for the cost and effort of rebuilding. But the devastation this time was so complete, the owners of the George and Southwark's other inns were reluctant to pay for rebuilding. A special Court of Judicature was established to deal with the claims on each of Southwark's great inns, most of which were eventually rebuilt. Mary Duffield of the King's Arms had her annual rent reduced from £66 to £8 and her lease extended to forty-eight years in return for rebuilding the inn. Weyland appeared before the court in October 1677, and John Sayer was ordered to compensate him by a further nineteen-year extension on the lease, plus a reduction of the annual rent to £50 a year and one sugarloaf. Why a sugarloaf, I have no idea and have been unable to find out. Maybe the judge was feeling whimsical that day. Weyland finished the rebuilding before the end of that year, and the oldest parts of the current George Inn date back to this time.

The fire seems to have changed the emphasis in Southwark, almost to have chastened it somehow and forced it to become responsible. Through the eighteenth and nineteenth centuries its history becomes more industrial and commercial, and the stews, bear gardens, bullrings and playhouses fade from view.

But there was one exception, a final huzzah that would squeeze all that old debauchery into an intensive two-week period every year for almost a century after the flames. And it had the George and Southwark's other inns at its very heart.

*The insanity of Southwark Fair, as seen by William Hogarth
in 1733. In the bottom left-hand corner there's a skeleton of
a cat walking on its hind legs wearing a sword and hat.
This is troubling.*

Southwark Fair was first established in 1462 by a charter
of Edward IV, the original idea for what was then 'Our Lady
Fair' being a sedate celebration of the Nativity of the Virgin
Mary and an extension of the usual market, running from 7
to 9 September, solemnly opened by the mayor.

'Sedate.'

'Solemn.'

In Southwark.

Two hundred years later, Southwark Fair was still going,
mainly because it had mutated into a drunken carnival freak
show lasting a fortnight. In 1660, John Evelyn saw:

monkeys and asses dance and do other feats of activity on the rope, they were gallantly clad a la mode, went upright, saluted the company, bowing and pulling off their hats; they saluted one another with as good a grace as if instructed by a dancing master. They turned heels over head with a basket having eggs in it, without breaking any; also with lighted candles in their hands and on their heads, without extinguishing them . . . I also saw an Italian wench dance and perform all the tricks on the tight rope to admiration; all the court went to see her. Likewise, here was a man who took up a piece of cannon of about 400lb weight, with the hair of his head only.

Hogarth painted Southwark Fair in 1733, when the madness was at its peak. It's a famous work, and features in just about every book on Southwark history you will find. As with all Hogarth's great engravings, you really need a large and very high definition print to truly appreciate the level of detail he portrays. Your eye is immediately drawn to the main figures: strolling musicians, tightrope walkers, a man on a rope slide from a church tower, some minstrels on a platform or gallery outside an inn that is collapsing under their weight, and the revellers below who are about to be crushed to death. But look more carefully, and it gets truly weird: there's a tiny couple no more than eight inches high, and something that looks like a skeleton of a cat standing on its hind legs wearing a hat and sword.

Inevitably, the Fair brought out Southwark's rascalry in all its shades. Legal records from 1683 show that Mary Dorril was arrested at the Fair and was whipped for stealing a gown. Thomas Bostock was transported for the heinous crime of stealing a handkerchief. His defence was that he had been at Southwark Fair, and was therefore very drunk. The Fair had a reputation. When Samuel Pepys went in 1668, he left all his valuables with his faithful waterman, Bland, in the Bear-at-the-Bridgefoot, for fear of having his pockets cut. He watched puppet shows and saw the famous tightrope walker Jacob Hall, and afterwards was 'carried to a tavern' where music played and he got fantastically drunk with Hall himself, before another waterman, Payne, delivered him safely back to the Bear.

Obviously the Fair was great business for the inns, taverns and alehouses, and they played a full part in it. Their role as purveyors of drink was essential, not least in upsetting the by-now-routine Puritan gawkers. In 1619 Robert Harris complained, 'Go but to the town's end, where a fair is kept, and there [drunkards] lie as if some [battle] field has been fought.'

The Catherine Wheel – rare in that it was built on the west side of the High Street, quite a way down from the George near the Marshalsea and King's Bench Prisons – was another famous inn for carriers and waggoners, and would have been in the thick of the Fair. One year it boasted:

> The Gyant or the miracle of nature aged nineteen last
> June 1684 born in Ireland and of prodigious bigness
> that his like hath not been seen since the memory of
> man . . . He now reached 10 feet and a half.

Inn-yard theatre also made a welcome return when the Fair was on, even when theatre had become a royal and fashionable feature of the West End.[2] In 1728 John Gay's *Beggar's Opera* was performed at the Tabard during Southwark Fair. A little earlier, back in 1715, a pamphlet was published called *The Siege of Troy, a dramatic performance, presented in Mrs Mynn's great booth, in the Queens-Arms Yard near the Marshalsea Gate in Southwark, during the Time of the Fair, Containing a description of all*

2. The players moved north of the river in the seventeenth century. John Taylor's watermen were deprived of a huge chunk of their income, and harsh words were spoken.

the Scenes, Machines, and Movements, with the whole Decoration of the PLAY, and Particulars of the Entertainment. In the small amount of room left after this title had been printed, the author, one Elkanah Settle, boasted that the production was 'in no ways Inferior even to any Opera yet seen in any of the Royal Theatres; as Thousands of Living Witnesses, that saw it at its last performance, eight Years Since in Bartholomew Fair, will acknowledge.'

Southwark Fair, also known as Our Lady's Fair and Bartholomew's Fair at various periods of its existence, was suspended in 1630, 1636 and 1637 due to worries about the spread of the Plague, but managed to survive Puritanical zeal, finally being abolished in 1762 or 1763.

By now the great inns generally had firmly established themselves as centres of entertainment. Mr Powell, a cele-brated fire-eater, toured the inns of Wiltshire, charcoal-grilling beef and mutton on his tongue. Mr Nevill's noted mechanical model of woollen manufacture, containing 5,000 moving parts, could be seen at inns throughout the 1750s for a shilling a head.

Innkeepers expanded from hosting players and singers to become fairly serious theatrical promoters themselves, staging concerts, lectures, plays, recitals and exhibitions. The yards may have become too congested with coaches and waggons by this point to stage regular performances outside, but inns remained the only buildings to feature large assembly rooms. The Wells Musical Society gave concerts at the Mitre through-out the 1820s; Oates and Fielding set up a theatre booth at the George in Smithfield in 1730, and in 1760 Mr Yates of the Theatre Royal, Drury Lane, put on a performance at the Greyhound in Smithfield. Each of these last two were for Bartholomew Fair, which also took place in Smithfield, so it's likely that, at this time, similar things were happening at the George in Southwark too.

Despite inns being frequented largely by the newly leisured

gentry, some of the old traditions remained. Cockfighting was very popular among the upper classes, as were prizefights featuring trials of skill at the quarterstaff, sword and dagger and backsword.

Southwark was also well furnished for anyone who wanted to come and see fights for pleasure. Not all butchers were as diligent and well behaved as the Harvards, and many of them took an active role in organized fights. Their big rivals were, of course, the watermen. You had to be well built and fit to contend with the capricious currents of the mighty Thames, and this meant you could earn a little extra income from prizefights in Southwark pubs. In May 1667 Samuel Pepys went to see a prizefight in a Southwark alehouse between a Bankside waterman and a Borough butcher:

> upon a stool [I] did see them fight, which they did very furiously, a butcher and a waterman. The former had the better all along, till by-and-by the latter dropped his sword out of his hand, and the butcher, whether or not seeing his sword dropped I know not, but did give him a cut over the wrist, so as he was disabled to fight any longer. But Lord! to see in a minute how the whole stage was full of watermen to defend their fellow, though most blamed him: and there they all fell to it, knocking and cutting down many on each side. It was pleasant to see; but that I stood in the pit and feared that in the tumult I might get hurt. At last the battle broke up, and so I away.

In 1699 the diarist John Evelyn enjoyed a fight between a soldier and a 'country fellow', noting that the countryman 'did soundly beat the soldier, and cut him over the head'.

Fighting of one form or another was an everyday occurrence in the Borough, and the George was no exception. In 1662 one Edward King, citizen and draper of London, had leased some rooms at the George. For some reason he was thrown out by the innkeeper, William Streape, following which he got into a brawl with Streape, his wife Elizabeth, and several other people. By the time the matter came to court two weeks later, King, who was seemingly unable to take 'Leave it, he's not worth it!' for an answer, was still attempting to re-enter the George, and was being 'kept out by armed force to the great disturbance of the King's peace'.[3] Once again, agonizingly, the outcome of the court case is not recorded.

With so many lawbreakers in Southwark, at least there was somewhere convenient to put them. London dumped much of its prison population over the river, along with everything else it didn't want. We've already talked about the sanctuary of the liberties, but if you're already on the run for stealing, mugging or fraud, it can be a struggle to mend your ways. The Bishop of Winchester had so many criminals within his jurisdiction, which was known as the Liberty of the Clink, that he was forced to build a prison to cope with them. As well as robbers and thieves, the Bishop's prison was soon full of brothel keepers, pimps, prostitutes and punters (except, presumably, those that were working in the brothels he made money from). The prison soon became known simply as 'the Clink', and this would of course go on to become slang for prisons in general, giving a second, ironic meaning to the phrase 'The Liberty of the Clink'.

Following the decline of Southwark's stews and its regulatory absorption into the City, the Clink became more infamous as a debtor's prison. As a major economic centre full of speculators, investors and other types of gamblers, one of the most common crimes in London was defaulting on debt. It was standard practice for anyone who had fallen into debt

---

3. I love that whole language about 'keeping the King's peace'. In the context of this story, it sounds like the ruckus being created by King (the draper) in the street outside the George was so loud that *the* King was being kept awake at night by the racket, several miles away across the river.

to be sent here until they could pay it back, or Parliament declared them bankrupt.

There were so many debtors that Southwark needed more prisons to house them. The two most famous were built in the fourteenth century – the King's Bench in 1368, and the Marshalsea in 1373. Bizarrely, some debtors were able to live in luxury. It was normal to move your family in with you, and if you had the right connections you could furnish your quarters quite luxuriously. Inmates were allowed out of prison to work and earn wages to repay their debts. But if the people to whom you owed money were paying for you to live in style, the impetus to get back on your feet and make good just wasn't quite there somehow. Some inmates even sub-let part of their accommodation. Prisons were let out to private contractors – which I'm sure must always seem like a good idea at the time – who used them to make as much money as possible, in a system that was entirely corrupt.

If you didn't have money and contacts, however, conditions within the prisons were truly appalling: unsanitary and overcrowded, and many of the inmates were often close to starvation. When prisons were run purely for profit, there was no point spending money on those not able to earn the warders a few shillings in return.

The Marshalsea was particularly notorious, and was attacked by both Wat Tyler's rebels in 1381 and Jack Cade in 1450. By the time of the Gordon Riots in 1780 (of which more later) freeing the prisoners and torching the place was almost a sentimental tradition.

One of the Marshalsea's more significant later residents was John Dickens, imprisoned briefly for debt in 1824. Dickens wasn't a bad man, simply one who spent beyond his means. He moved his entire family into the prison with him, all except his son Charles, who was sent into service at a blacking factory near Blackfriars Bridge and had lodgings near the Marshalsea in Lant Street. Charles Dickens was only

12, and the experience of visiting his family in prison would affect him for the rest of his life. He based the character of Mr Micawber on his father, and based *Little Dorrit* on the experience of a debt-ridden family living in the Marshalsea, writing that the prison had stood on the high street 'many years before, and it remained there some years afterwards; but it is gone now, and the world is none the worse without it'.

The George will be forever linked to the Marshalsea not just because Dickens knew both well, but also on account of the actions of one man who sounds like a perfect Dickensian creation, but was in fact wonderfully real.

Edward Digby was the eldest grandson of William, Fifth Baron Digby in the Irish peerage. Edward inherited the title in 1752 when his grandfather, having outlived Edward's father, finally died at the age of 91. By this time the younger Edward Digby was already Member of Parliament for Malmesbury, but as his peerage was Irish he was ineligible to sit in the House of Lords, and was therefore allowed to keep his seat in Parliament.

Digby had a reputation as something of a dandy, and was always decked out in the very latest fashions. But at Christmas and Easter, something strange happened: he would become morose, and would leave the house wearing a distinctly shabby blue coat.

Digby's uncle, Henry Fox, First Baron Holland, was a prominent figure in the Whig government, and this furtive dressing-down behaviour raised suspicions in the mind of the older statesman. So he began to have Edward followed on these occasions by Major Vaughan and another friend.

The two men followed Digby into Southwark. At St George's fields, near the Marshalsea Prison, they lost sight of him. Stumped, they approached the prison and asked a guard if a man matching Digby's description had been past.

'Yes, masters,' the warder replied, 'but he is not a man, he is an angel, for he comes here twice a year, sometimes oftener, and sets a number of prisoners free. And he not only does this, but he gives them sufficient to support themselves and their families till they can find employment. This is one of his extraordinary visits. He has but a few to take out today. We none of us know him by any other marks but by his humanity and his blue coat.'

The friends then caught up with Digby and asked what he was up to. By way of answer, he took his inquisitors to the George Inn, where he hosted dinner with the prisoners he had just freed, just as he did every Christmas and Easter.

In my mind's eye these are the actions of a distinguished, middle-aged, noble gentleman. So it was something of a shock to discover that Edward, Sixth Lord Digby, died in 1757 after complications arising from a gallstone operation. He was just 27 years old, having been elected as an MP aged 21.

Having been rebuilt after the fire, the George Inn that Digby knew was the building we know today. He would have taken his guests to the coffee room, or more likely one of the private dining rooms scattered around the inn's three wings. The inns were bigger and more powerful than ever, but Southwark had lost its stews (though prostitution was still rife). It had lost its bear pits and bull-fighting rings, and the great Elizabethan theatres had been pulled down when the Puritans finally formed a government under Cromwell after the Civil War. The Puritans lost their influence when the decidedly libertine Charles II ascended the throne and rebooted the English monarchy in 1660. Despite or maybe because of the new King's more relaxed views on pleasure, Southwark no longer seemed to be such a focus of dark desires.

And though it had nearly destroyed it, this rebuild proved to be a symbolic as well as a practical change in the fortunes of the George. From this point on, its recorded history becomes clearer and more detailed, and tells the story of a place focused on serious business rather than idle pleasure. In a broader sense, accounts of hedonistic Southwark fade away, to be replaced by sober histories of the rise of industry and its attendant poverty and hardship. Within years, the coaching era would begin in earnest. And it was in this era – which may not be as much fun but is certainly more glamorous – that the George hit its prime.

CHAPTER NINE: OUR INN ENJOYS A GOLDEN AGE OF ROMANCE, HIGHWAYMEN, COMPLICATED TIMETABLES AND SORE POSTERIORS

The yard presented none of that bustle and activity which are the visual characteristics of a large coach inn. Three or four lumbering wagons, each with a pile of goods beneath its ample canopy, about the height of the second-floor of an ordinary house, were stowed away beneath a lofty roof which extended out over one end of the yard ... A double tier of bedroom galleries, with old clumsy balustrades, ran round two sides of the straggling area, and a double row of bells to correspond, sheltered from the weather by a little sloping roof, hung over the door leading to the bar and the coffeeroom. Two or three gigs or chaise-carts were wheeled up under different little sheds or penthouses; only the occasional heavy tread of a carthorse, or a rattling of chain at the further end of the yard, announced to anybody who cared about the matter that the stable lay in that direction. When we add that a few boys in smock-frocks were lying asleep on heavy packages, wool-packs and other articles on heaps of straw, we have described as fully as need be the general appearance of the yard of the 'White Hart Inn', High Street, Borough.

(Charles Dickens, *The Pickwick Papers*, 1837)

IN THE RICH GUMBO of English folklore, race memory, myth and national iconography, there are few more powerful images than the brightly painted stagecoach speeding through a turnpike.

The very names of the stagecoaches were designed to inspire this reverence: the *Defiance*, the *High Flyer*, the *Royal Charlotte* and the *Brighton Comet* left you in no doubt that this wasn't just transport – a word so boring that anyone showing the slightest interest in it is seen as, at best, a pretty serious geek – this was something sexy, something brave, high class and, above all, *fast*. In a world of greys, earth tones and perpetual fog, their bright red, yellow, gold and green seared the eyeballs. The trumpets announcing their arrival made your ears ring. And if there was anything in the country more dashing, more glamorous, more seductive than the stage-coaches themselves, it was the dark, mysterious highwaymen who daringly ordered them to stand and deliver, before relieving an excited lady's panting bosom of its jewellery and thundering off into the night.

Think about Christmas card designs: one of the most common images is the stagecoach speeding through a snowy landscape under a bright moon, men in frock coats and women with scarves and mufflers huddled down against the cold while the driver spurs on the horses with a long whip.

And what do you find inside a traditional country pub? Horse brasses on the walls, and framed pictures of stage-coaches. The better ones even have some accommodation in 'the converted stables' out back.

These scattered decorations and references still permeate our culture almost two centuries after the rapid decline of the stagecoach era. They're central to the costume dramas we can't get enough of. They're remembered in place names, pub names, bus timetables and the specific locations of urban train stations. What's so surprising, given the persistence of this imagery and its appeal in our national consciousness, is that the golden age of the stagecoach was so brief. The stagecoach rose to prominence in the early eighteenth century, hit the start of its true glory days in the 1780s, and was history by the 1840s. But during that brief period, the stagecoach transformed inns like the George, for a time, into arguably the most important businesses in the country. Inns were not just where you got on or off the coach; they facilitated the very functioning of the stagecoach system. And the innkeeper, far more than just a barman or hotelier, became one of the most influential and respected members of the community.

Of course, the George was an established inn for travellers for centuries before the glamorous stagecoaches came along, prospering thanks to a mode of transport that was somewhat less glamorous. I have two books on my desk in front of me now. There's *Stand and Deliver! A History of Highway Robbery*, by David Brandon, with pistols firing on the cover and a blurb from the *Sunday Telegraph* that reads, 'Robbery with glamour . . . extremely entertaining.' And then there's *The Rise and Rise of Road Transport 1700–1990*, by Theo Barker and Dorian Gerhold, part of a series called 'Studies in Economic and Social History', featuring a black-and-white shot of a waggon and horses and another one of an Esso fuel tanker. There aren't any newspaper quotes on that one. It's not exactly a like-for-like comparison – a popular history of highwaymen and an economic- and social-history textbook – but you couldn't make a fair comparison even if you wanted to, because waggons have never been given the popular treatment. There's no 1970s TV series starring Richard O'Sullivan as a dashing young waggoner carrying hops from Kent to Southwark, no country pub homage to the gently plodding, thick-wheeled, two mile-per-hour goods waggon.

But to many inns, the waggon trade was far more important than the stagecoach. Both were central to the George, but waggons played a much bigger role in its history. If you're ever tempted to dig deeper into the world of transport history, once you get past the understandable defensiveness of the poor road-transport historians (railways and even canals have had far more written about them) you discover that road ruled until about 1800. Both the Industrial Revolution and the rise of the mercantile class were facilitated by waggons and pack-horse trains, and they were also responsible for allowing London to become a financial centre, and for local economies around the country to flourish. Even when canals and coastal sea transport were common, waggons could do things these other modes couldn't. Water transport suited low-value, high-bulk items, but roads were more secure, faster and more flexible than water, and therefore suited the high-value, low-bulk items of the Industrial Revolution much better.

So before we get to the pistols, paintwork and heaving bosoms, I need to attempt something I don't think anyone has done before: I need to try to make the history of road transport sound interesting to a mainstream, balanced audience.

If you'd like to gain an insight into what roads were like for most of English history, it's really easy to do. Just grab yourself a ticket to the Glastonbury Festival, and hope it's a rainy one. Wait until the first few thousand people have gone in. Then load a wooden trailer with your tent, bong, cases of Stella, funny hats and ironic flag, and try to drag it along the main track.

You see, no one talks about this much, but it rains in this country. Quite a lot. And when it rains, it gets muddy. You forget, when we have tarmacked roads and cobbled streets, just how quickly packed earth can turn to mud, and how completely and utterly debilitating that can be. During the English Civil War, Cromwell's forces captured 800 horses, not in battle but 'sticking in the mire'. During winter, the roads were often impassable. During summer, the only safe passage was down the middle. Even in London, things were pretty poor. In 1736 Lord Hervey wrote, 'The road between this place and London is grown so infamously bad that we live here in the same solitude as we would do if cast on a rock in the middle of the ocean.' And he was only in Kensington.

There were the Roman roads of course, but after seven hundred years even they were poorly surfaced. Most roads were little more than rough tracks created over the years by goods carriers and cattle drovers. In Chaucer's time, travelling with anything more sophisticated than a train of packhorses was impossible. There's evidence of two-wheeled carriages soon after, and by the fifteenth century huge, lumbering waggons were common. These coexisted with packhorse trains, each remaining a common sight right until the railway age.

Waggons had to be built with wheels that were about ten inches wide, the theory being that the weight of them would press down the mud rather than churn it up, on the same principle as a modern steamroller. They were typically pulled by eight to ten horses, which were expensive to keep, because they ate a lot. In 1882 Stanley Harris, a nostalgic chronicler of the old coaching and waggoning days, provided a colourful description of the typical waggoner:

> A picturesque object was the old stage-waggon on the road with bells on the harness of the leading horses, and frequently the driver in his smock frock riding by the side on a small pony, with his long waggoner's whip, and a horn lantern hanging up in front to be lighted up when night came on.

The waggons were built with high sides, and piled high with heavy items such as coal or hops, but also lighter components for local industries such as wool, leather, animal skins for gloves, and exotic imports from the major ports of London, Bristol and Liverpool, with spices, tea and tobacco being distributed to local markets. Although it is surely not typical, Thomas Russell & Co operated a waggoning business between London and the West Country, carrying woollen cloth and sailcloth to London, and an eclectic mix back. Between 1816 and 1821 their cargo included springs for a coachmaker, bundles of trees, caged birds, hunting dogs, numerous pianos, gunpowder, feathers for wigmakers and upholsterers, a crate of marble urgently needed by a stonecutter, a panorama of the Battle of Waterloo, and a corpse.

Waggons often travelled in company, both for safety and for mutual assistance if they got stuck, which they invariably did several times a day. A bit of support also came in handy when, travelling down the middle of the road, you met someone coming the other way. Disputes over right of way on muddy roads were often settled by fists.

Many waggons carried passengers too – if they didn't exceed four miles an hour (and they very rarely did) they could take passengers without incurring excise duty. But given that the average speed of a waggon was closer to two miles per hour rather than four – slower than travelling on horseback or even on foot – there was a certain social stigma attached to sitting on the back of a lumbering waggon. Writing in 1617, Fynes Moryson claimed that 'none but women, people of inferior condition, Flemings, their wives and servants, used to travel in this sort', rather like Margaret Thatcher's supposed opinion of the people on the 149 bus.

An early waggon would manage somewhere between fifteen and twenty miles per day, meaning popular routes such as London to Exeter or Manchester would take the best part of a week. But despite it being so slow and difficult, the demand for the waggoning trade saw a dramatic increase as England urbanized. In 1650 just 9 per cent of the population lived in towns and cities. This figure shot up to 13 per cent by the end of the century, doubled over the next hundred years and stood at 40 per cent by 1850. The amount of stuff – and people – that needed to travel between towns and cities rocketed. And as the waggoning trade grew, so did the need for inns to cater to it. Soon there were inns in every town –

and at regular intervals between them, corresponding to the average distance a waggon could travel in one day. By 1577 – the first year we have an estimate of numbers – there were 3,600 inns across England, lining every major road, with clusters every ten to fifteen miles. For example, St Albans – the first night's stage out of London – had twenty-seven inns, and there would be smaller stops along the way, providing midday refreshment and a change of horses.

One of the major routes serviced by the George was the old Roman road to Dover. In 1577, William Harrison broke down that route into its main stages, albeit coming the other way. It seems like a fairly gentle stroll, but some went faster than others, and no one stopped at every stage. But it shows how travellers would have considered the journey, and where the major pauses were:

From Dover to Canterbury	12 miles
Canterbury to Sittingbourne	12 miles
Sittingbourne to Rochester	8 miles
Rochester to Gravesend	5 miles
Gravesend to Dartford	6 miles
Dartford to London	12 miles

Harrison is one of our most important sources on what the inns along these routes were like. He was a huge fan, telling us 'they abound in beer, ale, and wine, and some of them are so large that they are able to lodge two or three hundred persons and their horses at ease.'

It seems like the business of inn-keeping became incredibly competitive. According to Harrison, inns tried to outdo each other with the entertainment they offered, the quality of the linen (and how frequently it was changed), the beds and the 'beauty of the rooms', and the 'costliness of plate, strength of drink, variety of wines, or well-using of horses'. They even vied with each other over 'the gorgeousness of their very signs at their doors', spending as much as £30 or £40 (£6,000 today) on one sign out of vanity, pride in their wealth, and 'also to procure good guests'.

As soon as you arrived at an inn, the ostler would take your horse, walk it up and down as it cooled, and feed it. Appointed by the trustworthy landlord, these servants, 'in hope of extraordinary reward, will deal very diligently after outward appearance in this their calling'. Meanwhile another servant would show you to your quarters, light the fire and pull off your riding boots. The host would ask if you would like to eat at the common table – a good deal at somewhere between fourpence and sixpence. But if you were a gentleman, this was not the done thing – you'd eat in your room, and have free rein of the kitchen, choosing whatever and as much as you wanted. The host would hover, making sure everything was OK, and would regard it an honour if you asked him to sit down and join you.

Fynes Moryson was another fan. A student at Peterhouse College, Cambridge, Moryson, as students seemingly always have done, spent quite a bit of time travelling and then telling everyone about it. But rather than taking a gap year in India[1] he spent a great deal of time in England's coaching inns. Writing in 1617, he supported Harrison's observation that, though he might now have linen instead of flea-infested straw, some of the social customs of Chaucer's time still remained:

> The world does not afford such inns as England hath, either for good, cheap entertainments for guests in search of pleasure, or for humble entertainments for passengers, even in poor villages. These could eat at the host's table and pay accordingly. The gentleman might have his chamber, and eat alone or with friends. In the case of eating together, they might have plenty

---

1. In those days the journey to India took around six months, so a gap year would have afforded a day or two on a Calcutta dockside before coming straight home again.

of good meat, choice fish, and no more than sixpence
per man.

And anyone who has ever been annoyed by one of those
notices in every hotel room that says the establishment can
take no responsibility for anything that happens to your
possessions while you're their guest would love Harrison's
observation that if anyone lost anything while staying at the
inn, 'the host is bound by a general custom to restore the
damage, so that there is no greater security anywhere for
travellers than in the greatest inns of England.'

But the main appeal of the inn for Harrison – which is
extraordinary when we consider the spirit of the modern pub
– was that the nature of inns was not like that of hostelries
in other countries, where the host 'doth challenge a lordly
authority over his guests'. Here in England, 'every man may
use his inn as his own house, and have for his money how
great or little variety of victuals, and what other service himself
shall think expedient to call for'. That basic democracy of the
pub, the feeling that you are at a home from home, seems
somehow to have always been in the DNA of the English pub
even in its highest form, the inn.

That's not to say these places were completely idyllic.
Country inns were seen as somewhat more disreputable than
those in the towns, dens of gaming, dicing, dancing and
brawling, and havens for highwaymen and pickpockets. Even
Harrison voices a concern that, after giving such a solicitous
welcome, if an ostler or tapster felt badly treated they might
cheat horses of food or collude with robbers. He describes a
scam, which has the whiff of apocrypha about it, in which the
ostler weighs a man's purse while helping him down from his
horse, and tips off robbers which guests are worth following.

Even in a reputable city inn like the George, where the
innkeeper was a respectable figure beyond reproach, you had
to keep your wits about you. In September 1741 the *London*

Evening Post reported that 'a couple of sharpers' overheard a gentleman giving instructions to a porter carrying a portmanteau to the George. They 'nimbly stept before him, and one of them impersonating the Master, and another an Attendant of the Inn, without much Difficulty got him to deliver it to them, and mov'd off with it'.

'Of all in England,' claimed Harrison, 'there are no worse inns than in London.' He didn't elaborate on what was so wrong with inns in the capital, and he did say they were still better than any hostelry abroad. Perhaps they weren't quaint and welcoming enough for him: urban inns tended to be larger than their country cousins, so the giants of Southwark really were the behemoths of the traditional inn, perhaps lacking the romantic personal touch.

London was, of course, the epicentre of the waggoning trade, and the inns were vital to making it work. Inns didn't just offer board and lodging; they provided warehousing and office space, received goods on behalf of carriers on commission, linked up businessmen, and generally provided the nodes around which the entire waggoning business functioned. This required a huge degree of trust between waggoner and innkeeper, a symbiotic relationship that underpinned the entire British economy as it entered the Industrial Revolution. And we get one of our most valuable insights into how this all worked from our old friend John Taylor, the celebrated 'Water Poet' (well, not that celebrated).

In a poor man's version of the old adage about monkeys, typewriters and the works of Shakespeare,[2] a man who wrote

---

2. The idea that the complete works of Shakespeare *were* in fact written by an infinite number of monkeys with an infinite number of typewriters has not yet been presented as a serious theory by the anti-Stratfordian camp. I think this is a bit of a shame. Not least because there is a more cogent rationale and a greater degree of thinking behind it than many of the more popular conspiracy theories.

as much as Taylor was at some point, I suppose, bound to write a detailed account of all the major waggoning routes, their timetables and the London inns that catered for them. Taylor's *Carrier's Cosmographie*, published in 1637, is a twisted masterpiece, a triumph of meticulous detail framed by personal anguish. You could argue – so I will – that it invented trainspotting two hundred years before there were any trains. In the fashion of the time, the full title of the work was a page long in itself.[3] And before we get on to the relevance of it to our story, the opening pages are an enthralling and extraordinary litany of cantankerous bitching and wretched self-pity.

After finally getting the title out of the way, Taylor reveals that as usual, this work was paid for by subscription. Who would subscribe to a list of inns and a timetable of the waggons that use them? Early trainspotters in ruffs, hosiery and very sensible waterproof cloaks, clearly. Taylor thanks those who have paid him for this and previous works, and then lets rip at those who said they would pay and have not, suggesting that doing him out of a few pennies should be regarded as a crime worthy of capital punishment:

> I am well pleased to leave them to the hangman's tuition, as being past any other man's mending, for I would have them to know, that I am sensible of the too much loss that I do suffer by their pride or cousenage;

3. *THE Carriers Cosmographie. Or A Brief Relation, of The Innes, Ordinaries, Hosteries, and other lodgings in, and neere London, where the Carriers, Waggons, Footeposts and Higglers, doe usually come, from any parts, townes, shires and countries, of the Kingdomes of England, Principality of Wales, as also from the Kingdomes of Scotland and Ireland. With nomination of what daies of the weeke they doe come to London, and on what daies they returne, whereby all sorts of people may finde direction how to receiue, or send, goods or letters, unto such places as their occasions may require. As also, Where the Ships, Hoighs, Barkes, Tiltboats, Barges and wherries, do usually attend to Carry Passengers, and Goods to the coast Townes of England, Scotland, Ireland, or the Netherlands; and where the Barges and Boats are ordinarily to bee had that goe up the River of Thames westward from London. By John Taylor.*

their number being so many and my charge so great,
which I paid for paper and printing of these books, that
the base dealing of those sharks is insupportable.

He's not one to complain, but he asks us to feel sorry for him.
Not only is he out of pocket on paper and printing, he also
risked his life to write this timetable of road traffic. Why, the
experience was so traumatic, he was usually forced to get over
it by having a pint in a nearby inn:

> But the tedious toil that I had in this collection, and
> the harsh and unsavoury answers that I was fain to
> take patiently, from Hostlers, Carriers, and Porters,
> may move any man that thinks himself mortal to pity
> me. In some places, I was suspected for a projector; or
> one that had devised some trick to bring the Carriers
> under some new taxation; and sometimes I was held
> to have been a Man-taker, a Sergeant, or Bailiff to
> arrest or attach men's goods or beasts. Indeed I was
> scarce taken for an honest man amongst the most of
> them. All which suppositions I was enforced oftentimes
> to wash away with two or three jugs of beer, at most
> of the Inns I came to.

Elsewhere, he reveals that this may not have been such a
hardship after all, saying that in Southwark, 'The Taverners
are of my own finding and the vintners my own friends . . . it
is "Welcome gentlemen; a crust, and what wine will you
drink?"' But he still thinks we should be grateful for all his
hard work. He clearly hasn't enjoyed the task, and he signs
off in high dudgeon:

> Reader if thou beest pleased, I am satisfied; if thou
> beest contented, I am paid; if thou beest angry, I care
> not for it.

In the pages that follow, Taylor then attempts to give a timetable of the traffic at every major inn in London on a weekly

basis. And joking aside, we should be grateful that he did so, because he shows us how important the waggon trade was, and how, even then, it ran to specific, set timetables.

Ironically, there is a kind of poetry to it. He lists ten inns in Southwark catering for the carriers of Kent, Surrey and Sussex: the Falcon, the Catherine Wheel, the Greyhound, The Spur, The Queen's Head, the White Hart, the King's Head, the Green Dragon, the 'Tabard or Talbot', and the George: 'To the George in Southwark comes every Thursday the carriers from Guildford, Wonnersh, Godhurst and Chiddington in Surrey, also thither out of Sussex on the same days of the week the carriers of Battle, Sandwich and Hastings.'

Inns clustered around the major arteries into and out of the city, and their highest concentrations mirror the locations of mainline train stations today. Inns didn't quite share the influential societal functions of the City's taverns and alehouses, so they have been relatively overlooked historically. But they were vital in so many ways, important out of all proportion to their numbers.[4]

The inn serving a particular route naturally became the link between major towns on that route and the capital itself. Newspapers such as the *London Evening Post* went out of inns to provincial towns where their contents were eagerly devoured, and the drivers, waggoners and, later, coachmen along the route were vital sources of gossip. It worked the other way round too. The innkeeper and his staff would develop a good knowledge of, and relationships with, regular travellers coming into town via his establishment. When someone seeking their

---

4. The distinctions between inn, tavern and alehouse were getting blurred by now, but even as late as the nineteenth century an important legal distinction was maintained. One legal document attempted to clarify the issue, but somehow made something very straightforward sound quite complicated when it said: 'Every inn is not an alehouse, nor every alehouse an inn; but if an inn uses common selling of ale, it is then also an alehouse; and if an alehouse lodges and entertains travellers, it is also an inn.'

fortune arrived in London, the inn at the end of their route would be their temporary home while they presented letters of introduction and sought positions of employment. Later, after they had moved out into their own accommodation, the inn was their source of news from home, or even the destination of parcels of food, clothing and money from Mum back in the village.

Of course, as London grew, all this activity became more intense. Southwark was the hub for everyone and everything from Kent, Sussex, Surrey and the channel ports, and the bottleneck over London's only bridge grew worse. In 1722 tolls were introduced on the Bridge for the first time, in a desperate bid to regulate the chaotic traffic. Another innovation was that men were employed to force carts and waggons crossing the bridge to keep left, introducing one of the rules for which British roads remain famous. Commerce demanded progress, and the 1750s saw the houses on London Bridge demolished. The Great South Gate went in 1760.[5] The bridge had lost the features that had made it a tourist attraction for more than five hundred years, but it began to work much better at what it was always supposed to be in the first place – a bridge.

And by this time, the waggons had been joined by their more glamorous cousins.

Eventually, something had to be done about the condition of the roads. In 1696 the first Turnpike Act was passed, allowing the Justices of Reigate, Surrey, to erect a turnpike (a spiked barrier that could block the road) and charge tolls to pass through it. Money could be borrowed against future

---

5. The Coat of Arms of George II, which had adorned the gatehouse, was taken down and moved to a house in Axe Street, later Newcomen Street, a little further down Borough High Street from the George. The building later became a pub and the coat of arms was amended to that of George III. But the pub, the King's Arms, still displays it today.

income from these tolls and used to improve sections of the main road. Over the next fifty years, a patchwork of turnpike trusts grew to cover the whole country, each working on its own section of road. As well as improving the surface, width and drainage of the road, embankments, cuttings and bridges were built to level the gradient and make it easier for horses to pull vehicles. Although the canals being built around the same period were more efficient at transporting heavy goods like coal and steel on horse-drawn barges, the improved roads remained the best way of carrying lighter, more manufactured goods – as well as the growing number of people on the move.

The Coaching Age is generally held to have begun in 1657, when the Chester stage was inaugurated. The 'stage' part comes from the practicality that forced the coaches, just like the waggons, to undertake a journey in several stages, stopping in inns along the way for refreshment, fresh horses, and somewhere to sleep.

The earliest coaches declared their intentions right from the start. Decorated with golden cloth, embellished with wonderful carvings and ostrich plumes, from the outside they looked magnificent and regal. The experience of being inside one was anything but. Once, giving an audience to the French Ambassador, Elizabeth I complained she was suffering aching pains in consequence of having been knocked about in a coach that had been driven a little too fast a few days before.

Our old friend John Taylor was no fan. Despite the acute discomfort, coaches were stealing business from the watermen by offering a mode of transport up and down the banks of the Thames that may have been less comfortable, but was undeniably more glamorous and involved far less foul language. Taylor claimed that the coach 'had driven many honest families out of their houses, many knights to beggars, corporations to poverty, almsdeeds to misdeeds, hospitality to extortion, plenty to famine, humility to pride, compassion to oppression, and all earthly goodness almost to utter confusion', which may have been overstating things just a tad. But the Water Poet wasn't done yet: he emphasized his point in the only way he could:

> Carroaches, coaches, jades, and Flanders mares,
> Doe rob us of our shares, our wares, our fares:
> Against the ground we stand and knock our heeles,
> Whilest all our profits run away on wheels. . .

While we remember stagecoaches as fast and sleek, the reality of travelling in them remained a less-than-pleasant experience. In 1757 a 'new flying machine hung on steel springs' was advertised departing from the Golden Cross and calling at the George on its way to Brighton. Steel springs were a huge improvement on the springless, leather-hung vehicles that preceded them, and the average speed of coaches shot up to an unprecedented seven miles per hour.

Journey times could also be shortened by 'flying'. A flying coach or waggon was one that treated inns more like Formula One pit-stops than places of welcome and good cheer. Horses could do about ten miles at full gallop, so every ten miles or so those in a hurry would pull in at a pre-arranged inn, take quick refreshment while the horses were changed, and continue on their way, occasionally changing drivers as well so they could continue without pause. Flying waggons would continue day and night, but with poor lighting this was simply too risky for coaches, and they would have to pull in for at least some of the night. Nevertheless, journey times fell dramatically – the journey from London to York took four days in 1754, but a combination of flying coaches, selective horse breeding and better roads reduced this to a mere thirty-six and a half hours just twenty years later. The fares for such journeys were of course expensive – time has been money ever since the Industrial Revolution – and if you wanted to economize, you could go in one of the 'slow coaches' instead.

As journey times became quicker for the rich, and cheaper for the less well off, inns such as the George grew ever more popular and important.

This increase in speed set the scene for the arrival of the most romantic of all the images from the coaching era. Since its formation in 1635, the Royal Mail had prided itself on its mounted postboys providing the fastest link between two points. These riders would travel between 'posts', removing letters from one area and taking them to the next, where they would deliver some and hand the others to the next rider. What this system gained in speed it lacked in safety, and solitary riders carrying important parcels were magnets for robbers on lonely roads. By the late eighteenth century, people were starting to point out that the stagecoaches were actually doing the journey quicker. The Post Office was a monopoly, and it was an offence to send mail any other way. Nevertheless, so many people were using illegal private contractors that it was estimated the Post Office was losing £80,000 a year. In 1784 John Palmer, the Postmaster-General, proposed to the Prime Minister, our clock-hating friend Pitt the Younger, that the mail should travel by stagecoach. Unlike conventional waggons and coaches, mail coaches would have the turnpikes thrown open for them upon their approach, announced by the blast of a trumpet before the thundering of the hooves. They didn't have to stop for the comfort of passengers, only for the change of horses. That first year, one mail stage completed the 120-mile journey from London to Bristol in just seventeen hours.

Speed was seductive, and coachmen and their passengers became obsessed with breaking records. Soon the average coaching speed could be eased up to ten miles per hour, which was achieved by compromising on safety, and fierce competition that went as far as trying to run rivals off the road. In *Coaching Days and Coaching Ways*, Tristram Outram tells of great rivalries between coachmen who achieved individual notoriety, such as John Marchant of the *Manchester Telegraph* and Bob Snow of the *Defiance*:

> these men drove opposition coaches, in which speed was
> the one thing looked to, associated in a mild degree with
> a more or less reasonable amount of safety. And they
> drove furiously to beat the record – careful of nothing
> so long as the coach kept on its wheels, demi-gods whose
> steel nerves their passengers implicitly trusted, well
> knowing as they did that if those steel nerves had for
> an instant failed their owners, the whole stock and lot
> would have gone to the Deuce in an instant.

Even with sprung suspensions, insane speeds like this meant comfort was thrown out of the window and left in the coaches' dusty wake. Washington Irving, the 'first man of American letters', who travelled by coach a great deal in the early nineteenth century, remarked, 'There is certain relief in change, even though it be from bad to worse! As I have often found in travelling in a stagecoach, that it is often a comfort to shift one's position, and be bruised in a new place.'

A classified ad in *The Times* from 1833 boasted of a new coach, the *Paragon*, that left the George Inn for Hastings. The way the coach's owners sought to sell it to prospective customers tacitly reveals what the primary concerns of regular coach travellers must have been:

> The PARAGON, on a new principle for safety, and
> almost impossible to be overturned, and so constructed
> as to go with much more ease for the passengers ...
> the distance performed in 8 hours without racing.

This is what concerned you if you were one of the lucky ones who could actually afford to travel *inside* the coach. An earlier ad in *The Times* from January 1825 offered a 'reduced fare to Hastings' on the *Royal William*, a 'new and elegant' coach that started at the Blue Boar in Holborn, called at Piccadilly and Gracechurch Street, and finally at the George in Southwark before heading out of London. You could ride inside the coach for fifteen shillings, or outside it for ten. People would sit on the back or even the roof of coaches, which would have made for an interesting and eventful journey. Apart from sheer discomfort, eyes streaming in the wind and extremities going numb in the winter cold, this was a journey that could occasionally put you in mortal danger.

We get a great illustration of such dangers from arguably the most informative and certainly the most entertaining chronicler of the coaching age: Dickens. Bertram Matz, whose brilliant work as a chronicler of the George in the early twentieth century was an extension of his role as editor of *The Dickensian*, argued in 1921 that 'no writer has done more than Dickens to reflect the glory of that era, and the glamour and comfort of the old inns of England which in those days were the havens for the road to every traveller.' And within this great canon of work, *The Pickwick Papers* was 'perhaps, the most accurate picture extant of the old coaching era and all that was corollary to it'.

Even though it does not make specific mention of the George Inn, *The Pickwick Papers* is intimately linked with the George and is one of the best books you can read if you want to become familiar with the everyday reality of coach travel. Dickens's characters tear around the country so often on their adventures that pretty much any key scene happens in a coaching inn, and these scenes are linked together by coach journeys. Dickens isn't trying to provide a document of the coaching era, but he ends up doing so anyway. It's telling that many historians of the coaching era date its peak as 1828 – *Pickwick*, written in 1836, is set in 1827.

In one early scene, Mr Pickwick is rescued from a public beating by his cab driver[6] by the intervention of Mr Alfred

6. Cab – from 'cabriolet' – which was, like the post-chaise, another light, two-seater horse-drawn carriage.

Jingle, 'a rather tall thin young man in a green coat' who speaks in short, clipped sentences. He joins them on their journey from the Golden Cross Inn in Charing Cross to Rochester, aboard the famous *Commodore*. The Golden Cross had a low archway, and as the *Commodore* pulls under it, Mr Jingle warns the party:

> 'Heads, heads – take care of your heads!' cried the loquacious stranger, as they came out under the low archway, which in those days formed the entrance to the coach-yard. 'Terrible place – dangerous work – other day – five children – mother – tall lady, eating sandwiches – forgot the arch – crash – knock – children look round – mother's head off – sandwich in her hand – no mouth to put it in – head of a family off – shocking, shocking!

Of course, these practical risks were not the only dangers to coach travellers once they were out on the open road.

The highwayman is surrounded by an air of sexy mystique, a sense of widespread acceptance, and even approval, in some quarters, that would remain unmatched in terms of our perceptions of murderous thugs until the rise of the Krays. In reality highwaymen, like pirates, were no different from other robbers who used violence or the threat of it, but it's hard to imagine the New Romantics of the early 1980s writing number-one hits about muggers coshing people over the head in dark alleys, or Disney creating a theme-park ride based around housebreakers. Highwaymen have long been assumed to have an altruistic motive. The first, probably fictitious, highwayman was Robin Hood, who if he did exist probably never redistributed his booty among the poor. Highwaymen, according to historian David Brandon, had nothing but contempt for the poorest in society. Having come from similar backgrounds themselves, they believed in getting on your bike – or horse, rather – and using your initiative and enterprise to make something of yourself, and god damn anyone who was too weak or lazy to do so.

Such thieves had always lurked hidden along English roads. But they came to prominence in the eighteenth century when the rapid development of the economy saw a huge increase in people and wealth moving along those roads, and judicial, penal and policing systems could not develop quickly enough to keep up.

The scale and rapidity of these economic changes also help explain why the highwayman became seen as, rather than a common criminal, a dashing hero or, at worst, a likeable rogue. Highway robbery was seen by some as the manifestation of a dark side to the huge wealth creation we've been talking about in this chapter so far. Dick Turpin owes his lasting fame to William Harrison Ainsworth, a novelist who pretty much invented most of the details of Turpin's life in *Rookwood*, an 1824 account of the highwayman's adventures in which Turpin is compared to Lord Nelson and admired for his 'passionate love of enterprise'. But Turpin was already being mythologized in his own lifetime. He may not have given to the poor, but he sure as hell took from the rich, and that was admired by those being chained to machines to create the wealth they then saw the rich as hoarding. In a country increasingly obsessed by property, Turpin was striking back.

Whether they were feared or admired, Turpin and his like were a constant subject of conversation in the parlours and coffee rooms of great inns, and their spectre lived on long after Turpin's demise. In 1778, Boswell wrote of Samuel Johnson's concerns over encountering a highwayman, and what the consequences of that encounter might be, after announcing his intention to travel down to Streatham:

> Taylor: 'You'll be robbed if you do; or you must shoot a highwayman. Now I would rather be robbed than do that; I would not shoot a highwayman.'

Johnson: 'But I would rather shoot him in the instant when he is attempting to rob me, than afterwards swear against him at the Old-Bailey, to take away his life, after he has robbed me. I am surer I am in the right in the once case than in the other. I may be mistaken as to the man, when I swear: I cannot be mistaken, if I shoot him in the act. Besides, we feel less reluctance to take away a man's life, when we are heated by the injury, than to do it at a distance of time by an oath, after we have cooled.'

Boswell: 'So, Sir, you would rather act from the motive of private passion, than that of publick advantage.'

Johnson: 'Nay, Sir, when I shoot the highwayman I act from both.'

Boswell: 'Very well, very well. There is no catching him.'

Innkeepers were sometimes accused of fencing highwaymen's loot. This may well be true, but in the greatest inns it would be surprising if the innkeepers had the time or even the financial need to do so.

As road traffic grew, so did the stature and premises of the inns. And as it was the newly rich mercantile class who were staying in the rooms, practical needs such as increased privacy were matched by big investment in improving standards of aesthetics and taste. The New Inn at Exeter had a fine plastered ceiling in its Appollo Room [sic] created in 1689. The Antelope in Sherbourne had fine wainscoting and the majority of its 'twelve handsome bed chambers [were] hung with good papers'. When Daniel Defoe undertook his 'Tour though the whole island of Great Britain' between 1725 and 1727, he found his lodgings at Northampton 'more like a palace than an inn'.

As the only buildings with large assembly rooms and accommodating yards, inns also became the nerve centres of urban life, as notable within their communities as churches. The sheer scale of business that happened within the precincts of the inn was dizzying. Inns provided places of business for those without business premises of their own, including medical men, truss makers, tailors and tutors. Auctioneering developed as an occupation in the mid-eighteenth century, and the inn provided a safe place for sale rooms, distributing catalogues and exhibiting goods before sale, with no fixed costs or overheads, located at the nodes of the country's great transport system. And if you did fancy something a little more permanent, as they grew into huge complexes they had room to spare in the buildings around the yard. When the George burned down in 1670, it had an ironmonger, a flax warehouse and a wholesale grocer in its grounds.

For much of the eighteenth century, inns also remained the only places with assembly rooms, dining rooms and ballrooms. The public sphere was growing, and as well as established entertainments such as balls and banquets, wrestling, and badger- and bear-baiting, inns became the venues for public administration, hosting events such as quarter sessions and electoral hearings. The growing number of clubs, societies and trades unions used inns as their venues – only in the last years of the eighteenth century did purpose-built assembly rooms begin to appear to rival multi-purpose inns. And all this activity made the inn even more of a landmark, even more important as your first point of contact when arriving in the city. By the 1780s, a top-end inn was insured for the same value as a cotton mill.

This all meant the position of the Hanoverian innkeeper required a great deal of organizational flair. Many innkeepers went on to become aldermen and mayors and were among the richest men in town. When Defoe got to Doncaster, he found that the landlord at the Post House was also mayor of the town as well as postmaster, that he kept a pack of hounds, and 'was company for the best gentlemen in town or in the neighbourhood, and lived as great as any gentleman ordinarily did'.

Nowhere was the inn more important than London, and the grandeur of the stately Southwark giants immortalized by John Stow outshone all others.

In 1720, John Strype substantially updated and added to Stow's original survey of London. He described the George as a fine inn that had built up 'a large and considerable trade', although it lagged behind the Talbot and the White Hart. Both of these were by this time accommodating stagecoaches as well as waggons, but the George was still not a coaching inn.

Not many inns could accommodate both coaches and waggons – less than a third of those in London had the facilities for both. Whereas waggons could be backed in or out of the inn-yard, coaches needed to be turned around inside the yard. The George's inn-yard was long and wide enough to accommodate both backing-in and turning, but it had still not entered the coaching business.

Perhaps this was because the innkeeper was tired. Up to this point the George was still being run by Mary Weyland, the widow of the unfortunate Mark who'd had to rebuild the inn from the ground twice in a decade. She'd arrived in the inn married to Thomas Underwood, the licensee in 1668. When Mark Weyland died in 1692 she took over direct running of the inn, was still there in 1706, and probably later. The next recorded innkeeper was William Golding in 1733. I'd hazard that it's unlikely that Mary ran the pub until this date, but as she entered her dotage, it seems likely that launching into a new line of business – when the existing duties of the innkeeper were already so extensive – was beyond her.

Nevertheless, the inn was perfect for stagecoaches. Not only did the yard have the right dimensions, having been remodelled after the fire, it had the coffee room for more upmarket guests and the more basic taproom where the lower classes could be fed and watered out of sight. William Golding made the obvious, belated move, and the first stagecoach left the George in 1732 for Brighton, arriving at the Old Ship Inn in what was then Brighthelmstone.[7]

From here the business grew quickly. By the latter half of the century, a typical day's coaching schedule began with the 7 a.m. Maidstone post coach, which covered the thirty-four and a half miles to its destination in just four hours. The Cranbrook and Tenterden coaches left at the same time, and forty-five minutes later the *Union* left for its ten-hour journey to Dover via Margate, along with the Canterbury post coach. Scarcely a half-hour passed without another departure or two, all the way through the daylight hours.

Dickens gives us a typically evocative description of what it was like to catch one of those early morning coaches. Years before he featured the Golden Cross in *Pickwick*, he gave a factual account of what it was like to board an early morning service from the same inn when he was working as a young journalist. Once West London's busiest coaching inn, the Golden Cross stood on the exact spot now occupied by Nelson's Column. This tall, gothic building was demolished in 1827 to make way for the building of Trafalgar Square, which may have influenced Dickens's decision to set *Pickwick* in this year, so that he could include the vanished inn in his story. Dickens's first published book was *Sketches by Boz*, a collection of short pieces that were 'illustrative of every-day life and every-day people'. In the chapter on 'Early Coaches', he describes an incident surely based on his own experiences:

7. Fittingly, this establishment still also survives, as the Barcelo Old Ship Hotel.

It strikes 5.15 as you trudge down Waterloo Place on your way to the 'Golden Cross', and you discover for the first time that you were called an hour too early. You have no time to go back, and there is no place open to go into, and you have therefore no recourse but to go forward. You arrive at the office ... You wander into the booking office ... There stands the identical book-keeper in the same position, as if he had not moved since you saw him yesterday. He informs you that the coach is up the yard, and will be brought round in about 15 minutes ... You retire to the tap-room ... for the purpose of procuring some hot brandy and water, which you do – when the kettle boils, an event which occurs exactly two and a half minutes before the time fixed for the starting of the coach. The first stroke of six peals from St. Martin's Church steeple as you take the first sip of the boiling liquid. You find yourself in the booking office in two seconds, and the tap waiter finds himself much comforted by your brandy and water in about the same period ... The horses are in ... The place which a few minutes ago was so still and quiet is all bustle. 'All right,' sings the guard ... and off we start as briskly as if the morning were all right as well as the coach.

The George was one of eight Southwark inns to accommodate stagecoaches, but it grew to become one of the most important. And it kept up its waggoning business too: of seventy-six carriers operating in London in the early nineteenth century, fourteen used the George.

Classified advertisements and Borough rent books from the eighteenth century attest to the burgeoning importance of the inn and its resident innkeeper. The Parish of St Saviour's in Southwark, like all the others, charged householders and businessmen rates based on the value of their properties or businesses, to raise funds for the relief of the poor of the parish. In June 1748 William Golding was still the innkeeper at the George, and was charged a rate of £7 1s 10d – higher than any other property in the parish.

In 1743 one William Baldwin was advertising a post-chaise operation from the George, offering transport that was 'safe, easy, secure and well secured from the weather, upon as such warning for the post horses, at any hour of the day or night.' The post-chaise was a cheaper, lighter, two- or four-wheeled carriage that offered a link to the main stagecoaches or, for those that could afford it, a private service along the main stages, the eighteenth-century equivalent of a Lear jet. Post-chaise services were created by many innkeepers from around the middle of the eighteenth century, so it seems Baldwin would have been one of the first. Like all coaches, they depended on inns for stabling, provender, repair, and most of all, bookings. This lopsided balance of power applied to all coaching businesses, and shrewd innkeepers formed consortia to buy out coach owners. By 1720 most London-based coaching businesses were owned and run by innkeepers.

Curiously, it seems William Baldwin somehow expanded the other way. In the rate books from 1748 he's paying rates as a resident of the George Inn yard, but after 1755, when William Golding either retired or died, Baldwin takes over as innkeeper at the George. But while this brought a post-chaise service under the auspices of the inn, the George never followed other London inns in focusing solely on the coaching business. It couldn't – when Westminster Bridge was built in 1750 and other bridges soon followed, Southwark remained a vital stopping place for inward and outbound coaches, but was no longer the terminus. It was merely a stopping point on the way to or from inns such as the Golden Cross in Charing Cross, the City or Piccadilly. However, because the heavy, lumbering waggons weren't allowed on the Bridge, the George did remain a terminus for the waggoning trade. Shrewd juggling of both businesses ensured the inn's prosperity.

By 1767 John Sabb had taken over as guv'nor of the George from William Baldwin, who was still paying rates on business premises in the inn-yard and advertising as a hop merchant. Sabb appears as the contact name in a 1775 newspaper advertising the sale of a mansion house in Gravesend. Such ads illustrate the link between the London inn and the route it served – there's always one local name in the town where the sale is taking place, and an innkeeper such as Sabb in London to whom enquiries can be made. In 1778 Thomas Green took over, and his name appears constantly in the classifieds as a trusted person to whom enquiries over sales and auctions can be made, or lost property returned.

We have to return to Dickens for the best possible eyewitness account of what a working Southwark coaching inn looked like. The White Hart gets the credit once again, and provides the setting for one of *Pickwick*'s most pivotal scenes, in a passage that contains the atmospheric description at the beginning of this chapter. It could also serve just as well as a description of the George Inn – so much so that, as we'll see, there has been fierce debate as to whether the George is the inn Dickens was secretly referring to.

There's just one problem with Dickens's legacy though. Over the last two centuries many fans of coaching days and coaching ways have discovered *Pickwick*, and with agonizing predictability, have been inspired to write oversweet, overstuffed accounts of the golden age of coaching that resemble nothing more than a tribute band from a different culture to their idols, phonetically mouthing the sounds without understanding them or being able to play their instruments. It's easy to do: Ah! And here he comes now, the stout jolly yeoman, offering us good cheer and a room for the night. And so we ascend those creaking stairs beneath the ancient eaves and the Boots greets us with 'Cor Blimey, guvnor, as my old dad used to say, it takes three chickens to make a walnut out of a pair of those trousers and no mistake,' and we eat our fine repast and slip between the sheets to the sound of the clattering mail coach going along its brave way into the dark night and . . .

. . . and . . .

Hang on a minute, I just need to go and place my hands in a hot sandwich toaster and repeatedly slam down the lid as hard as I can.

There, that's better.

Fortunately, I have the self-awareness not to try to emulate Dickens's deceptively simple prose. Instead, I'm forced to quote him at length, and I have to close this chapter with the longest quotation of all.

Every single account I've ever read of the George Inn quotes the passage from *Pickwick* that first introduces the White Hart, and the inns of Borough generally. It really is a long quote, but there's not a word I can in conscience leave out:

> There are in London several old inns, once the head-quarters of celebrated coaches in the days when coaches performed their duties in a graver and more solemn manner than they do in these times; but which have now degenerated into little more than the abiding and booking-places of country wagons. The reader would look in vain for any of these ancient hostelries among the Golden Crosses and Bull and Mouths, which rear their stately fronts in the improved streets of London. If he would light upon any of these old places, he must direct his steps to the obscurer quarters of the town; and there in some secluded nooks he will find several, still standing with a kind of gloomy sturdiness, amidst the modern innovations which surround them.
>
> In the Borough especially there still remains some half-dozen old coaching inns, which have preserved their external features unchanged, and which have escaped alike the rage for public improvement, and the encroachments of private speculation. Great, rambling,

George Inn Yard, *1800, painted by J. R. Weguelin in 1885.*
Perhaps this melancholy lady is thinking about the
suspension on the coach she's about to board.

queer, old places they are, with galleries, and passages, and staircases, wide enough and antiquated enough, to furnish materials for a hundred ghost stories, supposing we should ever be reduced to the lamentable necessity for inventing any, and that the world should exist long enough to exhaust the innumerable veracious legends connected with old London Bridge and its adjacent neighbourhood on the Surrey side.

Dickens evokes Borough's inns beautifully, and when we see photos of them from the late nineteenth century we can see that he captured their atmosphere perfectly. But this description, supposedly evoking the very peak of the Golden Age of Coaching, is laced with what we would, a century later, begin to call nostalgia: a wistful, sentimental look back at an age that was, even at the beginning of Charles Dickens's writing career 175 years ago, already beginning to pass.

CHAPTER TEN: CONCERNING DRINK, HOPS AND POLITICS, AND HOW THE GEORGE INN BRINGS THESE ELEMENTS TOGETHER

> This year [1765] was distinguished by his being intro-
> duced into the family of Mr Thrale, one of the
> eminent brewers in England, and Member of Parlia-
> ment for the borough of Southwark. Foreigners are
> not a little amazed when they hear of brewers, distill-
> ers and men in similar departments of trade, held
> forth as persons of considerable consequence. In this
> great commercial country it is natural that a situation
> which produces much wealth should be considered as
> very respectable . . .
>
> (From *The Life of Samuel Johnson*, James Boswell, 1791)

IMAGINE, IF YOU CAN, that French cuisine was based not around wine, but around beer. Imagine if the world's greatest beer styles had originated from France. Top-quality restaurants around the world would have beer sommeliers, and cellars featuring the full array of the world's beer styles. Any Michelin-starred place would have several select vintages of the finest barley wines and Russian Imperial stouts. Classic beer styles such as 'North Africa Pale Ale', developed for troops in the French colonies, would be protected by law, and imitators from outside France would have to call their beers 'African-style pale ales'. The porter and stout brewers of

Bordeaux would be protected by Appellations Contrôlée, and would draw tourists from around the world to the visitors centres where you would be able to trace the history of the style, sample the rich, complex malts that make it so superior to wine, and buy a share of a particular brew.

None of this happened because these great beers were British creations. Instead of North African Pale Ale, the beers for colonial troops were porter and India Pale Ale, products of London and Burton-on-Trent. The vast majority of people in Britain aren't even aware of the global status these brewers once had, or how other countries, now rediscovering these styles and reinterpreting them, have created a global revolution in craft beer. We think stout is Guinness, an Irish invention, and IPA is simply the name of a beer.

The 2012 Olympics aside, we're very funny about celebrating our achievements as a nation. Post-colonial guilt? Post-imperial identity crisis? British self-effacing modesty? Who knows? But nowhere are we so down on ourselves as we are in food and drink. France has more European Protected Designations of Origin (PDOs) for its cheeses than the UK has for everything put together. Even Germany – a country few British people would associate with wonderful food and drink – has many more than we do.

This strikes me every time I visit Southwark. Because Southwark today is a virtual theme park of British history. We've talked about its obsession with horror and gore, but on top of that there's the *Golden Hinde*, and Tate Modern. There's Borough Market of course, which slightly undermines my argument, but that feels very 'now', with little celebration of the fact that the Borough has always been a culinary centre. And then there's Vinopolis, which celebrates the world of wine, a theme park devoted to a drink for which Britain has only a scant reputation. (There are some excellent English wines, but you have to search Vinopolis carefully to find mention of them.)

This hasn't always been the case. A hundred and fifty years ago, Southwark was already a magnet for tourists from around the globe, and they were coming here to see one world-famous attraction that was so immense, it covered the area where Vinopolis now stands, and where Bankside's theatres, bear pits and bullrings stood before that. The only evidence of it today is in a street name – Thrale Street – and a pub – the Anchor. It was celebrated by Charles Dickens in various works, and welcomed Edward VII, Napoleon III, Otto von Bismarck and Giuseppe Garibaldi through its gates.

So how come today virtually no one is aware that the Anchor Brewery was so celebrated, a wonder of its age? Why does Southwark have no tourist attraction telling people of its beery heritage?[1]

The Borough has had many intensive, smelly industries over the centuries, but making beer was the one for which it became world-famous. The George had some great beer on its doorstep. But the relationship between the inn and brewing, drinking and Southwark beer in general goes deeper than that.

Brewing in Southwark is at least as old as its inns and taverns, and the two were inseparable. We know the Tabard had its own brewhouse when it was owned by the Abbot of Hyde in the fourteenth century, and it's likely the George did too at some point. Many Southwark alehouses began life as breweries.

Rendle tells us that Southwark beer always had a strong reputation for being, well . . . strong:

> Our ale was nappy and strong, sleepy and heady, 'headstrong ale' as they called it; 'it kept many a gossip from the kirk', and was the cause of many offenders being presented for punishment by the church wardens,

---

1. There is Brew Wharf, a sort of annex to Vinopolis. But while its *serves* some very nice beers indeed, it doesn't *celebrate* beer, and certainly not Southwark's role in its history.

> whose duty it was in those days to look after the doings
> of their neighbours in church time.

This reputation stretches as far back as Chaucer. The Miller starts the pilgrimage so drunk he can hardly sit straight on his horse. He admits as much when he butts in to tell his tale, blaming the famous Southwark ale:

> 'Now hear me,' said the miller, 'all and some!
> But first I make a protestation round
> That I'm quite drunk, I know it by my sound:
> And therefore, if I slander or mis-say,
> Blame it on ale of Southwark, so I pray . . .

As well as being strong, these beers would have been dark and sweet, and were drunk as a matter of course by a population for whom drinking nasty, polluted water could have been fatal. Down the centuries legal records are littered with people being fined who 'loved best the tavern than the schoppe', and Rendle, who treated many brewery workers in his time as a local physician, claimed that a diet of three gallons of beer a day left them with 'a dreamy muddled look about their eyes, and they had a shambling sort of walk'.

The reputation of Southwark ale had begun to grow in earnest thanks to some of the immigrants to the UK who always found a welcome south of the river. They came from all over the world, but the one group that had a bigger impact than any other were the Flemish Protestants fleeing religious persecution in the lowlands that now form parts of Germany, Belgium and Holland. Many of them were highly skilled artisans, but when they arrived in London, the closed shops of the City's Guilds prevented them from living and working there. So they settled in Southwark, creating thriving trades as tailors, jewellers, sawyers, goldsmiths, dyers, builders, shoemakers and hatmakers. But none were more renowned than the brewers and alehouse keepers.

One descendant of the early arrivals was Nicholas Webly-ing, a tenant paying rent to St Thomas's Hospital. Weblying was contracted in 1578 to supply beer to the hospital, which was then better known as a refuge for the poor than a place for the treatment of the sick. A supply of good, fresh beer was deemed an important part of this duty of care, and hospital records show that the poor were entitled to 'every one, a day, three pyntts of bere for two months, a quart at dinner and a pint at supper, and after that their olde ordinary allowance which is 1 quarte'.

But things didn't quite go to plan – it seems Weblying's beer was 'too strong', and inspired the poor to 'go abroad, especially on Sabothe day, and abuse themselves in the taverns and ale-houses, to the great displeasure of Almighty God, and the misliking of the Governors'. Upsetting both Almighty God *and* the hospital governors was clearly out of the question, so the board ordered that 'no strong beer shall be allowed, and none fetched except a pynte at a tyme, by order of the physician'.

But strong beer was never the only drink served in the George. Early references to inns tend to emphasize the serving of wine to guests, and by the sixteenth century visitors like Sir John Mennis were enjoying sack and sherry, as well as wines such as Canary and Claret. French brandy was also popular, to the extent that when William of Orange came to the throne in 1688 on a wave of anti-Catholic, anti-French sentiment, Dutch gin consumption was actively encouraged at brandy's expense. The plan backfired when gin became so popular and cheap that it caused the worst epidemic of fatal binge drinking in Britain's history. By 1721 gin was being described by magistrates as 'the principal cause of all the vice and debauch-ery committed among the inferior sort of people', and it would take another thirty years of legislation to bring the problem under control. Far from being seen as part of the problem, beer, being more moderate in strength, was advocated as part of the solution.

Daniel Wight was a gin distiller when he bought the newly rebuilt George Inn in 1692, at which time this would have been a respectable and fashionable profession. But the ownership details of the George show that brewing was already more prominent in the Borough. Wight's son, also named Daniel, married Valentina Malyn, daughter of a Southwark brewer. The marriage record reveals that the George was just part of a whole host of different properties in Southwark and Fleet Street, so owning an inn was by now something that signified (and generated) wealth. And one of the trustees who signed the wedding agreement was another brewer, Edmund Halsey of the Anchor Brewery, just across the road from the George.

This most famous of all Southwark's breweries dates back to 1616, when James Monger the Elder built a brewhouse on a site in Deadman's Place, just yards from the Globe Theatre, newly rebuilt after it was destroyed by fire in 1613. When Josiah Child, a London merchant and director of the East India Company, took over the brewery in the same year as the Great Fire of London, it became known as the Anchor in celebration of his nautical connections.

Edmund Halsey was a distant relative of Josiah Child. He joined the brewery as a humble 'broomstick clerk', but rose rapidly to become both a partner in the brewery and Josiah Child's son-in-law.

As a successful businessman, his next move brings us indirectly to another intriguing role for inns such as the George.

For over a century, pretty much every MP for Southwark was a brewer. Halsey felt that Parliament was his calling, and stood for the seat in 1710. He was defeated, but when his opponent died unexpectedly later that year, he stood again. He won the ballot, but his new opponent, Sir George Matthews, contested the result and petitioned the House of Commons, claiming that Halsey had bribed voters – not inconceivable given that many had borrowed money from him in the past – and that the High Bailiff in charge of the election was in Halsey's pocket. The House resolved 'that Edmund Halsey is not duly elected', and furthermore, that the High Bailiff, 'Henry Martin, Esq. be for the said offence taken into custody of the Sergeant at Arms attending this House'. This wasn't the end of Halsey's political career, however. He was finally elected MP for Southwark in May 1722, and again in January 1727.

That Halsey was eventually forgiven and allowed back into the fold is unsurprising when you look at the scale of corruption in elections throughout the eighteenth century. Everyone was at it, and inns like the George played a key role in this seamier side of politics, just as they did in an official capacity. After all, wasn't it perfectly reasonable to suggest that anyone intending to vote meet at an inn before going to do so? It all seems so innocent in the many newspaper ads used to arrange these meetings. On 8 May 1734, the *Daily Courant* featured a notice that anyone living in London who was eligible to vote in the Election of the two Knights of the Shire for the county of Kent, but was unable to get to Maidstone to cast their vote, could send their names to one of a number of inns, including Mr Golding at the George in Southwark, where coaches and saddled horses would be ready for them at 6 a.m. on the day of the election. No mention was made of who was providing these horses or paying for them, or if transport was conditional on voting in a particular way. In 1790, anyone voting in the Livery of London elections who lived in or near Southwark was invited to breakfast with Sir James Sanderson at the George before proceeding to the Guildhall to poll for Alderman Watson – a little more overt, that one.

Other, similar notices were common throughout the eighteenth and early nineteenth centuries. But we have two of our favourite chroniclers of Southwark life to thank for showing us what these meetings were really like.

In 'Canvassing for Votes' (1754–55) William Hogarth depicts Whig and Tory agents outside an inn or tavern, both attempting to bribe a farmer for his vote while drinkers look on. Another piece, the more famous 'An Election Entertainment', is a hilariously grotesque parody of the Last Supper: Whig candidates have organized a supper for supporters in a tavern or inn, while Tories riot outside. Inside, musicians caterwaul away, a potboy pours booze from a small barrel to top up a bowl the size of a small bath, and a man who looks disturbingly like Robbie Coltrane loses his wig. One man looks greenish and ready to chunder, a mountain of discarded oyster shells in front of him, while another reels from a brick thrown through the window by the rioters outside. Everyone is smashed. Hogarth's brilliant depiction of body language and facial expression tells us that this feast has been going on for some time.

In *The Pickwick Papers* eighty years later, Dickens gives a satirical account of an election in the fictional borough of Eatanswill, fought between a Mr Fizkin and Samuel Slumkey. Pickwick and his party are neutral, but out of politeness decide to support their host, who supports Slumkey. Slumkey's agent, Mr Perker, asserts that the contest is a 'spirited' one:

> We have opened all the public-houses in the place, and left our adversary nothing but the beer-shops – masterly stroke of policy that, my dear Sir, eh?' The little man smiled complacently, and took a large pinch of snuff.
>
> 'And what are the probabilities as to the result of the contest?' inquired Mr. Pickwick.
>
> 'Why, doubtful, my dear Sir; rather doubtful as yet,' replied the little man. 'Fizkin's people have got three-and-thirty voters in the lock-up coach-house at the White Hart.'
>
> 'In the coach-house!' said Mr. Pickwick, considerably astonished by this second stroke of policy.

'They keep 'em locked up there till they want 'em,' resumed the little man. 'The effect of that is, you see, to prevent our getting at them; and even if we could, it would be of no use, for they keep them very drunk on purpose. Smart fellow Fizkin's agent – very smart fellow indeed.'

Essentially, each side tries to get as many people as drunk as possible until their votes are cast. Pickwick's servant, Sam Weller also makes a few extra bob 'pumping over independent voters' with the two waiters up at the Peacock. This entails dragging comatose men to the water pump to revive them, for which Sam gets a shilling a head from the election committee of the candidate who takes their votes. Such things are deemed necessary, according to Weller, because at one election gathering in the Town Arms, the opposing candidate bribed the barmaid to 'hocus' the brandy and water of the voters by lacing it with laudanum: 'Blessed if she didn't send 'em all to sleep till twelve hours arter the election was over.'

Brewers, politicians and inns, locked together in a co-dependent relationship to win the favour of voters/customers . . . why can't it still be like the old days?

Given Southwark's reputation for dodgy dealings in general, you have to wonder what Edmund Halsey did that was bad enough to get himself disqualified. Perhaps his only crime was getting caught.

Edmund Halsey died with no male heir, and the brewery came under the control of his nephew, Ralph Thrale. A handsome, industrious man, Ralph found time between being Southwark's MP and serving as both High Sheriff of Surrey and Master of the Brewers' Company, to continue to build the brewery. Upon his death in 1758 *Grand* magazine described him as the greatest brewer in England.

The same couldn't always be said for his son, Henry, a friend of Samuel Johnson's, whose wild experiments to brew beer without malt or hops nearly bankrupted the brewery when it finally came under his control.

Nonetheless, the Thrales became famous for their Intire Porter. Porter was the first industrial beer, the first to be produced on a large scale that made it more economic for inns, taverns and alehouses to buy beer rather than brew it themselves. From the Thrales' time onwards, inns down the High Street such as the George would have bought their beer from the Anchor Brewery.

Porter was dark, rich and satisfying, and was commonly anywhere between 5 per cent and 7 per cent ABV. Modern recreations of the style conjure up hints of chocolate, coffee, caramel and nuts, followed by a dry finish – which we'll come back to shortly. And Porter made the Thrales their fortune. It was very much a drink of the people, and it was most likely the beer of choice for most visitors to the George from the early to mid-eighteenth century.

But Anchor's main claim to fame was its Russian Imperial Stout, a heady export brew beloved in the court of Catherine the Great of Russia. Often inky-black with strong notes of coffee, chocolate, liquorice, port and even tobacco, it's a bold dark bruiser of an ale for which Southwark was once world famous.[2]

If you talk to a beer geek about strong stouts and porters they'll start talking to you about the dark, chocolaty malts that give the beer its colour and body. But for that nice balance and dry finish, these beer styles also required large concentrations of hops. Which was handy, as the Anchor Brewery sat

---

2. The descendant of Anchor's Imperial Russian Stout, Courage Imperial Stout, was finally discontinued in 1993. But the brewery that inherited the Courage brands, Wells & Young's, brewed it again in 2011, and are promising to re-launch it in the UK. It's the perfect beer with which to read this book, but drink it slowly – in the best Southwark tradition, it's heady stuff.

in the hop-trading capital of Britain – a trade in which the George played an important role.

Though hops were introduced to English brewing by Flemish traders,[3] by 1590 English hops had begun to take preference in London brewing. Hops grow best in the temperate climate of southern England, and Kent in particular had long been known as the 'Hop Garden of England'. First they came up by waggon, then by boat around the coast and up the Thames, and finally by rail into London Bridge Station.

The Bridge Foot also made a good place to trade them. The official hop market was over the Bridge, but there was little point trying to take large loads across the Bridge to the brewers in the City. And anyway, following the rise of the Anchor Brewery, Southwark was one of the most important brewing districts in the city. Vast amounts were used locally, and brewers from around the country would come here to buy their hops for onward transport.

In 1710 a duty was placed on hops and the trade became more regulated. As the popularity of porter and stout grew, so did the hop trade, and it centred on Borough, whether the authorities liked it or not. Trade between factors took place officially through exchanges and warehouses, and unofficially in inn yards. John Pleasant, a hop merchant acting for a brewer, and Isaac Beeman, a factor selling hops, both had their offices at the George. Others, whose offices were in the High Street, also used the inn-yard for warehousing. As one writer commented, 'from September to the end of December the sweet smell of hops hung heavy in the yard'.

Maps of London from the eighteenth and nineteenth century show Southwark as little more than an amalgamation of long inns built around their yards, brewery complexes and

---

3. Hops were present in British beer before the Flemings popularized them: but it seems they were just one option in a big mixed bag of flavourings along with plants such as yarrow and bog myrtle.

hop warehouses. On the west side of the High Street, the Anchor Brewery expanded to cover over a dozen acres stretching down from Bankside, obliterating entire streets like Globe Alley, named after the theatre. On the eastern side, in and around the coaching inns, there were as many as twenty-four buildings for the warehousing and sale of hops along a stretch of road less than a fifth of a mile in length – and that's not counting the offices in inn-yards such as the George. Southwark revolved around the making and selling of beer.

But this being Southwark, the business was not without its risks. In 1780, this epicentre of London brewing came close to being destroyed.

That year, Sir George Gordon gathered a large crowd of Protestants at St George's Fields, Southwark, with the intention of marching on Westminster in protest against the new freedoms granted to Catholics in the Catholic Relief Act of 1778. But he seems not to have taken account of where he was. Gather a large crowd in Southwark, and they were going to do as they pleased. Instead of marching on Parliament, they decided to spend a week rioting, killing Catholics and burning down their chapels and houses, and anything else they didn't like. The King's Bench, Marshalsea and Clink prisons were largely destroyed (because you had to, it was tradition – every self-respecting rebel had done so for centuries). The George and other coaching inns escaped the fury of the mob, but not the Anchor Brewery. No one objected to the brewing and selling of beer – quite the opposite – but there were more personal scores to be settled.

Henry Thrale had long been sympathetic to the Catholic cause, and suddenly his vast brewing complex was a target. According to the *Gentleman's Magazine*, the mob came direct from the Marshalsea prison, swelled by released prisoners who carried their chains with them. The Thrales had scarpered, and it was left to John Perkins, the cool, collected Chief Clerk, to save the day. As the mob approached, he spotted the chains

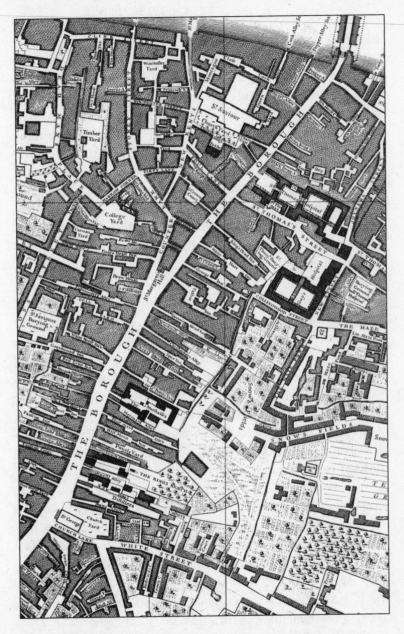

Detail from John Rocque's map of London from 1749. Look closely, and almost every side street turns out to be an inn-yard.

and observed that 'it were a shame that men should be degraded by so heavy a load; and he would furnish them with a horse for that purpose.' This stopped the rioters in their tracks: this is not how it was supposed to happen. According to James Boswell, Perkins then distributed fifty pounds' worth of meat and porter. By the time the troops arrived, the rioters were toasting Perkins and the Anchor Brewery rather than putting it to flame, and they departed cheerfully. Hester Thrale wrote of the 'astonishing Presence of Mind shewed by Perkins in amusing the Mob with Meat & Drink & Huzzaes, till Sir Philip Jennings Clerke could get the Troops'. Those troops were there, heavily fortifying the brewery, when the rioters briefly thought about returning once the beer and meat had run out.

But it was all too much for Henry, who died 'of apoplexy' the following April. Hester sold the brewery to the Scottish-American financier David Barclay (as in Barclay's Bank). Barclay recognized the value of John Perkins, and gave him a share in the equity in return for his agreeing to stay around and run what was now the Barclay Perkins brewery. The deal was worth £135,000 (around £8.5 million in today's money), and led Mrs Thrale's devoted friend Dr Johnson to utter one of his most often-quoted pronouncements: 'We are not here to sell a parcel of boilers and vats, but the potentiality of growing rich beyond the dreams of avarice.'

And he was right – the price soon started to look like a bargain as the brewery's output soared and its premises expanded. There are many references to Barclay's beer in the novels of Charles Dickens, for example: in *The Old Curiosity Shop* Dick Swiveller claimed that there was 'a spell in every drop against the ills of mortality', and in *David Copperfield* Mr Micawber had a job at the brewery in mind when he was 'waiting for something to turn up'.

'Except perhaps the very centres of government and trade,' wrote Dr William Rendle, 'no spot in London might so worthily excite feelings of curiosity and wonder as these few acres.'

In 1850, however, one visitor to the brewery was given a reception that fell somewhat short of traditional British hospitality.

In 1848, political revolution swept through Europe as people started demanding troublesome things like democracy, basic human rights, and freedom from tyranny. If you needed a man to quash such troublesome demands – and the Austro-Hungarian Empire certainly did – you could call the Austrian Marshal Haynau. He murdered rebellious Hungary's top thirteen generals after they had surrendered to him, and brutally put down a revolt in the Lombard city of Brescia, leaving maimed and wounded men lying in the streets and ordering that any women going to the aid of the wounded should be whipped. Even his own army hated him. A former commander of his wrote that Haynau 'knows the rules of military service but seeks glory in sharpening those rules so that he could proceed against men he doesn't like. These men he torments with calculating hatred . . . Because of his moral failings everybody in contact with him wishes to see him go, for no one likes to be in his company on military service.'

When the army finally succeeded in getting rid of Haynau, he decided to do a bit of travelling. This was to prove a bad idea for possibly the most hated man in Europe. After narrowly avoiding being lynched when he was recognized in Brussels, he came to England and on 4 September 1850, paid a visit to Barclay Perkins with an aide-de-camp and a translator.

When the brewery clerks saw the visitors' book and realized who their latest guest was, word spread quickly around the brewery. One eye witness wrote, 'Before the general and his companions had crossed the yard nearly all the labourers and draymen ran out with brooms and dirt, shouting out "Down with the Austrian butcher," and other epithets of rather an alarming nature to the marshal.' This quickly escalated into a full-on flogging. Haynau's clothes were torn from him as he fled, only to find that the aforementioned mob had gathered in the street outside. They surrounded him and dragged him down the street by the moustache. A woman threw a pair of scissors out of a window to cut off his famous whiskers. He tried hiding in a dustbin, but was dragged out of it by the beard. He was pelted and struck 'with every available missile'. And worst of all, some cad 'struck his hat over his eyes'. Finally, he managed to run and hide . . . in the George.

Imagine my surprise and delight, dear reader, upon discovering that the George Inn had a starring role in this caper. Imagine my incredulity that no previous chronicler of the old inn had placed this account front and centre in their work. And imagine my inconsolable grief when I read: 'He ran in a frantic manner along Bankside until he came to the George public-house where finding the doors open he rushed in and proceeded upstairs into one of the bedrooms, to the utter astonishment of Mrs Benfield, the landlady.'

The George Inn isn't on Bankside (though if you Google 'George Inn Bankside' you do get our George). And the George Inn never had a landlady called Mrs Benfield. But census data from 1851 shows Mr and Mrs Benfield running the George *public house* on Bankside.

There was another George in Borough. Right next to the Anchor on Bankside.

And it was in this George that the 'Hyena of Brescia', the 'Hangman of Arad', frightened Mrs Benfield ('I thought he was a madman'), asked Mr Benfield for a brandy via his translator ('I'll be damned if he have any brandy here!') and cowered in a bedroom until Inspector Squires of the Southwark police came to rescue him, borrowed one of Mr Benfield's old hats in a lame attempt to disguise him, and rowed him across the Thames in a police boat to the safety of Somerset House, jeered by the crowds on Bankside.

Reactions to the incident were mixed, with the right-wing press decrying the barbaric actions of 'all the choicest specimens of the rascalry of the Borough', while the foreign secretary, Lord Palmerston, refused to apologize to Austria, claiming the brewery workers 'were just expressing their feelings at what they considered inhuman conduct by a man who was looked upon as a great moral criminal'.

Even the lovely Dr William Rendle, a man so kind-hearted he hardly killed anyone in all his years as a surgeon, remember, said it was 'a cruel punishment no doubt', but that it was also the perfect example of the term *vox Populi, vox Dei*. 'Moral homeopathy', the 'cure of cruelty by cruelty, or more mildly, that which is known as poetical justice, administered by a mob'.

In 1865 the supremacy of brewing in Southwark seemed complete when the grand Hop Exchange was built at the top of Southwark Street. Its magnificence illustrates the importance of the trade: around forty cast-iron Corinthian columns stand in a gentle curve away down the street. The main entrance is two storeys high, with wrought-iron gates depicting hops, friezes above them showing hop-picking scenes, and a mighty stone eagle staring south, towards the hop fields of Kent. A large dealing floor provided a naturally lit single market for hop factors and merchants, and suites of offices above gave them a base of operations. Southwark would remain the centre of the British hop industry until the middle of the twentieth century.

For those at the heart of the Hop Exchange, business had never been better. But various hop merchants and factors chose to stay in the George Inn yard and run their businesses from there. Skylights were installed in the roof of the George, and its attics were turned into showrooms where factors could show off their wares. But only a few years after the Hop Exchange opened, the factors in the inn-yard were filing for bankruptcy, unable to compete with the efficient magnificence across the road. They were just the latest casualties though, in an inn-yard that had become deserted and downbeat, if not quite as derelict as its neighbours. By the time the Hop Exchange opened, most of Stow's fine old inns were decrepit hulks, forgotten and unloved, made irrelevant by changes that erased the golden age of stagecoaching as quickly and efficiently as a pen stroke. The George was about to face its darkest hour, and would not survive in any recognizable form.

CHAPTER ELEVEN: IN WHICH THE ROAD OF STEEL REPLACES THE ROADS OF THE ROMANS, AND THE INNS OF THE BOROUGH SUFFER A TERRIBLE FATE

We who have lived before railways were made belong to another world. It was only yesterday, but what a gulf between now and then! Then was the old world. Stage-coaches, more or less swift, riding-horses, pack-horses, highwaymen, knights in armour, Norman invaders, Roman legions, Druids, Ancient Britons painted blue, and so forth – all these belong to the old period. But your railroad starts the new era, and we of a certain age belong to the new time and the old one. We who lived before railways, and survive out of the ancient world, are like Father Noah and his family out of the Ark.

(William Makepeace Thackeray, *Roundabout Papers*, 1863)

ON 4 APRIL 1817, the *Liverpool Mercury* reported on an inquest that had taken place at the George Inn, Borough, on the body of an unknown 'mendicant' (beggar) of about sixty-six years of age. A porter named Johnson told how he had found the body in a hay-cart opposite the Talbot Inn. The dead man was almost naked and appeared starved. Several chimney sweeps identified him, 'having seen him in great distress and begging'. The recorded verdict on the poor wretch was 'Died by the visitation of God'.

If it seems strange that an inn would be the venue for an inquest such as this, remember that inns were large public spaces in an age before municipal town halls, libraries and other public buildings which, when they appeared, were usually financed by rich philanthropists (often brewers). This inquest gives a vivid impression of grim life in the Borough two centuries ago, but it's just one of the many events and functions that kept the inn bustling. The George was a regular venue for auctions of property including horses, fleets of barges, phaetons,[1] even large freehold country estates. It was the meeting place for both committees organizing elections and campaign meetings for the candidates. There were estate sales of deceased persons, and in 1789, the landlord was advertised as taking orders for Mr Ryman's cardiac tincture, a 'most excellent medicine' that cured disorders of the head and stomach, especially 'putrid bile', languors, faintness, hiccups, wind and 'griping in the bowels'. The ad claimed that 'Mr Green of the George Inn Borough will transmit any orders by the Reigate Coach, for persons who desire to have the Medicine from Mr Ryman's own house'.

Thomas Green, who ran the George from 1781 to 1809, was clearly someone you could trust. Classified ads in late-eighteenth-century newspapers are full of people who have mislaid their pocket books or silver watches, begging anyone who finds them to return them to Mr Green at the George. Such ads had long been common in London, but they soared in number under Green's tenure. He ran a pub everyone knew and used, and was evidently regarded as one of the most trustworthy and reliable people in the community. The George and other inns like it were the town halls, community centres, noticeboards, eBays and drop-in centres of their day.

Thomas Green retired in 1809, and no doubt at his

---

1. A small, nippy, horse-drawn carriage – the Regency equivalent of, say, a Vauxhall Astra.

recommendation, the Aynscombe family leased the George to his niece, Frances, and her husband, Westerman Scholefield. 'The Scholefields, when they took the George in hand in 1809, worked with spirit, and evidently meant to make it succeed, as they did,' Rendle tells us. In 1825, *Tavern Anecdotes by One of the Old School* describes the George as:

> a good commercial inn in the Boro High Street; well-known, whence several coaches and many waggons depart laden with the merchandise of the metropolis, in return for which they bring back from various parts of Kent, etc. that staple article of the country, the hop, to which we are indebted for the good quality of the London porter.

Residents in the best rooms were treated to magnificent four-poster beds that required a mounting block of three steps to climb up to them. The galleries were adorned with fresh flowers and the inn-yard was a constant bustle. Waggons loaded and unloaded their cargoes, and the inn acted as a booking office for coach passengers and a sorting office for the dashing post coaches – a function that proved to be a portent of what was to come.

The day began early, with the first stagecoach to Battle and Rye calling at the George at 5.30 a.m. The first waggon didn't leave until seven, but of course it had to be loaded before then. The last one didn't leave until gone nine in the evening, and the last coach of the night would pull into the yard even later. Businesses around the yard included a shoe factor and a painter, but by far the most important were the hop merchants. The 1841 census lists forty people sleeping there: the staff of the inn itself, James Dodson, a hop factor, and James Dawson, a labourer, with their respective families. Guests at the inn included a timber merchant, an upholsterer and a labourer.

In 1830, Westerman Scholefield put up a notice listing coach and waggon departures through the week:

GEORGE INN, SOUTHWARK.
W.S. SCHOLEFIELD.

The following coaches set out from the above inn:

Maidstone, Malling and Wrotham, four times a day.
Folkestone, Hythe and Ashford, 6 every morning;
Mon., Wed., and Sat. evening.

Tenterden, Cranbrook and Staplehurst, Sun., Tues., and Thurs. mor.

Wateringbury, Teston and Mereworth, daily.
Brenchley, Matfield Green, and Peckham, Tue., Wed., and Sat. afternoon.

Deal, Dover, Margate, Ramsgate, and Canterbury, twice a day.

Rochester, Chatham, and Gravesend, four times a day.

Orpington, St. Mary Cray, Chiselhurst, and Eltham, Mon., Wed., Sat. afternoon.

Hastings, Boxhill, Battle, Robertsbridge, Lamberhurst, Tunbridge, Sevenoaks, Worthing, Horsham, Dorking, Brighton, Cuckfield and Reigate, daily.

Waggons.

Lewes, Alfreston, and Saeford, Tue, Wed and Saturday.

Brighton and Cuckfield, Wed and Saturday.

Emsworth, Havant, and Petersfield, Tue and Friday.

Tenterden, New Romney, and Staplehurst, Thursday.

Folkestone, Sandgate, Hythe, Ashton, Wednesdays.

Coaches in Southwark, 1826.

Worthing, Angmoring, Horsham, Reigate, and Gatton, twice a week.

Dorking and Leatherhead, three times a week.

Igtham, Wrotham, Kingsdown, Lingfield, Cowden, Cobham. Estree, Kingston, Brenchley, Horsemonden, West Wickham, and Beckenham, weekly.

The George was in its prime. But perhaps competition was already tough. Scholefield signs off the notice with a sincere thanks 'to his Friends & the Public in general for their past favours, and to acquaint them that he has neither spared the pains nor expense in the improvements to the opportunity of soliciting their future encouragement, trusting they'll find Beds, Wines, Spirits, Stabling to their perfect satisfaction'.

Westerman Scholefield died in 1836 – the year Dickens wrote his nostalgic paean to 'rambling, queer, old' coaching inns. So perhaps he already sensed the end was coming; 1828 is regarded as the peak of the stagecoach era because that's when the larger horse-drawn omnibus began to replace the short-stage carriage. Scholefield's wife, Frances, would carry on running the George until 1859. She therefore witnessed what her husband missed, and may have been thankful he was at least spared the experience of another innovation that would sweep away the stagecoaches and the coaching inns with breathtaking speed.

Steam engines date back much earlier than most of us are aware. They were first recorded in the first century AD, although admittedly there was then a bit of a hiatus before Thomas Newcomen invented an engine driven by steam for pumping water out of mineshafts sometime around 1710. It took another century for someone to figure out how to use steam engines to make a vehicle move, and a little more time to figure out that a steam locomotive might be more suited to rail than road. In 1825 the world looked on in awe as George Stephenson outran horses with his locomotive on the opening day of the Stockton and Darlington railway, reaching the dizzying speed of twelve miles per hour. But even the best engines were unstable and liable to explode or literally run out of steam, and most of the trains were still pulled along the rails by horses rather than locomotives. Open access to the railway made it a completely untenable system, with punch-ups between rival train operators creating even worse delays than leaves on the track or the wrong kind of snow. But when the world's first steam-hauled and twin-tracked railway opened between Liverpool and Manchester in 1830, the path to the future seemed as clear and straight and fast as the tracks themselves. It would take a while for rail tracks to link up the entire country, but within a decade there were links between most major cities.

The London and Greenwich railway was the first to open in the capital. Hugely ambitious, it traversed a low-lying area full of housing, industry, roads and creeks on a viaduct almost four miles long, comprising 878 arches. The line opened from Deptford to Bermondsey in February 1836, and in December of that year it reached London Bridge, the first and oldest of London's permanent train stations. Two years later, the line reached Greenwich at the other end.

The railway was massively over budget, and the first London Bridge station had to be a basic affair. The platforms were built so low that a scandal ensued when it became apparent that ladies stepping down from the trains were forced to show their ankles, and sometimes even a bit of leg. Men started to hang around the station in the hope of getting a glimpse, and some of the railway's staff were accused of staring a little too closely as they helped the women down.

Other railways soon followed, with different companies opening up lines to Croydon and, soon, the south coast. The London Bridge viaduct grew wider to accommodate as many as eleven lines, and the station was rebuilt on more impressive dimensions. In 1858 a writer for the *London Evening News* breathlessly described the arches that were 'suspended in mid-air, more wonderfully than the Hanging Gardens of Babylon,' in a station 'looking down from an altitude of seventy feet upon Tooley Street and sending forth its convoys along an elevated route which lifts them above the chimney pots of Bermondsey'.

By 1854 this station was welcoming ten million passengers a year. As it grew and sprawled it completely swallowed whole streets, some of which still run beneath it today, as tunnels full of faintly upmarket fast-food and souvenir stands. With millions more journeys terminating at London Bridge, the bridge itself saw a colossal increase in traffic: a census in 1859 calculated that in one 24-hour period, the bridge was crossed by 20,498 wheeled vehicles and 107,074 pedestrians. It soon became obvious that the bottleneck from Southwark into the City, even though it had been eased by the building of other bridges across the Thames, had reached crisis point. The onward journey into the City from London Bridge was by horse-drawn bus or cab, or on foot, and apart from the congestion, people who had experienced speeds as fast as thirty miles per hour on their way into town found this far too slow and tedious. So in 1864, a new viaduct and bridge was opened to carry trains onward, across the river from London Bridge station to Charing Cross. It ripped through Southwark on ungainly viaducts, across the Bridge approach road, past the church, over the market and away to the west, tearing up working-class housing and displacing residents as it went, leading one observer to rant that 'nothing uglier, nothing more objectionable in an artistic point of view, could possibly have been designed. It is a pity that there should exist such an utter disregard among our railway authorities . . . for anything that is not strictly utilitarian.' Further extensions to Cannon Street and Blackfriars soon followed, transforming the map of Southwark in a way you'd find familiar if you've ever let a child near a beautiful picture with a fistful of felt-tip pens.

The trains with their smoke and noise, and huge, imposing viaducts, completed a picture of Southwark as a place of poverty, overcrowding, filthy industry and pollution. For so long a convenient repository for London's seedy, dark pleasures, Southwark was now just a dumping ground for the dirty industries the City needed, but didn't want in its back-yard. This was where 'sea coal' came in by boat from the north of England, and where finished goods could be sent off around the Empire. Coal-fired furnaces required by indus-tries such as glassmaking had been banned in the City itself because of their filth, but they were deemed perfectly fine for Southwark. Then there was hat making.

I've got nothing against hats – Southwark was famous for making them for hundreds of years – from fine beaver hats, to silk hats, to the new invention by Thomas Bowler, who worked in Southwark Bridge Road. The Bowler hat was originally designed for the hunting gentleman as a more practical alternative to the top hat, and it became hugely popular as the must-have headwear of the Victorian working class. It was even – you won't believe this, but it's true – the most popular hat in the old American West, far more so than the Stetson or the sombrero. In 1841 there were an incredible 3,500 hat companies in Southwark employing more than 23,000 people.

The only problem was, a by-product of hat making was poisonous mercury, which was poured into the Thames and its Bankside tributaries along with all the rest of Southwark's industrial oomska. Sarson's vinegar works, Crosse & Black-well's pickle factory, Day & Martin's shoe-polish factory and Epps Steam Cocoa mills were just some of the other industries crowding the streets of the Borough, their vast diversity united by a single common thread: somehow they all managed to discharge noxious pollution into the atmosphere and the water supply.

Little of the wealth created by these industries flowed down to the workers. In 1865 the medical journal the *Lancet* investigated conditions at a workhouse in Mint Street, Southwark, and was repelled by what it found, describing the area as:

> A densely crowded district on the S.E. of the Thames, with a population of 55,510 and is surrounded by every possible nuisance, physical and moral. Bone-boilers, grease and cat-gut manufactories represent some of them, and there is a nest of thieves, which has existed ever since the days of Edward III.

In Charles Booth's 1891 *Survey of Life and Labour of the People in London*, Southwark and Bermondsey were identified as the only districts where over half the population lived in poverty. The consequences were stark: in the mid-nineteenth century, the average life expectancy for Southwark was just 20 years for artisans, well short of the 43.7-year average for the rest of London.

The railways helped all these industries thrive, concentrating production, intensifying demand, and opening up new markets. For Southwark's brewers, the country and the whole world was made newly accessible. The hop merchants could get up from Kent and back in the same day.

And the effect on the coaching trade was instant: there was simply no need for it any more.

Trains were faster, cheaper and more comfortable, and stagecoaches were obsolete. The last Royal Mail coach was withdrawn in 1864, and if that sounds like a late date to you, perhaps it will sound less so when you consider its route was from Wick to Thurso. Only thirty-four years after the first proper railway was opened, steam trains had replaced coaches in even the most remote parts of the country. The last London Mail coach service – between the capital and Norwich – went as early as 1846. With the coaching trade vanished, Southwark's great inns were, at a stroke, bereft of purpose.

But they didn't go down without a fight. In 1850 the Great Northern Railway announced in all London newspapers that it was ready to carry general merchandize to and from London and all across their railway system. Goods could be booked in at a number of receiving houses, and the list of these houses was a list of London's former great coaching inns, about a dozen of them, reduced to warehouses for railway traffic and lined up in the classified ads like rounded up outlaws.

The inn was now a place to pick up and deliver parcels, book train journeys, passages on steamers and hotel accommodation – a post office, ticket office and travel agency all in one. Some innkeepers saw where things were going and leapt into this new mode of business. William Chaplin at the Swan and Two Necks in Lad Lane (now Gresham Street) and

Benjamin Worthy Horne at the old Golden Cross in Charing Cross had already enjoyed huge success running some of the major stagecoaching companies out of their inns. When they saw the end of the stagecoach writ large, instead of becoming sentimental they combined, and pitched to become the sole parcel agents on the London-to-Birmingham railway. The coach to Birmingham used to leave from the Golden Cross. Now the omnibus to Euston Station and the Birmingham train did the same.

But even when inns completely changed their function – and were pulled down and replaced by purpose-built ware-houses and offices in some cases – they often retained their old names, a link with an age that had suddenly and for ever passed. In Borough High Street, the Dun Horse became the warehouse for the South-Western Railway, the Catherine Wheel (or rather its site) for the Midland, the Nag's Head for the Great Western – and the George for the Great Northern.

The humiliation was complete when the greater mobility afforded by the railways led to a boom in hotel building. The first British hotel was built in Exeter in 1768, and was named, simply, 'The Hotel',[2] from the same French root that gave us the hostels and hostelers who were eventually Saxonized to become inns and innkeepers. It's retrospectively obvious that if you wanted to create a new form of travellers' accommo-dation that was bigger and grander than the inn, you'd go back to the French. Hotels were still very rare by the early 1800s, but inevitably they were soon common near railway stations, including the great London termini. None was finer than the Midland Grand Hotel at St Pancras, built in 1874 by Sir George Gilbert Scott. Not to be outdone, the railway companies at London Bridge built the Terminus Hotel at the front of the station. Seven storeys high with 150 bedrooms,

---

2. It's still around today as the Royal Clarence Hotel. It describes itself as 'Exeter's oldest hotel', seemingly unaware that it is Britain's oldest too.

it mocked the suddenly tiny-looking coaching inns down the street. The hotel failed and closed in 1893 – but not before almost all Southwark's inns had disappeared.

The inn, so long a multi-faceted, multi-functional jack-of-all-trades, found itself in the mid-nineteenth century as a curious anomaly. There were coffee houses, alehouses and taverns to drink in, hotels to sleep in, restaurants to eat in, auction rooms to hold auctions in, and village halls, town halls, corn exchanges and council chambers to meet in, hold balls in, or perform inquests on beggars in.

On 29 April 1854, *Berrow's Worcester Journal* reported that a man named George Ryland had 'committed self-destruction by hanging himself with a piece of thin rope-yarn, in a shed belonging to the George Inn, Southwark. The deceased was of cheerful disposition, and no cause is known for the deed.'[3] Ryland may have appeared cheerful, but he was a waggoner by trade. No one ever knew why he did it, but isn't it quite likely that he saw his livelihood disappearing before his very eyes? It must have been awful for waggoners with premises in the inn-yards to watch with increasing horror the quantity of goods being delivered to be taken on to the trains, knowing they could never compete on price or speed of transport over long distances.

The railways would have touched the lives of everyone living in Southwark, and the tenants of the George were no exception. In 1857, just outside Blackheath Station the railway signals failed, and two trains collided. Among the injured was a small boy called Alfred Dawson, son of James Dawson, the labourer living at the George with his family named in the 1841 census. Young Alfred was lucky in that he only suffered cuts and bruises. In total there were thirty injured, and eleven

---

3. In one of many unintentional-and-impossible-to-foresee examples of comic juxtaposition in old newspapers, the next story down tells us that a man called Ronald McDonald has caught a three-foot-long otter.

fatalities. Standing in the deserted inn-yard, James Dawson must have thought: you never got this with the stagecoaches.

This wouldn't be Dawson's last brush with the trains. A year later, he was charged with violating South East Railway Company bye-laws when he jumped from a train that was still doing five or six miles an hour as it pulled into New Cross station. The guard warned him not to but he jumped and fell, and would have gone under the train were it not for the help of a witness. The judge felt his near-death was sufficient punishment, but still fined him ten shillings plus costs as a warning to others.

The stables James Dawson saw when he opened his door each morning were defunct, but somehow business at the George still carried on. Frances Scholefield leased some of the back-stable yard to Guy's Hospital, which stood right by the back of the inn. This relationship developed, and in 1849 the trustees to the heirs of the Aynscombe family, who had owned the George for a century and a half, sold the inn in its entirety to the Governors of Guy's. As part of the sale process, they drew the map that gives us our most detailed guide to how the George looked in its prime, detailing the bars and hop merchant's offices in the front yard, and the stable yard to the rear. The sale was agreed, and Frances Scholefield continued to run the George under its new owners.

Why did Guy's want a coaching inn? They didn't: they wanted the land it was built on. Guy's began to demolish the stabling and build over the back half of the yard, continuing the hospital's expansion in what was now a crowded part of London where land was at a premium.

Oddly, it may have been the loss of part of the inn that saved the rest of it. Under Frances Scholefield the George continued to survive in its somewhat reduced state. Photos from the 1850s to the 1870s of contemporaries like the White Hart and the King's Head show Dickens's 'rambling, queer, old places' falling into complete disrepair, almost ruins in some cases. But possibly because there was less of the George to look after, it remained in better condition.

There was still the rump of a waggoning trade. The railways didn't yet reach every single point on the map, and even where they did, someone had to get goods to the train station. The George somehow managed to gather what scraps of trade were left around it, and indeed one waggoner in particular, John East, would come to play a key role in the survival of the George, as we'll see later.

While you could now easily get to London and back in the same day for meetings, there was still the occasional business-man who saw the need to stay overnight. The census for 1851 shows that the George hosted some guests even after the stagecoaches had completely vanished and the inn-yard was being used as a railway booking office. Fifteen stayed the night the census was taken, including a sailor, a customs-house clerk, an architect, a commercial traveller, two waggoners, a carrier's driver and his guard. The staff included the redoubt-able Mrs Scholefield, still running things at seventy-six years old, as well as a barmaid, cook, housemaid and tap boy. In addition, the Dawsons and Dodsons – who it seems were related to the Scholefields – were still resident in the inn-yard, with various family members working as shoemakers, ostlers, and a warehouseman in the hop trade on behalf of Barclay Perkins.

Rooms on the north side of the yard were leased out to businesses such as the Great North Railway and to Beeman and Hotchkins, hop merchants. They weren't needed as bedrooms or stables anymore, and in 1853 the beautiful balustrades on the north and east sides of the yard were removed and the galleries boarded up – it was more practical that way. Messrs Evans and Company, hop merchants, took rooms on the south side.

Ironically for an inn built specifically for the receipt of travellers, local trade also became increasingly important to its survival. The George did a thriving lunch trade to dealers and merchants from the Hop Exchange and the market, and to local residents.

So this was the context in which George Corner delivered his celebrated lecture to the Surrey Archaeological Society in 1858. Southwark's great inns still stood, but in some cases only just. Whenever we hear about the destruction of old buildings that once inspired awe, admiration and love, that summed up an age we have lost and want to reclaim, we ask why? Why did they have to go and destroy it? Why couldn't they see the value and preserve it for future generations? We imagine some heartless corporate wrecking ball, cynically swinging, ignoring the pleas of lovers of old pubs. But the difficult truth is that these buildings outstayed their welcome. By the time the coaching inns were finally demolished, they were neglected places in deep disrepair. Photographs of the Tabard/Talbot from around this time (it was known by either name at this point) show sagging rooflines and broken windows. Barrels and baskets are piled up in the yard alongside broken old carts, and a few labourers look suspiciously at the camera. The building looks like it's given up. Like it no longer belongs, or cares.

In 1859 Frances Scholefield finally retired, well into her eighties. George Grinslade had been renting some of the stables in the yard for years, and he took over the lease for the whole property. He obviously invested in the service and kept the buildings presentable – pewter mugs with his name as licensee engraved on them were still in use at the George almost a century later. Unlike some of its neighbours, business at the George just about survived.

But while it survived, it hardly thrived. In 1840 the rateable value of the premises was £360 per year. Five years later this had fallen to £284, and it continued to fall. As we've seen, the hop businesses in the yard started to suffer too, as the new Hop Exchange across the road sucked everything in. In 1869 Evans & Co., hop merchants of the George Inn yard, filed for bankruptcy. The following year the partnership of J. Preston and J. Morton, also hop merchants based at the George, was dissolved.

As the hop merchants withdrew, the railway companies advanced, taking an ever-greater proportion of storage and office space within the inn-yard. As the railway traffic grew, so did the amount of goods being brought by waggon into the inn-yard to be loaded onto trains, or to be sent into London after being unloaded. Waggoners like John James East kept the inn-yard a busy place.

The trouble was, an ever-decreasing amount of the business had to do with the inn itself. In July 1873 the *Builder* magazine lamented the passing of the great coaching inns and described the 'quaint courtyard' of the George, 'now filled up with railway vans, and the building covered more or less with huge bills and posters, not a little surprising to those who for a moment can forget the present, and live in the past in these fast disappearing places'.

Eventually, inevitably, the Great North Railway Company approached Guy's Hospital with a view to buying the George. The Governors of Guy's had by this time walled off and filled in about half the old stable yard. In 1874, they sold what remained of the inn to the GNRC for around £11,000.

Again, the railway company wanted the land rather than the building itself. The George was in a great location, but it hadn't been designed as a railway goods depot, and that is what much of it had now effectively become. A new entrance to the main yard was built to accommodate the huge horse-drawn goods waggons as they delivered up to a hundred tons a day. A stout, ugly wall of railway sleepers was erected in front of the inn itself, to protect it from the traffic.

The plans for the demolition of most of the George Inn ironically give us our best view of it before that demolition took place. These plans still exist in the National Monuments Archive, and for someone who has spent so much time at

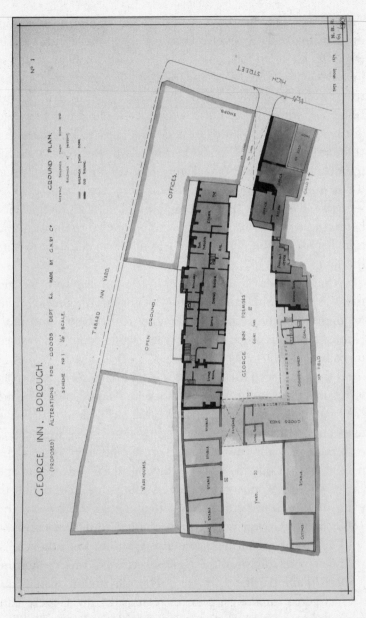

Plans drawn for the partial demolition of the George by the Great North Railway Company in 1879. Eventual demolition would go even further than shown here.

the George, they are both beautiful and chilling to see. The draughtsmanship is lovely. Drawn some time around 1879, the parts intended for demolition are shaded pale grey. These include what remains of the rear stable yard and the east wing, which is mostly a goods shed apart from a small private residence, while on the north wing there's another goods shed (formerly stables) and a coal shed. The parts to be spared are coloured dark grey. The south wing – which is what remains today – consisted of a small taproom, a large kitchen which today makes up most of the taproom, the small, curious servery – which was then the main bar – with a small parlour behind it, a dining room where the old coffee room was, and a scullery behind it. Then there was an office, and two private dwellings.

What comes as a surprise to anyone familiar with the inn today is that a substantial section of the north wing remains on these plans too. Offices belonging to Beeman's hop merchants, a parcels office and a private dining room are marked up to be saved.

If they had seen the plans, this would have come as a relief to the members of the Four O'Clockers. Named after the time they convened, this gentleman's dining club imposed heavy fines on any member who showed up late. There were many culprits – probably more than there would have been if the fines didn't go directly towards buying more wine. From the early 1860s they only ever met in the dining room of the north wing of the George, and enjoyed doing so throughout the 1880s, as the George enjoyed a prolonged stay of execution.

The rest of Stow's eight fine inns were not so fortunate.

That same edition of the *Builder* from 1873 reveals that the Tabard/Talbot was up for sale. The particulars of that sale are revealing, showing again the vast scale of the great inns even in their faded decline. The sale comprises a dwelling house; a tea-dealer's shop and cellaring below; the inn yard extending back from the street to Guy's; the booking office of the Midlands Railway Co.; and the 'Talbot' Public House. The inn itself comprised a spacious bar and parlour, kitchen, scullery, skittle ground, paved yard and good cellarage; two floors of bedrooms and a warehouse above; a range of stabling for cart horses and hop stores over the same, another dwelling house, two more stables with lofts over, a stable with a cabinet maker's shop above it, and a shed with a tiled roof. The whole was valued by the Great Northern Railway Company at £20,000 – almost double what they ended up paying for the George a year later. The future of the inn is made quite clear at the end of the sale particulars, which suggest the space is 'now available for a first class theatre, hall or public building'.

The Talbot Inn remained unsold at the asking price. In 1878 it was demolished amid substantial public outcry, and replaced by warehouses. An ornate, flashy Victorian gin palace was also built on the site and was, unashamedly, called the Tabard. A glitzy public house with no food and hardly any seating, the new Tabard and places like it were designed purely for 'vertical drinking' and the focused consumption of alcohol. Chaucer's genteel inn was supplanted, its name stolen by a common alehouse that *Piers Plowman*'s Gluttony would have fallen madly in lust with.

Sentimental Victorians suddenly realized this was the last chance to see these monuments of a bygone age. In 1884 Percy Fitzgerald visited Borough High Street for a piece published in the *Magazine of Art*. 'Nothing shows the changes that are almost weekly taking place in London, and transforming the city so much, as the rapid disappearance of its old inns,' he wrote. 'Only eight or ten years ago these were nearly all in existence, unaltered and undisturbed ... Four only of the old pattern remain and their days, or hours in one case, are certainly numbered.'

The King's Head stood 'ruinous and forlorn, with its two ancient galleries or balustrades in a sadly tottering state'. The White Hart had clothes lines strung across its galleries, from which 'squalid women look down and survey the intruders'. Most of the inn would be demolished later that year, and replaced by warehousing.

And yet the George, by contrast, had 'a bright and bustling air of business. It is a not unpicturesque courtyard . . . The galleries are gay with paint and plenty of flowers; and altogether one might seem able to take one's ease in one's inn here very fairly.'

The Society for Photographing Relics of Old London, as its name might suggest to more alert readers, captured the same atmosphere in priceless, stunning black-and-white photography. Formed in 1875 the society, which included William Rendle's collaborator Philip Norman, wanted to create a record of inns it knew were about to vanish. Its first project was the Oxford Arms in Warwick Lane in the City, which it captured in all its wonky, grimy glory before it was demolished the following year. The photos of the White Hart and King's Head show derelict wrecks, while the George and the Queen's Head still look respectable. Figures in tall, stovepipe hats bow their heads in wary greeting to the camera, thumbs tucked into waistcoat watchpockets. The buildings themselves stand like punchdrunk fighters, or ancient knights with withered skin and sunken eyes beneath their rusty armour.

And finally, after being introduced to him what seems like centuries ago, we meet Dr William Rendle in the flesh, so to speak. It's 1888, and he visits the George making studious notes for his book on the Old Inns of Southwark. I imagine this gentleman in his early seventies, still tall and unbowed. I don't know why, and I'm almost certainly mistaken, but in my mind's eye he sports long mutton-chop whiskers, a pale-blue frock coat and shiny black top hat, perhaps slightly old-fashioned for the age, for he is a very old man, the doctor. He greets the landlady with the utmost courtesy and permits himself to be shown around the inn, asking questions in every room, exclaiming 'Oh really!' and 'How fascinating!' at every answer,

Pictures taken to record the passing of the great inns around
1880 show a marked contrast. The George (above) is still neat
and bustling; the famous Tabard (below) nearly derelict.

occasionally dropping sheaves of yellowed old records and crumpled notes as he fumbles for a pen to make new ones. He spots that Robert Hill, stationer, has the freehold of number 71 Borough High Street, a house that sits over the gateway to the inn yard, and when he comes to write up this chapter this will lead him into a six-page digression about all the old printing presses that 'have been grouped around this spot since 1620 or before', and how among all its other facets, the Borough was once a major centre for the printed word.

Retracing his steps a little, he observes that the George is the 'least altered' of the great inns, and that the old taproom is still used by carters and van drivers. 'The parts of the inn not devoted to important business are mostly occupied by people who frequent the very bustling Borough Market close at hand.' He observes that the remaining galleries on the south side are 'often made pretty in summer with flowers', and that the surviving stables have movable partitions called bales, for varying the width of the accommodation, as was often necessary in the time of waggons, and round, smooth balls to prevent horses closely stabled from chafing one another.

'But alas,' he cries, 'like the rest, the glory of this inn is departing! Its fate is sealed, it will soon be pulled down altogether.'

As we say goodbye to Dr Rendle, a constant companion whose observations we have shared since the time of Chaucer, I wish there was a way to let him know that the future doesn't quite work out like that.

When the wrecking ball finally came in 1889, it went considerably further than the plans of a decade previously. The north dining room and the offices formerly occupied by Beeman's joined the rest of the north wing, the entire east wing, and all the stables and warehousing of the rear court- yard as rubble. All that remained of the George was the south wing and a few outbuildings in the northwest corner. The distraught Four O'Clockers disbanded in grief rather than move elsewhere. Purpose-built warehouses sprang up around the yard, with a big weighing platform outside the depot buildings. And so the George went from being an inn arrayed around an elegant courtyard with stables to the rear, to a pub hidden deep inside a railway goods yard, soon to be forgotten by passers-by on the eternally busy street out front.

It's strange now to think about the complete transformation the railways brought about. From around the 1850s until motorcars became popular in the 1930s, Britain's roads were dead. Imagine if you can what it might be like today if things had continued along this path, if the railway branch lines had remained open and railways had evolved in such a way as to keep their role as the dominant mode of transport. Imagine if light cars and vans were used just for short-distance trips to the station and back, because everyone had a station near them and train travel was quicker and cheaper than road travel could ever be. There would be no motorways, much less pollution, hardly any drink-driving fatalities, and best of all, no Jeremy Clarkson. What a wonderful world that would be! The train may be the villain of our story about the George, but its golden age wasn't much longer than that of the stagecoach.

The rise of the motorcar, when it came, did nothing to revive the fortunes of coaching inns, but it did give birth to a new generation of inns of a sort. On major roads like old Watling Street, revived and remodelled as the A2, huge red-brick edifices rose by the road side, as it became fashionable to put on your driving gloves, load the family up and take the car out for a bit of a run at the weekend. These new inns were considered grotesque by traditionalists, and while I'd like to say 'but actually, from a modern perspective they're beautiful' – no, sorry, unlike the beautiful Victorian gin palaces, once hated and now seen as architectural stars, the surviving roadside inns of the 1930s are still grotesque.

You can still see them down the A2, through south-eastern London suburbs like Dartford and Bexley Heath, only now that the A2 is a concrete corridor from London to other places, and now we think a little differently about drinking several pints of beer while driving, they're no longer inns. They're Holiday Inns, Tesco's and Burger Kings, each one garishly branded, as ill-fitting in these distinctive old buildings as Lady Gaga in a Matalan frock. As Bertram Matz wrote in 1921:

> We certainly are coming back to these roadside inns
> in the present age of rapid motor transit; yet we are in
> too much of a tearing hurry to make the same use of
> the old inns as they did in the more leisurely age.

And that should be it – this should be the last page of the story of the George. As Stow's fair inns for the receipt of travellers one by one lurched forward, staggered and fell, the George really should have followed them. And perhaps it would have if not for the landlady and her daughter who greeted Dr Rendle on the day of his visit back in 1888, and told him their tales of the inn.

Earlier in the nineteenth century, John James East, who inherited the waggoning business established at the George by his father, John East, hired a man called Marlborough Fleming to work for him. Fleming, late of the Royal Artillery, was the illegitimate son of the Fifth Duke of Marlborough and a servant girl from Blenheim Palace (which may be worth bearing in mind when we get on to the exploits of his descendants). Fleming had a daughter, Amelia, and when he died in 1843, John James East was appointed her legal guardian until she came of age. She married a jeweller called James Murray and moved to Scotland, but when he died prematurely, Amelia Murray moved back to London and John James East, taking a position as housekeeper in the new 'mansion' he'd moved into in Albion Road, Stoke Newington.[4]

In 1870 George Grinslade, innkeeper at the George and relative of Amelia Murray, died. The tenancy of the inn was in the hands of the trustees of his estate, of which Amelia was one. Grinslade's wife Mary Ann wasn't interested in carrying on and moved out to a house in Lambeth, complete with servants, until her untimely death two years later at the age of 48. The terms of Grinslade's will were that Amelia Murray, who had shown a head for business, should take over the running of the George, but not until 'your responsibilities towards John James East have ceased, by virtue of his passing from this life'.

The following year East sold the place in Stoke Newington and moved his family and the Murrays into the George. East's sons John and Charles were apprenticed to learn the innkeeper's trade but had a fiery relationship with their sometimes brutal father, and both ran away to become actors, with John M. East later finding some fame as a stage and silent-movie actor and theatre impresario. But Amelia Murray and her daughter Agnes, who was eighteen when the family moved into the inn, showed immediate aptitude for the trade. When John James East died in 1878, the terms of the will were effected, and Amelia Murray became proprietress of the George Inn.

By the time Dr Rendle was being entertained by her, Amelia Murray had 'stamped her own personality' on the George. She had known the inn for years, and was very proud to be associated with it. Back in my mind's eye again, I can

---

4. My wife used to live in a flat on Albion Road and I go down this street every day. It still has the original Victorian houses on it, but it's hard to think of them as mansions. But I'm quoting a descendant of the East family, who we'll be looking at properly in the next chapter, and this is somewhat typical of his overstatement.

see Mrs Murray and her daughter, Miss Murray, taking delivery of the doctor's book, back when it smelled of fresh ink from the presses rather than the dust and incense of my copy now. I can picture them turning eagerly, but not too obviously, to the section on the George, and reading it in silence with impassive faces. I'm watching them as they get to the 'Alas! Its fate is sealed' part. They lean back, fold their arms, turn to each other and say, 'Oh really? Well, I think we may have something to say about that.'

CHAPTER TWELVE: CONCERNING A MOTHER AND DAUGHTER, TWO BROTHERS, AND THE CONDITION OF NOSTALGIA

> Things ain't what they used to be and probably never was.
>
> (Will Rogers (1879–1935), American movie actor, cowboy, vaudeville artist, humorist and commentator)

DINNER AT THE GEORGE on Christmas Eve began with the Gresham singers performing part-songs. Then, the men stood and applauded in their frock coats, boots and breeches, the women in long, flowing gingham dresses, as the boar's head was ceremonially brought into the room, accompanied by a jester, and a traditional carol was sung. The boar's head was served with a spiced walnut salad, and this course was followed by haunch of venison, then game pie, and finally apple posset with round cakes and orange jelly. Old English ale and cider were drunk, and afterwards long, thin churchwarden pipes were smoked as the guests assembled in the inn's panelled sitting room to watch an ancient mummers play about St George and the Dragon, performed with puppets.

Back in the lounge afterwards, everyone gathered to see the Yule log placed on the fire with customary ceremony. The lights were lowered, and snap-dragon was quickly passed among the guests. This Christmas Eve custom, popular from the sixteenth century to the nineteenth, dictated that a bowl full of brandy was lit, and had raisins dropped in it. The guests had to quickly pluck the raisins from the brandy and eat them, trying their best not to get horrific facial burns as they did so.

Then the wassail song was sung as wassail (mulled cider or beer) was served. And right on cue, outside the window carol singers could be seen assembling in the inn-yard. They were wearing traditional old-English costumes and their leader was a fiddler in a beaver hat. The singers were admitted to the lounge and welcomed by the assembled company. Everyone sang, danced the Roger de Coverley, and finished with the national anthem and 'Auld Lang Syne'.

It was the perfect occasion, and could have come straight from 1843's *A Christmas Carol*. The only slightly odd part is that this dinner actually took place in 1936. The inn-yard outside was a goods-receiving yard for the railway, and there were no stagecoaches waiting in it.

The event was noteworthy enough to receive a full write-up in *The Times*. The account ends with a gentle rebuke, suggesting that the Dickens Fellowship – for that is the company that was enjoying the dinner – were perhaps behaving a little foolishly and should be grateful that they were in fact living in the modern era:

> Outside the inn there were no coach and impatient horses with jingling harness waiting to take the guests to Dingley Dell. The pavements were wet and glistening. Perhaps the guests were thankful for the facilities provided by London Transport to take them on from a world of make-believe and sentiment to the realities of 'Christmas Present'.

A hundred years before this dinner, when Dickens was writing about Southwark's coaching inns, he was already being nostalgic about them. Now, in turn, people were being nostalgic about Dickens. This dinner was but one example of something that was spreading rapidly across Britain throughout the 1920s and 1930s – a desperate yearning for an imagined past, an almost unbearable sense of loss, driven by progress in a world that seemed to have gone mad. It was a kind of sickness in society, and the George Inn found itself at the very heart of it.

Of all the strange and eccentric characters I encountered while researching this story, my absolute favourite, the one who stands head and shoulders above the rest (literally in most cases) is Agnes Maria Amelia Murray. There are one or two photos of her standing in the doorway of the George. She was a formidable woman: tall, severe, often dressed in black with her favourite brooch at her breast.

Agnes's first brush with the newspapers gives a strong hint of her character. In 1898, reports spread across the country of a burglary at the George Inn. Henry Shatter, 16 years old and abandoned by his parents, used to work at the George and knew where the valuables were kept. One night he slept in a goods van in the yard, and in the early hours of the morning saw his opportunity to slip in.

At around 7.15 a.m. Agnes Murray was woken by a noise, and called out 'Who's there?' She then saw the lad fumbling with the latch to her bedroom, trying to get out. Our stereotypical image of a late-Victorian lady is such that we might imagine that, if she woke to find a strange man in her room, she would either scream the house down or faint dead away. Not our Agnes. She leapt from the bed, grabbed him by the collar and dragged him down the stairs, where she handed him off to a watchman. When they searched his pockets they found £3 18s 2d, and jewellery belonging to Agnes worth over £30. When Police-constable 389M arrived to take the boy into custody, he said, 'I have had nothing to eat since Sunday. I knew where the keys to the pantry were kept, and I went to get them. When I got into the missus's room, someone moved, and I crept under the bed. When the missus went to sleep again I tried to get out, but the door creaked and betrayed me.'

When her mother, Amelia, died in 1903, Agnes promised to continue as manageress 'as long as I am fit to do so'. She was true to her word and would go on to spend her entire life in the pub from the day she arrived aged 18. Later that year, she was advertising the George in newspaper classified sections as the 'last of the old coaching inns'.

Newspapers began to write more about the George, and they began writing about it in a different way, with a new tone. Probably the earliest example of this was in 1899, when the *Daily Graphic* was happy to inform its readers that reports that the George was about to go the way of all Southwark's other coaching inns to make way for 'that modern abomination, the gin palace', having aroused the ire of 'antiquarians and lovers of Old London', were false. The paper celebrated the inn, 'standing with a kind of gloomy sturdiness amid the modern innovations which surround it'. But even with this apparent stay of execution, they were not optimistic for the long term:

> Considering the ground values of that district it would be injudicious to foretell much longer life for the interesting relic, and I would therefore suggest that those who are unacquainted with the hostelry should lose no time in making a pilgrimage to see the last of London's galleried inns, for which the Borough was at one time particularly famous.

Many 'lovers of old London' began to do just that, and sentimental accounts of visits to the George began to appear with increasing frequency in national and international press as well as locally.

The *Daily Chronicle* in 1903 set an early example of the tone, when a journalist was delighted to stumble across the George and enjoyed a midday 'ordinary' in the coffee room

for 1s 11d – 'where else would you be charged so odd a sum?'
He goes on to tell us the meal:

> includes the privilege of carving your own portion
> from the joint and helping yourself to vegetables, ad
> lib, followed by cheese, also unlimited, the whole in a
> spot invigorated with the breath of the hop – Borough
> is the headquarters of the hop trade – after such a
> meal you may pull a rope bell and a smart chamber-
> maid will show you round the 'rambling queer old
> place' . . . 'Oh, to think', says the aged landlady – the
> place has only owned three since the beginning of the
> last century – 'of the herds of cattle and flocks of sheep
> that have been roasted before that fire.'

In 1906, Charles G. Harper in his book, *The Old Inns of Old
England*, explained the appeal of the place:

> It is pleasing to be able to bear witness to the thriving
> trade that continues to be done in this sole ancient
> survivor of the old Southwark galleried inns, and to
> note that, however harshly fate, as personified by
> rapacious landlords, has dealt with its kind, the old-
> world savour of the inn is thoroughly appreciated by
> those not generally thought sentimental persons, the
> commercial men who dine and lunch, and the com-
> mercial travellers who sleep there.

The George was being celebrated as a sole, great survivor,
something of interest to 'lovers of old London'. But at the
same time it was no museum: it was a working pub, a practical
place, and to its regulars it was all about no-nonsense food
and drink. Commercial travellers still enjoyed lunch there, but
thanks to the trains and the increasingly common motorcars,
there was no need to stay overnight. Ironically, an inn that
built its business for centuries as a place 'for the receipt of
travellers' began to survive directly on local custom.

The 1901 census shows just one guest staying at the George, along with Mrs and Miss Murray, three servants and a long-term lodger. The surviving buildings in the inn-yard were home to just one family, belonging to Albert Stewart – a railway worker. Many of the rooms stood empty, the attics deserted and dusty. Nevertheless, Agnes kept the huge four-poster beds made and ready, and sat patiently in her parlour behind the main bar, waiting for guests to arrive.

Some of the old functions of the inn survived, and it remained a popular venue for clubs to meet. While there were many clubs, restaurants and civic buildings for groups to choose from now, the George was probably cheap and usually available, and always had good food and drink readily at hand. In 1898 'The Most Secret Brotherhood of the Rolling Stones' switched their regular dinners from Stone's Chop House in Haymarket to the George, writing invitations to dinner with childish glee:

HUSH !

Beware of Spies !

This is to be delivered into your hand by a trusty messenger.

Beware you are not observed !

To make all secure, be careful to follow these instructions before you open this:

(a) Draw the Blinds !

(b) Sack the Cook !

(c) Get under the Table !

(d) Double lock the door !

(e) Hide the Drinks !

(f) Stuff up the Key-hole !

(g) Shut down the Register, so that when you read this aloud to yourself in the dark you be not overheard.

*****

From the sacred head centre to our Sisters Murray
  greeting !

It is ordered that you do on the fourteenth of February
  next report yourself at the sign of 'The George'
  High Street Borough, exactly as the clock strikes
  the hour of seven-thirty-one.

Fail not at your peril!

He who does, is a traitor to the cause and shall die the
  death.

Present yourself at the wicket door, knock thrice and
  stand [drinks] and give the counter-sign to the shop
  walker whence you will be shown by the secret
  staircase to our presence there to discuss:

(a) The fishy behaviour of certain Renegades and
   track the same to their sauce.

(b) Many will be condemned to the steak and
   d'ungeons.

(c) A lot will be drawn and each one's cup will be
   full of Bitter-wo!

(e) A Red Herring will be drawn across our tracks.

(f) Another Unity Brotherhood will then be
   introduced.

Vengeance having been meated [sic] out the oath of
  secrecy will be sworn. Your mission will be accom-
  plished and three days grace allowed.

The Psalm of Fraternity will next be sung 'Of Wesir
  Rolling Rapidly'.

Each member of the Brotherhood must then render
  an account and he will lawyer-like recite his acts
  and be judged by his deeds and weeds.

Strike while the iron is hot!

The cause is just!

Death to Traitors.

Hush-sh!

P.S. Rolling Ties and Intriguing Breeches will be de
  Rigueur.

For decades, the 'Old Chums' met there for supper on the first Saturday of each year, journeying from around the UK to drink and smoke churchwarden pipes. The Twelve Club, a dozen major buyers from West End stores, met for dinner at the George for a few years around 1910, celebrating their venerable venue on the back of the dinner menu:

> Here within these walls, hoary with the rime of centuries, hover the shadows of the past. Memories crowd one another, anxious to keep us in mind of their little past in the Drama of Life. The old wainscot yet rings with the boisterous laughter of a bygone pageantry, and the rollicking roysterer still elbows the prim puritan of Stuart days. Courtly knight and dame, ruddy squire and hardy yeoman pass before us, and the spirit of past welcomes from bygone Bonifaces mellowed with the ringing voices of children, long since of the dust, cast that glamour which is always the presiding genius among these ancient relics of our glorious Country's history.

London was being erased and rebuilt. The world of the stagecoach, the world of Charles Dickens, had all but passed from living memory, and there was a growing yearning to somehow hang on to it. For the first time, people began to visit Southwark in search of its past: in 1911, a party of Americans made national news when they came looking for the London of Shakespeare and Dickens. *The Times* reported that they lunched on chops and tomato sauce at the George, before visiting the site of the Marshalsea, 'now partially redeemed' and turned into a public garden.

And then the First World War happened, and changed the way we viewed nostalgia for ever.

If this was progress, then we wanted yesterday back, please. The notion that all this change was leading us inexorably to a better, brighter future was seriously challenged for the first time since the start of the Industrial Revolution, and we had to come to terms with the fact that an ever-accelerating, increasingly interconnected world could be a dangerous and unpredictable place. The certainties of the past became even more appealing, and our longing for them became ever more intense. In the 1920s the word 'nostalgia' appeared in its current usage for the first time.[1]

Harvard professor Svetlana Boym has written the only real academic examination of nostalgia. Her fascinating, often beautiful book tells how nostalgia in its original form was thought to cause 'erroneous representations' where patients confused past and present, real and imaginary events. When nostalgia becomes a more widely spread sense of loss, Boym suggests that this loss 'does not necessarily suggest that what is lost is properly remembered and that one still knows where to look for it'. One doctor called it a 'hypochondria of the heart' that thrives on its symptoms. It was caused by the constant acceleration of progress. At the start of the Industrial Revolution the way we regarded time itself had changed from something cyclical and constantly renewed to a straight line marked by numbers, timetables and schedules. Progress was simply accepted as a dominating ideology, something that wasn't even up for question or debate. Maybe Pitt the Younger, with his apparent hatred of clocks, had a point after all.

---

1. The funniest thing about the common misquotation of old Will Roger's comment on the past, 'nostalgia ain't what it used to be', is that it's factually correct. The term 'nostalgia' was first used by Johannes Hofer, a Swiss doctor, in 1688, and is derived from Greek *nostos*, meaning 'returning home', and *algos*, meaning 'pain' or 'ache'. He coined it as a description of homesickness among Swiss mercenaries fighting in France and Italy. At the time, this was seen as a debilitating condition, a real illness that prevented the troops from fighting and could even lead to death. It was treated by medicine, rest, or even a return home, and troops suffering from it were often discharged.

Today we wallow in nostalgia, and time has become, if not cyclical again, then certainly more fluid, allowing us a pick-and-mix approach to everything from political ideology through fashion and music to He-Man action figures, Camp Coffee or white dog poo, depending on your age. So it's astonishing to think how subversive it must have been when people first dared to suggest that things might just have been better in the past, a feeling partly attributable to the fact that we didn't have tanks, machine guns and mustard gas back then.

Looking through volumes of press cuttings, it's fascinating to see visitors and journalists beginning to discuss the George in nostalgic terms at the very moment writers like Boym tell us the term took on its current meaning. Every account of the George from this period is nostalgic in tone, but doesn't use the word because it hasn't quite been coined yet in this particular currency, referring instead to the 'sentimental remembrance' the country was feeling for a vanished past that it couldn't quite remember and had probably never been. And Charles Dickens was the talisman of this past. He had described that vanished world so vividly, so vivaciously, that it seemed to live on in his pages. He wrote about the city as it transformed from the age of coaching inns, public executions and strolling players into the smoky, sooty, modern industrial metropolis. The George belonged to him – a last, physical, tangible link to his world. The place was catnip for nostalgists, the perfect antidote for the soul bruised by crushing modernity.

'Give, oh! Give me yesterday!' cried the writer (and favourite of Miss Murray) E.V. Lucas in his essay on the George in his 1913 book *Loiterer's Harvest*:

> This bitter cry is on the lips of every lover of London,
> faintly heard amid the din made by the pick-axes of
> the demolishers and the cranes and the trowels of the

contractors. But the wish can never be granted; at the most we can by hunting for it cherish for a moment an illusion, and here and there, in the few sanctuaries of antiquity and beauty that remain, cheat ourselves that time has run back and the serener past again is ours.

The George has been 'mercilessly reduced,' he says, 'although what remains is perfect. It is Dickens in essence.'

To picture the scene properly, we have to remember that the whole of the Borough had changed beyond all recognition from a generation before. It was now home to heavy manufacturing and food-processing industries, as well as every imaginable support industry to the docks just down the river in Rotherhithe. In *The Taverns of London*, published in 1927, H.E. Popham painted a vivid picture of what it was like to walk down Bankside towards Southwark from Blackfriars Bridge:

> To get the correct atmosphere of the locality it is as well to walk along the side of the river from Blackfriars Bridge – not along modern Southwark Street – but close to the water, by the wharves, under the cranes, over the ropes, and round the barrels, stumbling over a chain every hundred yards, and incidentally getting a glorious view of St Paul's Cathedral. Although we are almost in hail of the Bank of England, yet we have in spirit left it far behind, and are now down at the heart of things, where the actual work is done, and connection established between the Mother City and every other part of the world. Not on paper but in stern reality; where the things that you actually touch have been or will be handled by some stevedore at Valparaiso or Sydney or Tokyo. Silk hats and patent boots are not for Bankside nor Bankside for them. Coats off here, for there's heaving to be done.

To Bertram Matz, editor of *The Dickensian*, the George was a spiritual home:

> Set in an historic neighbourhood associated with Shakespeare and the players and, in more modern times, with Dickens and his characters, it has become the rendezvous of a continual flow of literary and antiquarian enthusiasts who never miss an opportunity for a visit to its enticing old-world rooms and exterior ... Americans, and country and London ramblers round old London, stand agape on their first introduction to the old galleries as soon as they come in view; whilst their astonishment and delight know no bounds as they proceed from bar parlour to coffee room, up the ever clean wooden stairs to the galleries above and into the various bedrooms furnished with the furniture of polished and rich mahogany of the olden days, which would turn any and every dealer in antiques green with envy, and do, we believe, frequently.

The 'amiable and good-natured proprietress', Miss Murray, 'is ever ready to welcome visitors, not merely because she has good wholesome English food and drink to dispense, but because she loves the old Inn and likes others to love it too.' The stories of coaching days she told her guests had 'such a fascination in these modern days of trains, motors and aeroplanes'.

For over thirty years the George had been the last man standing of the great coaching inns, and it was in a much-diminished state, obscure and hard to find, with a modest sign on the street covered over by railway notices. People didn't remember the old inn-yards any more – the former George Inn yard was now a railway goods yard. And why on earth would there be an old pub in a railway goods yard?

This question aroused the curiosity of a *Daily Mail* journalist in August 1921. He was looking around Southwark

Cathedral when he was approached by an American tourist who asked him where the George was, as it was 'the last surviving Dickens inn in London'. Dickens in his prime was, if anything, even more popular in the United States than he was here.[2] And by now, it was affordable for American tourists to come to Britain on holiday. In the wake of F. Hopkinson Smith's *In Dickens's London*, published in 1912, many now arrived in Southwark, had their senses assaulted by its noise, industry and ugliness, and said, 'Well, where is this Dickens inn, then?'

But what is, or was, a 'Dickens inn'? Our correspondent decided to find out, and managed to find the George 'in a railway goods yard within a stone's throw of London Bridge The Station'. The story he filed bore the headline(s):

LAST DICKENS INN.
WHERE CITY MEN STILL GO FOR ROAST BEEF AND DOMINOES.

---

2. For 160 years, the main example given to illustrate 'Dickensmania' in the States has been the story that, in 1841, as *The Old Curiosity Shop* neared its wrenching climax, crowds lined the docks in New York and as a new ship came in, yelled, wailed and begged those on board, 'Is Little Nell dead?'* However, this story has never been verified and is listed by the *Oxford Companion to Dickens* as 'unconfirmed'. One literary blogger, 'Caleb Crane', examined microfilms of the *New York Herald* from January to March 1841, when the news would have arrived, and found no mention of it – and the arrival of ships was always a big deal. Of course, if it were still the same today the crowds would be shouting 'Don't tell us if Little Nell dies! No spoilers!' And I've just revealed that she does, in fact, die at the end. If you are one of those readers who hates spoilers and is now angry with me for revealing this, I would just like to stress again that the book was written 160 years ago, so it's not really my fault if you didn't already know.

* It wasn't wrenching for everyone: although the author apparently wept as he wrote it, Oscar Wilde said, 'One must have a heart of stone to read the death of Little Nell without laughing.'

The George, he says, has been 'left untouched by the rude hands of "improvers" and "restorers" and is exactly as Dickens knew it.'

> There is a delightful absence of the commercial atmosphere – I was treated rather as a guest than as a customer – and all the old men who were having luncheon there seemed to be firm friends of the house. After the meal they settled down to a game of dominoes ... the fare, consisting of roast beef, bread, and cheese, was very simple and English.

A few days later, Ralph Edwards of the Tredington Rectory, Shipston-on-Stour, wrote to the paper to correct the journalist: the George was far from being just as Dickens knew it – it had been heavily mutilated since then. And it was now patronized by far more than just city gents. 'Mr A.H. Bullen, the celebrated Elizabethan scholar, always regarded it with peculiar affection, and seldom failed to stay there when in London during the last years of his life.'

But Ralph Edwards of the Tredington Rectory, Shipston-on-Stour wasn't the only one who was unhappy with the *Mail* story: Miss Murray herself was bloody furious.

Two days after the *Mail* story, the *Daily Graphic* sent someone down to the George to see what the fuss was about. He found a warm welcome for himself, but the place was in chaos. A party of American tourists filled the place, blocking the door, attempting to buy a bedpan that was hung on the wall, and trying to get the parrot to speak. But the inn wouldn't sell them the bedpan, and the parrot was keeping schtum.

'It is a newspaper that has done this,' fumed Miss Murray. 'We've got our regular customers, and they are quite good enough.'

'All my sympathies are with Miss Murray', writes the *Graphic* journalist. 'She knows the hop-dealers who visit her for lunch every day. One's own friends are always preferable to strange faces.'

Except . . .

If Miss Murray was perfectly happy with her regulars and resented souvenir-hungry tourists and inquisitive newspapers, why did she then go and have a series of postcards printed and distributed, one with a picture of her standing in the doorway of 'The George Hotel', the parrot in the foreground, with a caption reading:

> Ye Olde George Inn, Southwark
> (77, Borough High Street.)
> Where good olde English fare is still served as in ye
> Coaching Days.
> Proprietress – Miss Murray

To me, that reads an awful lot like the work of someone who definitely doesn't feel her regulars are quite good enough.

The George, though, was a place of delightful discovery. In 1921, the *Daily News* commented that there were men who walked down Borough High Street every day for twenty years who had never seen it. Again, this was something Miss Murray set about remedying in unsubtle ways. In 1926, another *Daily News* reporter described the 'narrow entrance to a yard into which the lumbering railway vans are continually passing', and the growing collection of 'smoke-grimed signs' that graced the side wall. First there was an old sign simply pointing to the George Inn. Then there was another, bigger sign, pointing to 'The Old George Inn of Dickens Fame'. And finally, the newest, biggest sign urged you to visit 'Ye Olde George Inn, the scene of Jeffrey Farnol's Great Romance, "The Amateur Gentleman".'[3]

---

3. Farnol's novel, now largely forgotten, features the George in several key scenes. The main character stays there when he arrives in London, and in the George Inn yard he tames and calms a wild horse.

And then there was that bloody parrot. Joey the parrot was a gift to Miss Murray from the writer H.M. Tomlinson (best known today for his first work, *The Sea and the Jungle*, which featured parrots). He was installed in the coffee room and came with a guarantee that if he didn't speak within three months, the dealer would exchange him. The date expired and Joey's beak remained zipped. The dealer, apparently, heard about this and came to the pub.

'No, you won't take Joey away,' insisted Miss Murray.

Was this a previously unforeseen sentimental side to the steely proprietress? Not at all. 'All the men who think they understand parrots come here to make him talk, some of them from as far away as Canterbury,' she said. 'He brings good trade to the house. That parrot that won't talk is the talk of South London. Indeed, and you won't take away Joey!' And so the taciturn parrot remained, perfectly suited to his mistress, until the inn changed hands after her death, and he retired to Brighton.

Agnes Murray was a very shrewd businesswoman, preserving the George as a well-kept secret while telling everyone about it, and insisting it was just for the regulars while doing everything she possibly could to lure in tourists.

And her greatest ally in all this was Dickens himself. Except he wasn't really an ally – at least, not in the way she claimed.

It's almost impossible now to appreciate just how popular Charles Dickens was in the early twentieth century, and the unique flavour of that popularity. Fans spoke of his characters as if they were real, because to them they were. They yearned for some kind of contact with these imaginary people, anything that could put them in touch with this world. Matz described *The Pickwick Papers* as 'a mirror of the manners and customs of a romantic age which has fast receded from us.'

And within the Dickens canon, the pecking order was quite

The one and only Agnes Murray, definitely NOT trying to drum up tourist business with the help of Joey the parrot.

different from today. A poll conducted by Penguin to mark Dickens's bicentenary in February 2012 found that, unsurprisingly, Ebenezer Scrooge is the most popular Dickensian character, followed by Miss Havisham, Sydney Carton from *A Tale of Two Cities*, the Artful Dodger and Fagin. *Oliver Twist* and *Great Expectations* between them provide the majority of the top ten. *Pickwick* is mentioned nowhere in the list, nor in the news coverage around the poll.

A hundred years ago it was quite different. *The Pickwick Papers* was, according to Matz, 'the most popular book in our language – a book unexampled in our literature'. It was filmed five times between 1913 and 1952, and was made into a long-forgotten TV series in 1985, but hasn't been adapted since, despite our love of costume drama and the regular adaptation of many of Dickens's key works. It's astounding, given the popularity it once had, that it comes so far down the pecking order today.[4]

Pickwick was published episodically. It was floundering until chapter ten, when Pickwick meets Sam Weller in the yard of the White Hart Inn, upon which it instantly became a publishing phenomenon and rocketed Dickens to fame. Weller was so popular he gave his name to the 'Wellerism' – when a phrase or saying is shown to be comically wrong in certain situations ('"So I see," said the blind carpenter as he picked up his hammer and saw') – and was even honoured with Sam Weller souvenir notebooks. When the White Hart was finally demolished, a surviving building within the new warehouse complex that was built in its place was opened as the Sam Weller Social Club in 1911.

Read today, Sam Weller is a very familiar stereotype of the cockney geezer with a heart of gold. But he's one who offers a skewed view on Pickwick's adventures, often expressed in comic phrases and proverbs. The narrator of *Pickwick* very gently makes fun of the main character's self-delusion – perhaps too gently, because the introduction of Weller makes this benevolent mockery much more overt, and therefore much funnier. In one introduction to *Pickwick*, the relationship between Sam Weller and Mr Pickwick is likened to that between Sancho Panza and Don Quixote.

When we first meet him, Weller is working as a bootblack

---

4. Or perhaps it's not too surprising. At the time of writing I'm trying out a new talk, a 'beer and book matching' event where I read passages from books that have a link to beer or pubs, and do a tutored tasting of beers I've chosen to go with each reading. Last time I did it, I chose what is commonly agreed to be the funniest passage in the whole of *Pickwick*. One person came up to me afterwards and said cheerfully, 'You know, you forget how unfunny Dickens was.' Or maybe it was just my delivery.

in the White Hart.[5] Dickens quickly realizes the comic
phenomenon he's created, and has Pickwick hire Sam as his
personal servant and occasional rescuer for the rest of the
periodically released book. Among his many other achievements, Samuel Weller rescued the career of arguably the
greatest novelist the world has ever seen, and he did so in a
Borough coaching inn.

After the White Hart disappeared, a number of Dickens
scholars began to suggest that when Dickens had written 'The
White Hart' and carefully described that inn, he was secretly
writing about the George. As early as 1888, Joseph Ashby
Sterry was dropping very strong hints in an article called
'Dickens in Southwark' for the *English Illustrated Magazine*.
He described the George as 'The most thoroughly Dickensian
hostelry from cellar to roof-tree that you could now find in
London', loving everything from 'the quaint passages, the
queer-shaped rooms', to the 'communicative green parrot,[6]
who seems to have a word to say to everybody, and whom I
fancy must have exchanged jokes with Sam Weller'. And then
he comes right out and says it:

> Moreover [the George] is especially notable as being
> the spot where Mr. Pickwick first encountered the
> immortal Sam Weller. The 'White Hart' is the name,
> I am aware, given in the book, but it is said that
> Dickens changed the sign in order that the place
> should not be too closely identified. I . . . had the
> opportunity of comparing both inns some years ago,
> and have no hesitation in saying that the 'George' is
> the inn where the irrepressible Alfred Jingle and the

---

5. In his first line, after a chambermaid says that number twenty-two wants
his boots, Sam replies, 'Ask number twenty-two whether he'll have 'em
now, or wait till he get's 'em', and the whole of 1830s England pissed itself
in paroxysms of uncontrollable, unceasing laughter.

6. Back then, it was obviously a different parrot.

elderly Miss Rachel were discovered by the warm-hearted, hot-tempered Wardle. If you like to go upstairs you can see the very room where Mr. Jingle consented to forfeit all claims to the lady's hand for the consideration of a hundred and twenty pounds. Cannot you fancy, too, the landlord shouting instructions from those picturesque flower-decked galleries to Sam in the yard below?

By the 1920s newspapers such as the *Daily Mail* were routinely repeating the claim that the George was 'said by authorities on Dickens to be, in all probability, the inn where Pickwick and Sam Weller met'. Allegedly even Dickens's son, Charles Dickens Jnr, believed this to be the case.

There is no doubt whatsoever that Dickens did know the George. He mentions it specifically in *Little Dorrit*, the book in which he turns his ire on the Marshalsea, where he used to visit his father. In Book One, Chapter Twelve, when the Dorrits are impoverished, Maggy refers to Little Dorrit's brother, Tip, suggesting that he goes into the George to write begging letters to Arthur Clennam. Miss Murray firmly believed that Dickens had been a regular customer, on the grounds that when she first arrived at the George one of the regulars, Abraham Dawson, an old carrier who lived in the yard and was Westerman Scholefield's nephew, claimed to have seen him in the coffee room regularly.

So if Dickens referred to the George by name in one book, why would he disguise it in another? J. Ashby Sterry argues that this was common practice for the author, citing numerous instances where he has changed the names of inns in other works. But Matz takes this claim apart – where Dickens did change names, he had specific reasons for doing so, and there were far more cases of him using the correct names for real places. In a letter to the *Daily Graphic* in August 1921, Hammond Hall insists, 'It was not Dickens's way deliberately to misdescribe a place which he identified with its real name. When he says the White Hart – and he says it four times in one chapter – he means the White Hart and no other.'

The Dickensian, in reviewing F. Hopkinson Smith's, *In Dickens's London*, stated, 'The "George" Inn is just a fine survival of the old days of which Dickens wrote and is similar, in many respects, to what the "White Hart" used to be. As such Dickensians have a great affection for it; there is no need to invent stories about it to justify their reverence.'

Matz agreed, writing, 'Let us leave it at that and retain our regard for the old inn for what it is, rather than what it is not.'

Of course, Sam and Pickwick met neither in the George nor the White Hart. Because they were not real people. They never existed. They were made-up characters. But to point this out in the 1920s would have probably resulted in a lynching from the balustrades of the George Inn. There is no better demonstration of the yearning, the desperate need to stay in touch with Dickens. This was an almost physical manifestation of a longing that also seemed to tear Sam Weller out of the pages and into reality. The George was the last Dickensian coaching inn still standing. Oh, it simply *must* be the inn Dickens described! Can't we all just say it is, and make it true?

Serious Dickensian scholars had no truck with such sentimentality. Matz and company wrote as if they simply couldn't understand why anyone would seriously *believe* Dickens had meant the George, as opposed to simply *wishing* he had. But in their many writings, they seem curiously reluctant to acknowledge the real reason why, for many people, it was genuine belief rather than wishful thinking. With so much evidence pointing to the White Hart (its name, for example) how could anyone seriously think it was the George?

Why, because Agnes Murray was telling everyone it was.

When Matz destroyed F. Hopkinson Smith's case for the George by pointing out that Smith admits he gained his information from 'any Tom, Dick or Harry', he chickened out of pointing the finger at the formidable Miss Murray herself. But Smith's account of his visit to the George makes it clear that she is the source:

> 'When you finish your coffee come up-stairs with me,' she broke in again, removing a Cheshire cheese as big as a bandbox in answer to a call for a portion of its contents from the next pew, 'and I'll show you the room where Miss Wardle passed the night when she ran off with Alfred Jingle, and the room where Mr Perker settled the affair for one hundred and thirty pounds of Wardle's money, and where Sam Weller first met Mr Pickwick.'
> 'And the English-speaking race as well,' I added.
> 'And the English-speaking race as well,' came the echoing laugh. 'It's just over our heads.'
> 'If you had your "Pickwick" with you,' she said, my coffee finished, 'you'd find that nothing has been changed in the bedroom.' This came with a sort of reproof. Not to put a copy of 'Pickwick' in one's pocket when visiting the 'George' was like being in Westminster Abbey during morning service without a prayer book.

Later, after being shown around the rooms in which the action in chapter ten supposedly took place, unchanged since that momentous day, Smith emphasizes the absolute certainty with which Miss Murray asserts her position:

> [These were] not the rooms, remember, in which the above events *were supposed* to have taken place, nor the room in which various admirers of Mr Dickens believe they *might* have taken place, but the rooms in which they really *did take place*.

Matz attacks Smith on the grounds that he provides 'no data' with which to back up his argument. In doing this, he's making the same mistake Miss Murray makes above – namely, forgetting that data or proof or certainty one way or the other are impossible to provide given that – and let me emphasize this point again, just to make sure it gets across this time – the book WAS MADE UP AND THE CHARACTERS NEVER EXISTED, whichever pub they were supposedly in.

But hang on: F. Hopkinson Smith then seemingly acknowledges the absurdity in both side's positions – and defends them:

> And here it will be just as well for me to inform my reader that if he entertains the slightest doubt of the truth of this and similar statements, and feels disposed to accentuate these doubts by indulging in loud and contemptuous poo-poohs, he might better puff them all out at this first chapter, and then close the book, for he will be treated to no other point of view should he continue to the end. Not to believe that Sam Weller and Pecksniff and David Copperfield, Peggotty, Little Dorrit, and all the rest of them lived and moved and had their being, would be like doubting that Santa Claus, Robinson Crusoe, and Peter Pan ever lived.

Oh all right, maybe I was being a bit too mean and cynical when I shouted at everyone just then. We do genuinely believe in characters we know are fictitious – or if not believe in them entirely, we completely suspend our disbelief. Isn't that the appeal of great fiction or drama? When we share Scrooge's delirious joy at simply being alive when he wakes on Christmas Day, or feel an adrenaline thrill of terror or sense of creeping dread when we read Stephen King or H.P. Lovecraft, when we feel grief at the death of Little Nell in *The Old Curiosity Shop* or Emma Morley at the end of *One Day*,[7] aren't those feelings as authentic as those we feel in the real

---

7. Whoops.

world, for real people? If we accept that they are, then we must also accept that it's perfectly sensible to have heated arguments about which real-world inn these fictitious characters supposedly inhabited.

There are so many wonderful, atmospheric accounts of visits to the George from this period that I have to give you one more.

One of the greatest pleasures of writing a book like this is having to go and dig into dusty old books and discover people like William Rendle and Bertram Matz. One man whose name, unlike theirs, is still recognized today is Henry Canova Vollam Morton. OK, that might sound just as unfamiliar. But as H.V. Morton, author of *In Search of England*, he's enjoyed a resurgence of interest among the kind of people who read and write humorous travelogues, thanks to his pioneering journey by automobile around a vanishing, changing country. Morton was also a distinguished journalist. He scooped the official *Times* correspondent in his coverage of the opening of Tutankhamun's tomb by Howard Carter in 1922, but is less well remembered for his columns in the *Daily Express* in which he explored London life. Still, these were popular enough at the time to be collected into a number of anthologies. One of these, *Nights of London*, contains an account of a night spent at the George in 1926.

Like many writers of the era, Morton draws a sharp distinction between inns and modern hotels. 'I hate arriving at a modern hotel to be shot up in a lift to a stereotyped room in which to the servants I become "Number 209",' he writes. 'Even a millionaire taking possession of the best suite in Claridge's cannot achieve the faintest ghost of the pleasure of arriving unexpectedly and importantly at an inn which, recognizing you as "the quality", flings itself into quick activity to give you the best it has ... it all gives you the feeling, impossible in the Ritz, that people are not only serving you well but that they are glad to do so.'

In this he was echoing Dickens, who lived long enough to see the transition from the coaching inn to the 'great station hotel' in which 'we can get anything we want, after its kind, for money; but where nobody is glad to see us, or sorry to see us, or minds (our bill paid) whether we come or go, or how, or when, or why, or cares about us . . . where we have no individuality, but put ourselves into the general post, as it were, and are sorted and disposed of according to our division.'

But this is the George Inn we're talking about, and it's hard to imagine Agnes Murray in the middle of an obsequious bustle of welcome. Morton, a great judge of people, could see the passion beneath the rigid exterior. Miss Murray was sitting in her parlour just behind the taproom bar, reading a book, when Morton arrived:

'Can I stay here?'
'Certainly.'
I learned afterwards how sincerely she loves this old inn of hers, so that I am now able to translate her smile into words. It meant: 'For five hundred years travellers have been staying at the "George" and the "George" is not dead yet! Of course you can stay.'

Miss Murray must have been delighted. Only two bedrooms remained in use by this time, both with their giant four-posters, and you can almost hear Morton giggling when he admits that he is the only guest at the inn. Later, Miss Murray tells him, 'Once we were busy with the hop merchants from the Hop Exchange near here. They used to come up from Kent and spend the night. But now they come up by motor and return the same evening. We do not have many visitors now. We do a luncheon trade, but no dinners.'

She doesn't know when the last coach called. But she remembers someone who does:

'I have no idea of the date, but once, many years ago, an old gentleman came here and asked for a room. When I told him that I could put him up for the night he said, "And it isn't the first time either! The last time I stayed here I came on the coach!" So, of course, I gave him the best bedroom. Ah, times have changed . . . all London has changed.'

'Except the old "George".'

'Well, I've tried to keep it as I always remember it.'

She then tries the usual Dickens scam on him, showing him the very desk where Tip Dorrit wrote his begging letters to Clennam – a remarkable feat, given that this scene is not even described in the book.

When Morton retires for the night, he's astonished by the great four-poster that takes up most of his room, and the three carpet-covered steps leading up to it:

It looks as though it should be mounted on wheels so that it could be drawn through the streets with a sultana lying inside on silk cushions. Or it looks, with the white sheets turned back, as if ready for the lying-in-state of a French president . . . [or] . . . it looks as though against its generous pillows should recline an eighteenth-century belle with a lace cap on her Greuze-like head. She would, of course, be sipping chocolate.

Writing in bed by candlelight, his thoughts inevitably turn to ghosts, and he fancies that the room itself is a living entity, watching him and sizing him up:

It seems to me that the shadows are like fingers pointing, that this old room is trying to say to me 'The time may come when you, and those who love London, may have to fight for all that is left of me!' and the knowledge that I would indeed fight hard places me in sympathy with the shadows, which no longer appear to watch doubtfully. I have made friends with this queer old room.

But to Morton, the strangest thing of all is that he is here, now, in the dizzying modern world:

> The candle has burned to the last two inches and it is nearly midnight. I cannot say that mighty bed invites me: it would never be so familiar. It looms before me like a state coach . . . I would dearly like to go out to the balcony and look down on the ghosts of the inn yard, but the floors creak and I might awaken the 'George'. The strangest thing about tonight is that I am in London in 1926!

In this way, Agnes Murray kept the George Inn alive. She did little or nothing to maintain the ancient building itself, but she built the fame of the inn, fed its soul, and created a legend.

She brooked no argument. Winston Churchill was a regular visitor. He once turned up for dinner with a bottle of quality port, explaining to Miss Murray that on his last visit, there was none. She served him with a quiet smile, and then presented him with a bill, which included 'Corkage: one shilling and sixpence'. On another occasion she was asked to make lunch for James Scullin, a former Borough boy who became the Australian Prime Minister from 1929 to 1932, and members of his cabinet. She replied, 'I have only a small leg of mutton for myself and the staff, but, if your friends come, I will gladly give them a glass of good sherry.' She received the deputation like a queen, wearing her favourite cameo brooch.

There are many other delightful stories I could tell you about Miss Murray, but I'm not sure they have much basis in fact. My first introduction to her was by her relative, John M. East, great-grandson of the old waggoning Easts who first brought Amelia Murray and her young daughter Agnes to the George back in the 1870s. In 1967 East wrote *'Neath the Mask*, the story of the acting dynasty spawned by the family that grew up in the George Inn yard. It's a colourful book and was among the first material about the George that I was able to find. But as I discovered more, I realized there was a good reason why East's account was so vivid.

Here's how East, in 1967, describes the arrival of the Murrays when they moved into the George Inn yard:

> Amelia Murray gazed about the courtyard itself. No smart young chambermaid called to her from over the balustrade of an upper sleeping gallery, neither did a bustling landlady make her appearance from an opposite gallery. But George Grinslade, the cheery and welcoming landlord, on hearing the sound of the wheels on the cobblestones, did peer at the visitors through the quaint panes of a low-sashed window, his hand busy with a pewter mug held close to a wooden spigot.

And here's a passage from F. Hopkinson Smith's *In Dickens's London*, written fifty-five years before, when he first meets Miss Murray herself:

> No smart young chambermaid called to me from over the balustrade of the upper sleeping gallery when I alighted from a hansom in the courtyard of this same inn, known then and now as 'George Inn', and gazed about me this morning in June – nor did any bustling old landlady make her appearance on the opposite gallery. There was a maid, of course, who might, and possibly did, cajole all the subsequent Sam Wellers of her time; and there was a landlady – a most cheery and comforting landlady, as I afterward discovered – who on hearing the sound of wheels peered at me through the quaint panes of a low-sashed window, her

hand busy with a pewter mug held close to a wooden spigot.

I subsequently found Matz's, Morton's and Rendle's observations on the George each woven into East's account as if they were his own. He faithfully repeats, almost word for word, the sketchy history first outlined by George Corner in his 1858 lecture, and then claims this history was in fact compiled by the elder John East, who 'made it his business to learn all he could about the history of the George Inn and details of his findings can be seen to this day in a faded notebook, with his name embossed on the cover'. He claims the Lord Digby story was one of John East's anecdotes which he used to entertain fellow visitors, even though he repeats it in the same words I found in older sources. He goes on to say, yeah, my great-granddad and Charles Dickens were best mates. Like *that*, they were. John James East apparently provided Dickens with all his transport needs, and Dickens visited East 'many times' in his private quarters at the George.[8] He apparently reciprocated East's hospitality by inviting him to dinner at the Trafalgar Tavern with Wilkie Collins and Harrison Ainsworth. He also claims to have invented scissors. OK, I made that last bit up, but it's contagious.

'Neath the Mask, as its title suggests, is theatrical in every possible way. I decided to track down its author to see if he could tell me any more stories, and discovered that, sadly, he passed away in 2003, aged 70. So where I've mentioned any of East's stories of Agnes Murray, I've verified them elsewhere.[9]

---

8. Census data shows no record of the Easts living at the George.

9. I also found on the Internet Movie Database that 'after a successful career as a broadcaster, stage actor and bit-part player in British television comedies', John M. East became a 1970s soft-porn star. He worked closely

An inn-yard performance of Shakespeare at the George Inn,
some time in the 1930s. Each year these performances
attracted national press coverage, and kept alive the
spirit of the arts on the South Bank.

As Agnes Murray turned eighty the George was something
of an institution. On Shakespeare Day in 1932, J.M. Barrie,
or Sir James Barrie as he was called by then, turned up to
watch the annual performance in the inn-yard. It was preceded by a procession to and from Park Street, the site of the
Globe, and an address by the Bishop of Southwark who

---

with porn legend Mary Millington, and his credits include *Hellcats: Mud
Wrestling; The Whitehouse Video Show*, in which he played 'Dirty Old Man';
Mary Millington's World Striptease Extravaganza (which he also 'wrote') and
Queen Kong: Amazonian Woman. Approaching the end of the colourful history
of the George Inn, this seems wonderfully, perversely appropriate – Sinful
Southwark exerting its influence one last time.

conceded that Stratford may have been Shakespeare's birth-place, but Southwark was where he 'mounted the ladder of fame and won his greatest triumphs'.

The tenor of the regular newspaper stories of this now famous old inn changed again in the early 1930s, with reports that the George was 'to be saved' gaining in frequency. In January 1933 *The Times* reported that what was now the London and North Eastern Railway had for the first time announced its commitment to preserve the inn. A few days later the *Evening News* followed up the story with a piece that excited them so much, they couldn't decide which headline to use, so ended up using four instead:

LAST OF LONDON'S COACHING INNS
THE 'GEORGE' TO RENEW ITS YOUTH
SHAKESPEARE USED TO GO THERE
SO DID DICKENS

These reporters spoke to people who had used the coffee room, with its red plush seats, old beer ads and Parliament Clock still keeping good time, every day for over fifty years. They asked Miss Murray about ghosts, and she replied that she had never seen one in the fifty-six years she had lived there (even though she'd actually lived there for sixty-two years).[10] The LNER claimed there were no plans for altera-tions to be made. 'At the present time it is in good repair . . . It is felt that alterations to the worn floors and old beams would at once change the character of the place, and it will only be as a last resort that such changes will be made.'

Agnes Murray never married. The constant presence of Miss Isabel May Barnes, a lifelong 'companion' who lived at the George as a 'servant', probably tells us the most likely

---

10. Agnes never seems to have had a good grasp of numbers. In the 1871 census, in which she is listed as a barmaid, she's 18 years old. But on the 1901 census thirty years later, somehow she's only 44.

reason for this. Although at various points in my research, I've also held the view that Agnes had given her heart to Charles Dickens, the man who used to sit just over there in the coffee room, but died three years before Agnes arrived at the inn, the man to whom no other could measure up. 'I should love to have met Mr Dickens,' she told F. Hopkinson Smith wistfully. 'I've seen a lot of men in my time, but there's none I'd rather have met than Mr Dickens.'

But it seems obvious to me now that Agnes was married to the George Inn, till death did they part.

That parting came on 30 October 1934 when Agnes Murray died, aged 81. She left £16,296 11s 2d, most of it to her companion Isabel May Barnes (John M. East was aggrieved she left nothing to the East family). For the first time in over sixty years, the railway company had to seek a new tenant.

Their advertisement was answered by Harold and Leslie Staples, who moved in in July 1935. The two brothers were shopkeepers from north London who had never run a pub before but were massive Dickens enthusiasts, an interest that earned them the nickname The Cheeryble Brothers, 'the twins of humanitarian activity, of benevolence, and private charity' whom Dickens created in *Nicholas Nickleby*. The chance to take over what was now generally referred to as a 'Dickens inn' was a dream come true for them, and they pledged to put all their energies into making it 'as near as possible what it was in Dickens' day'. 'The George was a haunt of Dickens, and we are convinced that it was the original of the White Hart in Pickwick Papers,' brother Harold told the *Daily Mirror*.

They didn't quite succeed in making it more like Dickens knew it, but did make several major improvements that actually made it less like it had been in Dickens's day. Agnes Murray may have loved the pub, but she wasn't as passionate about the comfort of its customers. There was no telephone, not even a bathroom. The brothers installed a phone, and had a new letterhead printed with the number on it, pointing out the Southwark exchange code:

'The George Inn'
AD 1676
London's last Galleried Coaching Inn
One Minute from London Bridge
'Phone HOP 2056

The old kitchen on the ground floor was made into a comfortable lounge and its open fireplace was brought back into use. A bathroom was installed and the main room on the first floor was restored to something like its former appearance, when eighteenth-century panelling was rescued from beneath so many coats of paint that, when it was removed, it weighed four hundredweights (448lb, or 204kg).

Sphere magazine turned up for that year's Dickensian Christmas dinner and was delighted with the results. 'During the past few months many Victorian excrescences have been removed, and by judicious cleansing and furbishing the rooms of the George are taking on an added attraction,' the magazine said.

'When we came in we found fine old furniture, and we are always making fresh discoveries beneath the lumber,' the Cheerybles told the journalist. They expressed their aim to restore the 'prestige of old English cookery', with dishes that were 'simple but perfect'.

The article concludes that they've done a great job: 'To stand outside when dusk has fallen and the lights are shining from these many-paned windows is to be greeted with a scene of great joy to the lover of antiquity.'

With the plays now happening out in the yard every Shakespeare Day and Dickens's birthday, the George was universally celebrated and never out of the papers. The Overian players, a bunch of local working men, made great use of what they had, with one paper describing how 'a dray serves as a stage, and a violinist at an open window as an orchestra. But on these occasions no London theatre has a more genuine gallery and pit.'

It was all going so well.

The LNER had stated its commitment to maintain and preserve the George, with no changes to be made to it without specific sanction. But this didn't include the end buildings on the south wing, formerly private residences used by families such as the Dawsons and the Dodsons, now railway offices. While the Staples brothers were improving the inside of the inn, next door the LNER was partially demolishing their offices with the intention of remodelling them. They'd previously said the structure of the George was fine, but as is so often the case with old buildings, and as anyone who has had a new kitchen and bathroom fitted in a terraced house in Stoke Newington and been quoted fifteen grand only to end up spending over forty at a time when they're skint because they've just spent most of a year working on their new book will know, as soon as you start taking up the floorboards, things can look very different. Shockingly, it became obvious to the LNER that the George was on the point of structural collapse. Extensive repairs were urgent and essential, and would mean the inn would have to be closed for some time. The Staples brothers, having spent a huge sum, now saw their source of income suddenly shut off. They couldn't continue, and left after less than two years of living their dream.

Just when its future seemed safe, the George was belatedly facing the same fate as its forgotten neighbours.

CHAPTER THIRTEEN: IN WHICH THE GEORGE INN IS SAV'D FOR THE NATION, AND A PRINCESS AND A BISHOP HAVE A LOCK-IN

> London has always been rebuilt, and demolished, and vandalized ... one of the characteristics of London planners and builders over the centuries, has been the recklessness with which they have destroyed the city's past.
>
> (Peter Ackroyd, *London: The Biography*, 2001)

'THE NATIONAL TRUST for Places of Historic Interest or Natural Beauty' was founded in 1894 and incorporated by an Act of Parliament in 1907 'for the purposes of promoting the permanent preservation for the benefit of the nation of lands and tenements (including buildings) of beauty or historic interest', after three philanthropic souls discovered a common interest in preserving buildings and public spaces for the people, protecting them from the eternal hunger of property speculators and developers. The Trust had modest beginnings, but grew quickly in a climate where there was such a keen desire to hold on to a vanishing past.

Perhaps the most bizarre story in the history of the National Trust is that of Ferguson's Gang, an anonymous group consisting – we think – entirely of women, who raised money and donated considerable sums to the Trust in the

1930s. They were known only by pseudonyms such as Red Biddy, Bill Stickers, Black Maria, and of course The Right Bludy Lord Beershop of the Gladstone Islands. They communicated in a fake cockney argot and were usually masked when they appeared in public. Despite or perhaps because of such eccentricities, they raised the equivalent of over £500,000, which allowed the Trust to buy such properties as the Old Town Hall at Newton on the Isle of Wight, and Priory Cottages at Steventon in Oxfordshire. Their first victory was Shalford Hall, which they bought themselves and then donated to the Trust. They delivered one cash donation sewn into the carcass of a goose, and another time 'Red Biddy' delivered one hundred pounds' worth of Victorian coins in a sack, dumping it on the secretary's desk before making her getaway in a taxi that 'The Nark' had positioned just outside. Although they're now all long dead, only one member of the gang was ever identified: in December 1996 the obituary of Margaret Pollard, a Cambridge University Sanskrit scholar, claimed that she had been Bill Stickers.

So the National Trust was accustomed to the unexpected when in March 1937 representatives of LNER effectively said, 'Congratulations! You are now the owners of an ancient coaching inn.' The railway company made a deed of gift of the George, but not the ground on which it stood or the yard outside, on the condition that it was retained as a working inn. While the LNER couldn't afford to make the urgent repairs themselves, over the past fifty years the place had clearly worked its magic on them. Perhaps a sense of guilt at the railways having destroyed Southwark's entire landscape of inns compelled them to save this last surviving fragment by any means possible – apart from spending vast sums of cash, of course.

'OLD COACHING INN SAVED FOR THE NATION' announced *The Times*, with a second, almost plaintive headline beneath, reading simply, 'A LINK WITH DICKENS'. The report told how the inn had become 'a popular place of pilgrimage for sightseers in London and of refreshment for many businessmen in the district'. And it now provided a fascinating subject of study. 'The beams are of white deal, an unusual type of wood for this purpose,' said an official of the Timber Development Association. 'We have examined the wood under the microscope and it appears to be in perfect condition although nearly 300 years old.' The same couldn't be said of the rest of the inn of course. 'A considerable sum is now needed to repair the ravages of time,' the newspaper continued.

And the big problem was, the National Trust didn't have that kind of money. As Mr Matheson, the Trust representative, explained at a meeting of the railway property board in March 1937, never before had the National Trust accepted a property 'on the chance of obtaining sufficient money to preserve it . . . They had no funds with which to buy it and indeed no funds with which to repair any structure.'

Before the gift was formally accepted, a plan to raise the money had to be worked out. The Trust began approaching breweries with a view to them taking on a long lease on the inn at a low rent in return for carrying out the urgent repairs needed at their own expense. After several months of searching with no interest shown, in July they began talking to Flower & Sons of Stratford-upon-Avon. This may have seemed like a random choice when there were so many brewers closer to Southwark, but Flowers had a good reputation for looking after old inns and for restoring and endowing historic buildings. And the Shakespeare connection didn't hurt either, at a time when the inn-yard performances of his work were regularly making national news.

In a letter to his solicitors dated 9 July 1937, Fordham Flower, chairman of the brewery, wrote that he shared the National Trust's interest in keeping the inn going, but it depended on how much the peppercorn rent would be, and how much the repairs would cost. With the bill initially estimated at £600, Flower believed the George would 'only be a commercial proposition for us if the rent is merely a nominal one'. He instructed the solicitors, Crossman & Block, to proceed accordingly.

The reply from Crossman & Block ten days later is littered with scribbled exclamation marks and question marks which create a perfect picture of Flower's reaction upon reading it. The Trust's solicitors said trade at the inn was increasing appreciably, so the rent should be more in the region of a full spice rack rather than a single peppercorn. No specific figure was mentioned, but a previous occupier (probably the Cheeryble brothers) had been paying £80 a year ('!!'). It was proposed that the lease should be renegotiable at stated points every few years by either party so this rent could be further increased if the pub started making serious money ('?!!') which they felt was highly likely once the public became aware that it was owned by the Trust ('When it becomes known that Flowers ale is there!!')

On the twenty-third, by which time he'd calmed down a little, Flower sent a curt response. He was 'astonished' by this change of tack, and questioned the Trust's supposed optimism, on the grounds that they'd found it so hard to find an interested party so far:

> In the first place we were approached privately by a member of the staff of the Trust with a view to assisting them to save this historic inn from demolition. We ascertained that certain London brewers had previously been approached but that they could not be persuaded to take any interest in the property on account of its bad position and entrance, and on account of the very small beer trade attached to it.

Flower had always understood that it would be a peppercorn rent, and wrote that if terms were any different, the deal was off. Yet again, having almost been pulled out of the fire, the future of the George was hanging by a thread.

Eventually a compromise was reached. Flower's would pay their peppercorn rent, but it would be reviewed every seven years so they could withdraw if the building proved unprofitable, and the rent could be increased if the money started rolling in. The Deed of Gift of the George was formally made on 6 December 1937, and the lease from the Trust to Flower's was signed the same day. The National Trust owned the building, with the LNER retaining 'the substratum and soil beneath the site of the said inn'. The annual rent paid to the Trust by Flower's was £1 per year, plus 5 per cent of the costs of drainage and a contribution to any maintenance or repair the Trust might undertake. The lessees agreed to spend not less than £700 'in putting the said premises in a state of structural and decorative repair to the reasonable satisfaction of the Surveyor of the National Trust'. The lease would run for twenty-one years, and the furniture, fixtures and fittings still belonged to the Trust. Flower's agreed to do an external paintjob every three years in colours to be agreed by the National Trust, and all internal decoration had to be approved by the Trust. Flower's were to carry on business 'only as an hotel tavern or licensed victualing house', and had to agree to 'carry on as far as possible and improve the existing goodwill of the premises as a Dickens Restaurant and public house'.

With all this finally agreed, there was one last party at the George before it closed for refurbishment.

Festivities were supervised by Sir Garrard Tyrwhitt-Drake – a crazy name for a crazy guy. Drake was a well-travelled businessman and philanthropist who loved animals. He was twelve times mayor of Maidstone, and was so fascinated by zebras that he had a donkey painted in black-and-white stripes so he could admire it from his manor house. He eventually founded Maidstone zoo in the grounds, as well as a museum of coaches and carriages. He published books including *Beasts and Circuses, My Life with Animals* and *The English Circus and Fairground,* and his hobbies included poultry farming and painting inn signs. It was this last hobby that drew him to the George, where he suggested ale garlands should be hung for Christmas.

Ale garlands stretch back to the days of the early alehouses, when they were hung outside the door to let everyone know a new brew was ready. As the streets became more crowded they were hung on poles or 'ale stakes', the forerunners of the first painted inn signs, and this was the medieval tradition Drake was keen to revive. Inevitably though, newspapers announced the decision to hoist ale garlands onto the galleries of the George as an attempt 'to maintain links with Dickens'.

Sir Garrard hosted the event, making a speech in which he celebrated the fact that inns had a good reputation, which meant anyone could now enter a public bar 'without losing prestige'. The garlands were made of winter berries and evergreens, and mounted on stakes that were pushed through the balustrades of the gallery. Ale conners from the City of London, whose traditional duty it had been for centuries to test the quality of new beer when the ale stakes were hoisted, turned up to perform their ceremonial duties clad in velvet hats and robes trimmed with fur. I'm sure the ale was fine, but this was a special occasion, and instead of mere beer the crowd was served with possets: rich, beer-based cocktails – although 'soup' may have been a better word than 'cocktail'. One posset, reputedly created by Sir Walter Raleigh back in the Elizabethan era, consisted of ale, three quarts of cream, mace, nutmeg, sherry and sugar, and was described as 'smooth and fragrant'. Another from Jesus College, Oxford contained strong ale, nutmeg, ginger, sherry and lemon. If nothing else, they'd have kept the cold out for those who didn't have furry robes.

And then the George Inn closed its doors. In February 1938, the *Daily Telegraph* reported that the planned refurbishment would keep the original features of the inn while enabling it to cope with modern conditions: 'Care will be taken to ensure that every part of the historic inn left by the vandalism which in the last century swept away half the original structure, shall be preserved as it was known to the wayfarer of the late seventeenth century.' With the addition of a few mod cons such as electricity and bathrooms, obviously.

No sooner had these repairs been finished than Flower's had to go into financial battle again. In August 1938, the local justices wanted to increase the rates paid on the premises, now that it had had so much money spent on it to improve its value. Flower's argued that they had indeed spent a great deal of money, but all this had done was keep the building standing rather than spruce it up. 'Practically every penny has been spent, not on major improvements, but on trying to prevent the structure from collapsing and ensure its safety and soundness for the period of our tenancy. The idea that major improvements have been carried out is ridiculous,' they protested. Most of the cash had gone on repairs to the roof, underpinning and strengthening the main walls and reconditioning the kitchen. Two of the long-disused bedrooms were converted into a self-contained flat for Charles Griffiths, the landlord who had taken over from the Staples brothers and whom Flower's kept on the payroll while the renovation work was done, as he'd been doing an excellent job. Steel girders were thrust through the cellar walls to take the strain from elm beams which had almost been eaten away by death-watch beetles. From the outside it looked just as it had before, 'and it has been impossible to undertake any expenditure calculated to improve the trading figures of the house'. Against the initial estimate of £650, these repairs cost over £1,000.

The only visible changes inside were the removal of the partition between the taproom and the former kitchen-cum-lounge created by the Staples brothers, the fitting of a service lift, and a new sign outside depicting George IV, king during the heyday of the coaching inn.

Not everyone was happy with these changes. On 29 August Richard Keverne wrote to the *Daily Telegraph* to ask, 'In the name of St George, why?' The object of his anger was the new sign featuring George IV. Standards were slipping. It wasn't British to replace an image of our patron saint with that of, er, a British monarch. 'One despairs when one realises that the National Trust is responsible for the new sign,' thundered Mr Keverne. 'The George is worthy of an honest sign, the best we can produce.'

But this was a trifle. The George Inn had been saved for the nation, its future assured. Surely, nothing could threaten it now?

And then Hitler invaded Poland.

In the summer of 1940, the German Luftwaffe attempted to destroy the British Air Force to pave the way for a seaborne invasion. In early September, they admitted defeat in this plan and switched their air power to other objectives: destroying Britain's armament-manufacturing base, and, later, adding to that the destruction of Britain's civilian morale. Intensive bombing of London killed two birds – not to mention 60,000 people – with one stone. Southwark – an industrial centre near the docks – was one of the Luftwaffe's prime targets within London. On the second night of the Blitz in September 1941, much of Borough High Street went up in flames, and the bombing continued thereafter, every night, for fifty nights.

The bomb-damage maps drawn up by the London County Council use a colour scheme from light to dark to represent the severity of damage done to buildings, overlaid with circles to represent the blast radiuses of V1 and V2 rockets. Damage in west and north London is relatively superficial, with just a few clusters of colour here and there. Around the City whole blocks, one after the other, are coloured purple – damaged beyond repair. In the Borough High Street, buildings in

Talbot Yard, King's Head Yard and White Hart Yard suffered severe damage, with some being destroyed outright, and in the case of King's Head Yard, pretty much everything was flattened. Somehow, right in the middle of all this destruction, the George Inn escaped. The maps show no damage at all, and a letter from Flowers in 1941 refers to 'blast damage minor in nature' while the building next door where the Tabard had once stood suffered severe damage. Total repairs to the George cost £400. Future Labour Prime Minister Clement Attlee, who reputedly dined on fish and chips at the George while the bombs fell around him, must have been a lucky charm.

The George played its part in protecting Southwark's citizens. We're all familiar with the images of cheery Londoners sheltering in tube stations to avoid the bombs. What's less well known is the heat, dirt, crime, disease, lice and discomfort associated with nights on tube platforms, not to mention the fact that the authorities initially did not grant permission for people to go down there. The old tunnel of the City & South London Railway, London's first tube line, was eventually brought into use as the Southwark deep tunnel shelter, able to accommodate up to 14,000 people. There were several staircases into it, and one of these was built in the cellar of the George.

After the war, as London counted the cost, former landlord Leslie Staples delighted at the George's continued, now nothing short of miraculous, survival, writing in *The Dickensian* in 1946:

> I was once told by an architect who had been intimately concerned with the building for many years that its construction was such that theoretically it is impossible to say why it did not collapse, and yet, not only has it stood for 270 years, it has done so despite the repeated bombing raids.

But Staples also has a grumble of his own: the lovely little lounge he and his brother created in the former kitchen next to the taproom was no more:

> There is a change for the worse ... A wall of the unique little tap-room, the like of which was not to be found in London, and seldom outside it, has been destroyed to enlarge bar space, quite destroying the character of the room ... How the National Trust can justify such a piece of vandalism in a building given into their care is more than I am able to explain.

Given that the National Trust's research has proven that this wall was not original demonstrates that, after a certain point, one man's act of vandalism is another's loving restoration.

The theatrical performances continued to take place on Shakespeare Day. In 1947, the perfectly monikered Melita Spraggs came to see a production of *The Merry Wives of Windsor* staged by what was now the Overian Masque Company, and wrote about it for the *Christian Science Monitor*, published in Boston, Massachusetts. 'All around', she wrote, 'wharves and factories stand on the sites of early theatres where Elizabethan drama first saw the light and Shakespeare's genius found expression.' Two years after the end of the war, the sky still showed through the broken roofs of 'bomb-splattered' railway sheds.

She had a hard seat in the inn-yard, perched on the edge of a railway dray whose floor was covered with hay and cabbage leaves. The stage was erected by the entrance to the yard, just beneath the galleries. There was a choir in the first gallery, and the upper one was crowded with prompters, press and other VIPs. Her account of the play is wonderfully atmospheric:

> As the evening sun set, the scene was one of gay informality. Cameramen perched precariously on the high driver's seat of the horse dray, on upturned oil

cans, on walls, on chairs or benches. Players mingled
with the audience when they weren't on stage.

But the most revealing part of her account is the main topic
of conversation after the play has finished.

Post-war London had a chronic power shortage, and the
Ministry of Town and Country Planning had just revealed
proposals to build a huge new power station on Bankside,
near the site of the old Globe Theatre. Dramatic views of St
Paul's from Bankside, newly opened up by the bombing,
would be obscured once more. Bankside's artistic past was to
be buried under yet another layer of heavy industry, and there
was a widespread sense that the destruction caused by the
Luftwaffe created the opportunity to rediscover this heritage
instead, to rebuild Bankside as a place for theatres in an age
when plays and players were somewhat more respected, and
unspeakable cruelty to bears, bulls and monkeys had long
been banned. The London County Council, the Borough of
Southwark, and the City Corporation strenuously opposed the
building of an eyesore power station on the site. Lord Latham,
leader of the London County Council, called it 'a grave
mistake which Londoners of today will deplore and those of
tomorrow find difficult to understand or to forgive'.

Miss Spraggs notes all this in her piece, and in doing so
reveals that the plays in the George Inn yard, doggedly staged
every year, kept alive the flame of the theatrical tradition on
Bankside. They provided a focal point of discussion and
resistance to the proposed Bankside power station, and helped
build the case for developing the arts on the South Bank.

But these protests proved futile. Between 1947 and 1963
the coal-fired Bankside Power Station was built. Its central
tower was limited to 99 metres, in theory so as not to
overshadow St Paul's or have too much of an impact on the
skyline. Questions were asked in the House of Commons
about the noise and sulphur and other noxious fumes, possibly

because the building was pretty close to Parliament itself. While it lacked the physical presence of the iconic Battersea Power Station, it would be pretty hard to argue that it was unobtrusive: it dominated Bankside. In the end though, having taken sixteen years to complete, it was operational for only another eighteen: it closed in 1981, after which it stood half derelict, a totem of Southwark's then declining industries.

But just a little further along the South Bank, that commitment to reviving and celebrating the arts that still clung on in the George Inn yard finally found fuller expression. In 1951 the Labour government staged the Festival of Britain. The idea was to give the population a sense of recovery in the aftermath of the war, and to promote Britain's contribution to the arts, science, technology, industrial design and architecture – and the centre of it all was the south bank of the Thames. A few hundred yards west of where the bear pits, theatres and stews had once stood, the festival site cleared a large area of warehousing and poor housing to create a public space featuring the 'Dome of Discovery', the futuristic metal Skylon tower, and the 2,900-seat Royal Festival Hall, built on the site of the old Lion Brewery. Over 8.5 million people visited the South Bank site in just five months, half of them from outside London. But the Conservatives clearly thought this attempt to make people feel a bit better and celebrate British achievement was an awful idea, or at least a Socialist one, which to them was the same thing.

When he returned to power later that year, Winston Churchill's first act as Prime Minister was to order the closure and demolition of the site. Only the Royal Festival Hall, which hosted rather un-Socialist events such as classical-music recitals, was spared. In the 1960s the RFH was joined by Queen Elizabeth Hall and the Purcell Rooms – two further music and concert venues – and the Hayward Art Gallery to form the Southbank Centre which, while managing to be spectacularly ugly, is the most important centre for the arts in the UK. The link to the George is a tenuous one, but the inn now finds itself once again within walking distance of London's riverside entertainment complex. And this time, you don't have to hire a waterman to get to it.

Back when the Festival of Britain was still in its planning stages, London County Council did an architectural survey of London's buildings to assess what was left after the war. A 1947 audit of the George (published in 1950) produced some beautiful plans, with the architects taking time to sketch some of the surviving features such as carved stair banisters and lintels in great detail. Bedrooms on the first floor were still in use even now. Downstairs the taproom had been opened up to be the main bar, and the old coffee room served as a restaurant.

An inventory of contents taken in 1958 reveals a careworn building occupied by centuries' worth of detritus, but still much loved and cared for. Six oak wine and spirit barrels in the cellar had direct feeds to brass taps on the bar, alongside the mahogany beer engine with its ivory hand-pulls that was already an antique, serving beer into ancient pewter tankards. The inn was no longer offering accommodation, but the mighty four-posters remained in what were now staff bedrooms, each complete with its own 'mahogany three tread bed step commode'. The long attics, once hop showrooms, were now full of crap: a useless swing-frame dressing mirror, four mahogany-frame dining-room chairs beyond repair, two toilet basins, and prints of Dickens and his characters. 'Much of this furniture is now in poor shape,' says the report, 'and some with wood-worm was cleared out when the new Manager came in about two years ago. The old carpets were worn and moth eaten.'

That new manager was Frederick Martin, a former sailor born in Sunderland who came to the George in 1956. He was a big man from the Harry Bailly mould, and soon gained a reputation for his plain-speaking bluntness. One Sunday in 1960, he gained brief national fame when the regulars at the

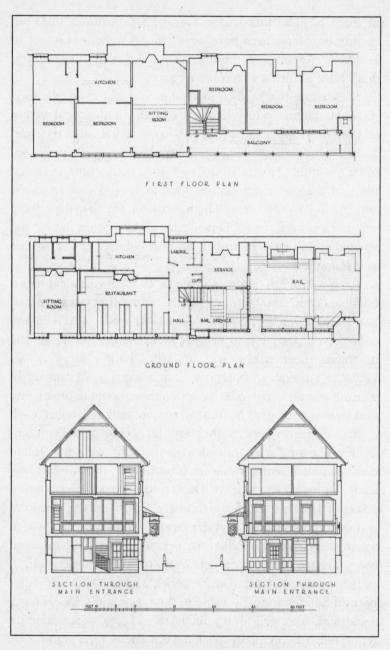

FIRST FLOOR PLAN

GROUND FLOOR PLAN

SECTION THROUGH
MAIN ENTRANCE

SECTION THROUGH
MAIN ENTRANCE

Plans from the Survey of London, 1950.

George had their Sunday lunch disturbed by a visitor no one except Martin and a few handpicked staff were expecting.

People must have been wondering why Fred Martin was wearing a morning suit and his wife, Winifred, who was recovering from an operation over the wall in Guy's Hospital, was home for the day. The waitresses were wearing smart green gingham dresses, but they did that every Sunday, because the American tourists loved that kind of shtick. But for the guv'nor of the place, this attire was most unusual. Then, at 1.30 p.m., after the end of an ordination service across the road in Southwark Cathedral, in walked the Right Reverend Mervyn Stockwood, Bishop of Southwark, in his full cerise cassock. He ordered a pint of bitter and stood anxiously among the regulars, obviously waiting for someone. Again, this was an unusual sight, but not a completely new one. 'I always come here to lunch after ordination services, and quite often at other times,' said the bish. 'It is very handy.'

And then, in walked his guests: Princess Margaret and her new husband Anthony Armstrong-Jones (later Lord Snowdon), who had also been attending the ordination service. The Princess wore a frock and jacket of navy-blue silk and a hat of white curled feathers, trimmed with dark-blue ribbon. Mr Armstrong-Jones wore a blue suit and wine-coloured tie. They were ushered upstairs to the panelled dining room – rather posher than the downstairs restaurant – and sat down to Sunday lunch.

What did they have? 'We gave them lobster instead of prawn cocktail,' said the plain-speaking Mr Martin, 'otherwise they had the same as everyone else,' namely the 7s 6d table d'hôte menu of clear soup, roast beef and Yorkshire pudding, followed by apple tart, Welsh rarebit and mushrooms on toast. Chef John Steinberg, of Bexleyheath, carved the joint at the table in the best British tradition. I'm not sure 'everyone else' was served sparkling Moselle and a 1935 claret with their Sunday roast by sommelier John Small, but as far as the food went, it was typical pub fare for the time. The royal party even had to contend with the pub cat, Two Bobs, trying to steal food from the table. He had to be shown out by the waitresses three times, and eventually stalked into the court-yard in disgust.

Clearly the *Daily Mail* and the *Daily Express* found the idea of a princess in a 'London Public House' quite extraordinary. Recounting his conversation with the bishop, a journalist from the *Mail* 'suggested that it seemed unusual to entertain a princess in a pub'.

'That,' replied the bishop, 'is an idea 100 years behind the times.'

Now I know what you're thinking. If they only arrived at 1.30 p.m., and had a meal stretching to four or five courses, they would have had to eat very quickly, because in those days pubs were required to close at 3 p.m. on Sunday afternoons. And indeed, they were only just tucking into the apple pie when 83-year-old George Birch, a former soldier sporting a winged collar and waxed moustache, entered the room and called time in the traditional fashion: 'My lord, ladies and gentlemen, it is now time. By Act of Parliament you must all leave the building. Thank you, and may God save the Queen.'

And this is where the story takes a sinister turn. Because despite time being called in such an elegant way, the diners simply ignored the old soldier and carried on eating and drinking. Eventually Princess Margaret and Mr Armstrong-Jones left an hour after the pub had closed, and the bishop went back upstairs to finish his drink.

Yes, that's right: a princess – the Queen's own sister, no less – and a senior member of the English Church, knowingly and wilfully broke the Queen's law. And after Mr Birch had gone to such lengths to maintain it in the proper fashion, instead of simply turning up the lights and trying to take your drinks from you as most pubs do today.

This flouting of the law of the land was widely reported in the national press, and yet despite scouring many newspaper archives, I can find no mention of the princess or the bishop being questioned by the police. Mr Martin was allowed to continue as landlord of the George and faced no disciplinary action whatsoever.

I don't know – anyone would think there's one law for princesses and bishops, and another for the rest of us.

In 1962, having somehow survived his blatant contravention of licensing law, Fred Martin got a new boss. This was a period of rapid consolidation in the British brewing industry, when shrewd speculators realized that brewers still thought of themselves as brewers, and their 'tied' estates of pubs as being of secondary importance, the outlets where they sold their own beers. Looking at these publicly listed companies from the outside, speculators like the Canadian entrepreneur Eddie Taylor saw that many pubs had not been revalued since before the war. In his eyes, they were vast property portfolios with a far less-valuable brewery growing out of the back. He started buying up breweries rapaciously to get his hands on the pubs, and in many cases dispensed with the breweries themselves. It soon became apparent that the only businesses to escape would be those who grew big enough to avoid his clutches by emulating him. In 1962, Flower's Breweries Ltd was taken over by Whitbread & Co., who formally took over administration of the George in 1967. Around this time, what was now British Rail finally left the George Inn yard, with Guy's Hospital taking over most of it. But the George acquired the two cottages next to it that had been railway offices for nearly a hundred years, and whose rebuilding in 1937 first uncovered the mortal danger the whole building was in.

The lock-in loving princess wasn't the only celebrity visitor to the George in this period – it had become an essential stop on many London sightseeing tours. *Woman's Realm* magazine came for lunch in 1965, and reported that the landlord kept an excellent cellar specializing in port, Madeira and sherry, to accompany the menu of jellied eels, steak, kidney and mushroom pie, fruit pie (served with lashings of cream), and Dover sole and smoked salmon 'for more sophisticated tastes'. Set lunch cost 6s 6d weekdays, 9s 6d on Saturdays and Sundays. And you could always be sure of a welcome from Mr Fred Martin (not a warm welcome, note, just a welcome). The magazine gushed that recent recipients of this welcome included actresses Elizabeth Taylor and Clare Bloom.

In 1973 a student writing a local-history project found a very warm welcome from Mr Martin. Mike Pierrot describes the landlord as having 'a smile as broad as his considerable girth'. An avid snufftaker, it takes a will of steel not to describe Martin as 'Dickensian'. He told the student that he could easily sell souvenirs of the George, but he preferred to keep the place as a simple pub rather than making it an overt tourist attraction.

Mr Martin extended a different kind of hospitality altogether to some newsworthy visitors in 1974. In 1963, seven beer drinkers who were increasingly disgruntled with the poor quality of beer from big brewers such as Whitbread had formed the Society for the Preservation of Beers from the Wood. Its aims and activities were pretty much identical to those of CAMRA, the Campaign for Real Ale, which was founded in 1971, but it didn't have as catchy a name, so while it attracted several thousand members, it remained much smaller.[1]

By the early 1970s both organizations were using highly effective tactics to draw attention to the decline of traditional

---

1. It's still going today, with a website that proudly declares 'we embrace new technology', a link to a Facebook page and even a jokey acknowledgement of the unwieldy name. But given that it has accepted that wooden barrels are a thing of the past, you'd have to ask them what the difference is now between CAMRA and SPBW.

cask-conditioned bitter in pubs and its replacement by harshly pasteurized and artificially carbonated keg beers, which the SPBW referred to as 'sealed dustbins'. They would stage pickets and mock funerals at pubs where cask ale's traditional hand pumps had been replaced by the tiny illuminated plastic boxes of keg-bitter pumps.

It's hardly surprising, given the George's beauty and venerability, that a group of its core beer drinkers were SPBW members. These pin-striped city gents (the stereotype of real-ale drinkers being fat old northern blokes in flat caps has never been an accurate one) got wind of a plan to rip out the George's 100-year-old beer engine and stop selling cask beer. They decided to protest against this outrage, and started a week-long picket outside the pub.

The picketing of the George soon drew the attention of both the local and national press, much to the frustration of Fred Martin. Brian Wilcox of the SPBW's 'action committee' declared that this move put the George under threat once more, and expressed his disappointment that the National Trust was prepared to 'stand by and allow this removal of part of our heritage'.

The reason this made Mr Martin so angry was that there were in fact no plans to rip out the beer engine at all. It was simply that Bass – which was admittedly a legendary and much-revered beer – was coming out because it was a guest beer from another brewery, and the reciprocal deal between Bass and Whitbread was coming to an end.

'We are selling draught beer and we will always go on selling draught beer,' Mr Martin told journalists and photographers from the *Guardian*. 'If you are taking photographs and publishing them you are committing libel because this is private property,' he added, ejecting the journos from the building before they had a chance to correct him.

The following day, the *South London Press* found the SPBW's Brian Hill handing out leaflets to passers-by and asking them to sign a petition to save the traditional pint. He had now seemingly accepted that the beer engine wasn't being ripped out, but he still wasn't happy. 'This is an erosion of the status quo,' he complained. 'If the Bass goes from the George, we go. There will only be Trophy and Tankard, which is a keg beer.'

Mr Martin, apparently happier to talk to journalists today but still 'more than irritated' according to one, was losing his patience. 'Look I've had enough trouble over this. I told some regulars that the Bass would be finishing when a reciprocal trade agreement expires. But as long as they are brewing draught beer I will serve it up. There's no question of taking out the hand pumps.'

The SPBW then announced that it would call a truce the following Sunday, and go back to the George to finish off the final cask of Bass. It's perhaps surprising that they simply assumed Mr Martin would let them back in. Whether or not he did so is not recorded.

In the mid-1970s Fred Martin retired. He had come to the George in 1956. He'd survived an illegal lock-in with Princess Margaret, and a picket by pin-striped city gents. But when the George had to be closed again for extensive refurbishment, like the Cheeryble brothers forty years earlier, he decided it was time to go.

The *South London Press* had announced improvements costing over £25,000 back in 1973, including the installation of male toilets inside the pub to replace those in the inn-yard, and the conversion of the downstairs restaurant into a bar, with a new kitchen upstairs, and a new dining room for private parties. 'We can only do what the National Trust allows us to do and everything is being done with their co-operation and approval,' said Thomas Holt, retail director for Whitbread. 'No money has been spent on the George Inn for a very long time.'

But for some reason the work had to wait, and the inn

finally closed in 1976, reopening the following year. The two cottages had been incorporated into the fabric of the inn, using materials of a similar age wherever possible. (You have to look quite closely at it today to notice how new this section of the pub is.) The George now offered three bars on the ground floor, two restaurants and an aperitif bar on the first floor, and a third restaurant on the floor above that.

And one other thing had changed: the way pubs were run. The George had a long history of landlords who clearly loved the pub. While they always remained subservient to the old inn's own personality and spirit, for people like the Grinslades, the Scholefields and the Murrays, all the way through to Fred Martin, the George was a labour of passionate love. Most British pubs were at this point still owned and run by the breweries that supplied their beer, but after the heady rush of acquisition activity that peaked in the 1960s, they were starting to realize that property – the pubs – was a greater asset than the beer itself. Some pubs are free of any brewery relationship, and in these freehouses the landlord reigns supreme and defines the place. In brewery-tied pubs, the licensee may be a long-term leaseholder with a serious chunk of his own money invested in the place, or a tenant who still has a degree of autonomy but acts under closer supervision of the brewery to whom he pays rent.

But after all that consolidation, the big pub-owning companies owned far more outlets than ever before, and a new breed of pub manager, with loyalty to the company rather than the specific pub, started to emerge. Managed pubs are today the fastest-growing model of ownership, and regulars sometimes complain that, to a manager, running a pub is a job rather than a passion. This is often unfair – there are many managers who strain at the corporate leash and push for greater individual entrepreneurship, people who one day want to run their own pub and are seeking to gain experience, or simply people who fall in love with the pub they've been placed in charge of. But managers are subject to a greater degree of corporate control and supervision, and many managed pubs lack the soul of a place where the gaffer lives upstairs and sees the pub as an extension of his or her own personality.

It seems that, after reopening, the George became more of a managed house. Between 1977 and 1985, it had four different licensees, each staying for no more than a couple of years. It's hard to figure out why, because no records whatsoever from this time survive today. In the London Metropolitan Archive, where I found the blow-by-blow account from the 1930s of the George's acquisition by the National Trust and the tense brokering of the deal with Flower's, there was very little thereafter, apart from a printout of a chilling 1993 email from a Whitbread member of staff reading:

> I have come across a Deed packet relating to the George Inn 77 Borough High Street, London SE1, the most recent document being a Lease from the National Trust to Flower & Sons Ltd dated December 1958. Have you any suggestions as to who may like to take these from me or shall I hire a shredder!
> Thanks
> Jennifer

These documents were saved. But the original deeds to the George Inn, last seen in 1950, are missing today – the National Trust has no idea if they still exist. And Whitbread, one of the 'Big Six' breweries in Britain, would go on to systematically and purposefully destroy its entire archive when it sold its brewing arm. Nick Redman, who worked for years as Whitbread's full-time archivist, could only stand and watch with tears of anguish running down his face when his life's work was thrown into a skip in front of him a few years ago. I contacted Nick, who now hunts whalebones for a living (honest), to see if he had any recollection of the George.

'Getting the occasional email like yours is the time when I feel really sad about the closure of the archive, and the loss of that great resource,' he replied. 'Today's Whitbread will have nothing I am afraid, and no interest either. I have nothing. With hindsight I should have "liberated" stuff. But there it is.'[2]

The only recorded mention I can find of the George Inn from the early eighties is a restaurant review written in 1982 by Stan Hey for *The Times*, and it warms the heart. He reflects on how few places there are called the Patrick, the Andrew or the David ('what does that tell you about the English mentality?') and congratulates Whitbread on avoiding the worst excesses of period tat, with a sign reading 'to the privies' the only clanger. There are two restaurants: the George, which offers a set three-course meal for £4.40, and the Coaching, which has beamed ceilings, leaded windows, and an à la carte menu offering 'more expensive simplicity' in the shape of steaks, Dover sole, chicken Kiev and veal escalope. But my favourite part of the review is Hey's description of the clientele: 'overseas guests escorted by the sort of homely businessmen who wear cardigans under their suits'. Hey also loves the staff, 'friendly ladies who ooze maternal concern for your appetite, and who kept addressing me as "young man". I left a large tip . . .'

But around the same time, there were some less than pleasant meetings taking place in the George. Beer writer Roger Protz, possibly the best-known campaigner for real ale there's ever been, was attending a CAMRA committee meeting in Southwark on St George's Day one year in the early 1980s, and given the date, he decided it would be appropriate to have a pint in the George afterwards. He'd already encountered a very drunk man dressed head to foot

2. I did contact Whitbread. Nick was right.

in black leather, staggering down the street. And on entering the George, he saw many other men in similar attire, mingling with women in evening dress and men in black tie and disappearing with each other to one of the upstairs meeting rooms. This seemed inexplicably strange until Protz was standing at the bar and realized that the man-mountain standing next to him was Martin Webster, a leading figure in the National Front, and that the gathering of leather-clad thugs and moneyed couples upstairs was a fascist celebration of St George's Day. Protz – a former editor of the *Socialist Worker* – has never really gone in for the 'discretion is the better part of valour' idea. He turned to Webster, a man known for both his hatred of 'Commies' and his immense physical bulk, and said, 'Good afternoon, Comrade.'

The massive neo-Nazi stared at Protz for several seconds before replying, 'Good afternoon . . . *Comrade*,' at which point Protz's colleague, Tim Webb, murmured in his ear, 'Go. Right now.'

Protz returned to his senses, left the pub and was running by the time he neared the gates of the inn-yard. A bus was passing. It was going in the opposite direction to where Protz needed to go. He boarded it anyway, and didn't look back.

The pattern of short-term managers changed soon afterwards, either by luck or design. John Hall was operations manager of the prestigious Regent Palace Hotel in Piccadilly when Whitbread came and headhunted him to take over as licensee at the George in 1985. What may have seemed like something of a step down on the career path was anything but for Hall: he described it as love at first sight. Portly, bald and moustached, he looked like an ex-army officer from a hundred years before. He moved into the manager's rooms on the second floor with his wife, Rosemary, and Great Dane Toby, 'a dog of powerful presence and a Hound of the Baskervilles bark' according to nervous journalists who met him, and began getting to know his new love.

Hall hosted some interesting guests. The following year Steve Williams, now of the Pub History Society, was working in London for British Telecom on Stock Exchange deregulation: 'I found it quite unusual that here in London, all the engineers went to the pub at lunchtime, but of course I had to follow them. One day we were sitting in the yard and noticed all the windows in the taproom were blacked out, and there was a trailer in the yard. Then, the trailer door opened and out stepped Rik Mayall, made up with a hunchback and one eye, and Robbie Coltrane in a filthy vest and miner's helmet.'

The Comic Strip film, *Strike*, in which English alternative comedians play Hollywood actors playing the roles of the protagonists of the 1984–85 miners' strike, is available today on YouTube, and features the taproom of the George portraying a Hollywood studio portraying an ancient pub in the Welsh Valleys. Apart from the one-eyed miners and crones sitting by the fire, it looks exactly the same in the film as it does today.

John Hall worked with the National Trust to explore the history of the George, and working with historian Dr Judith Hunter, uncovered some genuinely new pieces of the jigsaw for the first time in almost a century. They managed to pull together a much richer effort than any previous booklet, and the National Trust publication *George Inn: an Illustrated Souvenir*, launched in 1989, is still on sale at the inn today.

Hall saw Borough – particularly Bankside – undergo a rapid transformation that left it almost unrecognizable from the fading industrial area it had been throughout most of the twentieth century. Back in the sixties London Bridge began to crack, and a new bridge was commissioned in 1967, and completed in 1973. It's as bland and uninteresting as the first bridge was beautiful and eccentric.[3] The mighty Park Street

---

3. The original second bridge, which occupied the space between the

Brewery, once owned by the Thrales and then by Barclay Perkins, ceased brewing in 1981. The brewery that had once been a global tourist attraction was demolished to make way for housing. The hop industry disappeared as brewing declined, and the magnificent Hop Exchange restyled itself as 'Bankside's premier corporate hospitality and party venue' with office space above. The food factories closed down as employers like Sainsbury's moved elsewhere. The docks, out-dated and facing stiff foreign competition, were defeated by the 1950s, and took many associated industries with them. By the 1970s and 1980s, Bankside was little more than an abandoned wreck right in the heart of London, and the rest of Southwark still languished in Victorian slums. Gradually, people drifted away to the new council tower blocks deeper in South London.

Then, in 1989, the year the *George Inn* booklet was launched, the remains of the Rose Theatre were uncovered following the demolition of a 1950s office block. Archaeologists revealed a structure based on a fourteen-sided polygon, with a floor sloping down towards the stage to permit clear views from the back.

This ignited a renewed interest in Bankside's theatrical heritage. In 1949, American filmmaker Sam Wanamaker had come to London looking for the remains of the Globe and was, justifiably, astonished to find no permanent memorial to it or to Shakespeare himself on Bankside. He managed to gain permission from the Council to stage plays in a tent theatre, and established a Shakespeare museum in an old warehouse.

---

medieval and new bridges from 1831 to 1967, was sold to American businessman Robert P. McCulloch for two and a half million dollars. McCulloch had it shipped to the States, with each brick individually labelled and the whole exported under the label 'large antique'. The reconstructed bridge now stands at Lake Havasu City, Arizona, as the centrepiece of an English theme park that features a Tudor-period shopping mall.

In 1993, after twenty-three years of fund-raising and research, work finally began on building a replica of the Globe. Meanwhile, the destruction of the Anchor Brewery revealed the remains of the original Globe Theatre beneath the brewery car park – the new site was only yards away. The project to recreate the Globe wasn't without its hiccups: Southwark Council was reluctant to give up the land, claiming it was the only place in the Borough where they could store their municipal dustcarts. But objections were overcome and building began in 1992, with designs based on Hollar's 1638 panorama of London and Hentzer's interior drawings among other sources. Tragically, Sam Wanamaker died the following year. But his dream came to fruition when the Globe Theatre opened in 1997, featuring the first thatched roof to be put on a London building since the Great Fire of 1666.

John Hall stuck around and watched the Borough redevelop as a yuppie playground. As the 1990 recession hit he played host to several 'golden handshake' parties for newly redundant City bankers. Sometimes they threatened to get out of hand but this six-foot-three, twenty-stone former rugby player took them in his stride. He loved his inn, and wanted to see bedrooms reintroduced – there was space for ten, he claimed, and the inn was in a perfect location. But it never happened. The George remained as it was, while all around it property developers began buying up the derelict land left behind by forgotten wharves and factories, and turning old industrial buildings into luxury apartments. Millions of pounds of public money, plus lucrative private contracts that were supposedly intended to regenerate the area, certainly made Borough a more pleasant place if you could afford it. But a 1996 survey revealed that half the existing inhabitants had seen no benefit whatsoever from the millions poured into the area.

Hall's passion was rewarded in 1995 when the George was named London Pub of the Year by the *Evening Standard*. The judges of the competition included such luminaries as Willie

Rushton, Tim Rice and, of course, Carol Thatcher. Their reactions to the place were telling. Sir Tim felt discovering it was 'a wonderful surprise'. You really did feel the link with the sixteenth and seventeenth centuries. Carol Thatcher said its façade must be the most enchanting in London, and Willie felt it was an old friend. Hall sat for photos with Toby outside in the old inn-yard, both of them visibly bursting with pride. Whitbread's internal newspaper celebrated the award, noting that the George had hosted parties for the Duke of Westminster, Charlton Heston and Patrick Duffy, with other notable guests over the years including Dwight D. Eisenhower, Gary Cooper, Elizabeth Taylor, Liberace and Judy Garland. One family had travelled from Cheltenham to London every week for fifty years just for a drink. 'People love the atmosphere here,' said deputy manager Peter Dunn, 'this place has special qualities.'

Today, the watermen are long gone, replaced by pleasure craft, floating pubs and tourist attractions. Docks gave way to shining towers full of bankers and other financiers, who spend their money in restaurants and brasseries that gain their cachet from the heritage and architecture of the wharves that stood here before them. With the Globe Theatre, the Clink Prison, London Dungeon, Vinopolis and the replica of the *Golden Hind*, Southwark, particularly on Bankside, is a tourist haven, a dramatically cleaned-up version of the pleasure gardens of old.

Even the controversial Bankside Power Station, so hated by those who wanted to revive the area's artistic reputation after the war, eventually became part of the solution rather than the problem. Attitudes to its architecture softened. While property companies wanted to tear it down as part of their redevelopment of Bankside, a campaign grew to have it declared a listed building. Then, the Tate Gallery drew up plans to convert it into an art gallery. It was an inspired choice: a building on the banks of the Thames with great views across London, close to St Paul's across the river. The £135 million conversion began in 1995, and on 11 May 2000 Tate Modern opened to the public. It is now Britain's national museum of modern and contemporary art, and draws five million visitors a year, a triumph of public thinking and civic planning by any standards. After its initial (literal) wobbles, the Millennium Bridge opened just outside it to create a new link to the City north of the river, and refocus our entire perception of what London is all about.

In 2001 Whitbread pulled out of pubs and bars to focus on hotels, and its 3,000 pubs became the Laurel Pub Co. But by August 2004 Laurel had sold its 432 'non-high street' pubs – including the George – to Greene King for £645 million. George Cunningham, licensee for about eight years after John Hall retired and moved to Cornwall, left the following year and was replaced by Scott Masterson, the current licensee. The George survives, walking a delicate balance between theme park museum and working pub. Having had its glory day as a haven for travellers, today it still caters for people a long way from home, who have come to see the sights and reconnect with the age of Dickens or Shakespeare.

'Some of the alterations, particularly those of recent years, may be seen as regrettable,' wrote Judith Hunter in 1989, 'although it is through adaptation and modification through the course of its history, that the building has maintained its continuity of purpose.' The George has survived partly by luck, partly thanks to the incredible characters who were drawn to it and committed to it in long relationships. But more than anything, it's survived because it is adaptable.

Stewart Brand is probably one of the few genuine geniuses alive today, and his book *How Buildings Learn* is quite possibly the only architectural tome I will ever read voluntarily. Brand is one of those thinkers who is truly original, who can't be categorized or compared to anyone else, and he thinks about, well, everything. In *How Buildings Learn* he argues for the principle of 'adaptive architecture', where buildings that are made from low-cost materials to standard designs are familiar and easy to modify, and are therefore more successful in the long-term than innovative statements of an architect's vision. Buildings are not 'finished' once they've been built; they evolve to suit the needs of the people who use them. If they cannot evolve, chances are they'll be demolished.

This is the thing about the George. Even if we just think about the building as it has stood since 1677, it was built with bigger rooms that were then subdivided, and most of those rooms have changed their functions over the years. The main kitchen was once where the taproom now is, then moved behind what used to be the coffee room, before moving upstairs. That coffee room became the restaurant and is now the main bar. As Brand would have it, the George is a structure that allows simple transference and change. To the untrained eye, from the outside the George is preserved as it ever was. But beneath the unchanging whole, the inside is constantly adapting and refreshing, replacing its constituent cells.[4] The George had become a focus for nostalgia by the end of the nineteenth century, and has performed that function ever since. But to provide this consistent, unchanging experience, it has had to change constantly and dramatically. Rather like Southwark itself.

But then that's what pubs do, generally, and that's why after first emerging in their recognizable state eight or nine hundred years ago, pubs will be around centuries longer than those currently predicting their demise. Writing these final lines as the George creaks and groans with age and the Shard approaches its zenith, if I could live long enough to collect my winnings, I'd place a rather large bet on which of these two buildings will still be here in five hundred years' time.

---

4. Just like the Sugababes.

EPILOGUE:
A DRINK AT THE GEORGE INN TO-DAY

I do hope the fire's you are having in London has not touched the George Inn. I was there in 1970 and had the BEST Kidney and Beef Pie. In 2008 I found the Inn by myself. It had changed a LOT. And no Kidney and Beef pie:-(

(Review of the George Inn on www.pubs.com,
posted 13 August 2011, a few days after
violent riots erupted across London)

MY OWN INTRODUCTION to the George was less than salubrious.

It was 2007, and with two books under my belt I'd started to get various talking-head bits on TV. In May, the BBC's *Culture Show* phoned and asked if I would film a long section of the programme with them about the Great British pub, and they chose the George as the location for reasons which are hopefully obvious by now.

It was my highest-profile TV spot to date, and I was quite nervous. I thought the venerable inn would be atmospheric and quiet, but when we entered the taproom (because you *have* to film in the taproom – just ask Rik Mayall) there was a table of drinkers who had clearly been there for some time.

Filming proved tough – every time I started talking they would raise their voices to talk over us. The crew's runner offered to buy them pints if they'd be quiet while we filmed, and this seemed to go down very well. We made good progress, and were nearing the end of the interview when I started talking about the benign anarchy, the unpredictability of the pub. It's the reason why, in all those jokes, a man, a bear, a piece of tarmac or a lobster always walks into a pub. You could go out for a quiet drink on a Tuesday night and it might turn out to be a night you remember for years. Because in a pub, absolutely *anything* can happen.

As I said the words 'anything can happen', a deep, sustained *bowking* noise drowned me out. Behind me, one of the drinkers was vomiting into his pint glass. We were petrified, rooted to our places, waiting to see what happened next. We went again, from the top, but the same thing happened again. And again.

Zena, my interviewer, had to go outside. Then, mercifully, we were saved. A horrified barmaid swiftly ejected the group and set about clearing up the carnage. She cleared up everything apart from the offending glass, which sat alone on its table, exuding a kind of talismanic power, not to mention a powerful smell.

Eventually the barmaid came back. I didn't dare turn around to see what she was going to try to do. And then I heard the sound of a glass smashing wetly on the floor. We couldn't stand it any longer, and the whole crew collapsed into hysterical laughter.

'This is not funny!' the waitress screamed at us. 'This is horrible. I really, really do not think this is funny!' We tried to apologize, but it was no use – she told us to get out, and that was the end of filming. The BBC had been ejected from the George.

The item never did make it onto the *Culture Show*.

I mention this story now not just for a gross-out laugh – though that's reason enough – but because it kind of breaks the spell. When all is said and done, I suppose that if you go to the George today as an ordinary drinker rather than an obsessive, it's just a pub. It's a very good-looking pub – quite distinctively so – but it's just a pub. You can tell it's a very old pub and you can speculate on the history it must have had, but you get very little of that story simply by coming here for a pint.

Still, what's wrong with being just a pub?

We take pubs for granted. We think they'll always be there when we need them, unchanging, just how we left them. And if we don't visit them for weeks, months or years, and we come back and find them changed, we're outraged. If we come back and find them closed, we berate all the other people who should have come here more often and kept them in business.

In 2010 a pub close to my house in Stoke Newington shut down, changed ownership and reopened. Before the closure it was a spit-and-sawdust affair with a scattering of old drunks nursing pints of Guinness for hours and shouting at the racing on the bank of TVs bolted high on the walls, outside punching distance. No one was even that sure what the place was called: there was a sign outside saying it was the Jolly Butchers, across the windows it said it was Father Ted's, and on the wall outside it claimed to be Stokey's Bar. This pub gathered names in layers, like the grime on its windows. It stayed open well into the small hours, and when the place finally closed down Twitter came alive with sentimental recollections of 3 a.m. punch-ups.

It reopened as the Jolly Butchers – quite sure of its name now – with a bright airy space (all knocked through into one large hall reminiscent of medieval inns, naturally) and offered a range of eight hand-pulled ales and ciders, imported bottled beers and genuine lagers, and craft beers from the new wave of British brewers who are making beer exciting all over again.

The hipsters who fill the pub every night can routinely be heard saying it's a shame it's changed, because they loved the old place.

Some of them can even remember drinking in it once or twice.

This is the story of many urban pubs now. It makes me smile that it's nearly five hundred years since the George last changed its name, because it's obviously something of an exception. Pubs are in steady decline. We've just gone through a period where we were losing thirty to fifty a week, converted into housing, Tesco Metros or Burger Kings, or demolished to make way for car parks in areas where this is far more profitable than attempting to keep the building standing.

But in an industry that's brilliant at pessimism, as this book came to a close I was surprised to find that the number of weekly pub closures is falling. The people who monitor the situation are now predicting we'll have a small net growth in the number of pubs by 2014, as the economy finally recovers and pubs complete their latest regeneration, timelord-like, into some new format. The new ones that are opening are very different from the ones that are failing and dying. Some of them are like the Jolly Butchers, with a focus on great food and interesting beer. Others will reinvent the concept of 'the local' in different ways, catering to the specific needs of their communities. Some focus specifically on music, others on sport. Sadly, others will be like the Heel Tap on the other side of the George Inn yard, insecure and shallow like the people who drink in them. But pubs are alive; they evolve to survive. 'We're talking now about pubs closing down,' Professor Earnshaw told me when we were discussing the pub in literature, 'but we were having the same conversation when the railways came in and closed the coaching inn. Then the car came in and opened up country pubs for everyone.'

I nodded. Just like the constant rebuilding of London, pubs generally are in a long-term state of flux. How could they not be, when we are, as people?

'In *Barnaby Rudge*, which Dickens used to write about the Gordon Riots of 1780, there's an inn called the Maypole,' continued Earnshaw. 'The inn represents Old England, and there's something rotten at the heart of it. Eventually it gets looted and burned down by the Gordon rioters. But then it's rebuilt by a new generation.'

We will always need pubs. We will always love them. But, while they offer a basic formula that is at heart unchanging, thanks to central heating, electricity, television, double glazing, plasma screens, IKEA, Habitat, Ocado, Tesco, Jamie Oliver, broadband Internet, Wi-Fi, Facebook, Xbox, Sky and Twitter, the home is stealing many of the reasons to visit, and even the most dedicated fans of pubs find themselves going less often than they did.

Never again will we need a street full of pubs, with hardly any houses between the red lattices. But the Borough still doesn't do too badly on that score compared to other areas, and remains one of the best places in London to go for a beer. The Rake on Winchester Walk – named after the Bishop when it was at the heart of his Manor, now in the heart of Borough Market – is London's smallest bar, with possibly London's largest selection of beers. Vinopolis, under the arches of the railway viaduct heading over to Cannon Street station, has Brew Wharf, complete with its own on-site micro-brewery. The Barrowboy and Banker (a modern equivalent to the Bear-at-the-Bridgefoot, standing on the new London Bridge approach), the Market Porter, the Wheatsheaf (moved from its old home under the ugly new railway viaduct to the basement of the Hop Exchange), the Southwark Tavern (on the site of the old Cross Keys, and before that, Southwark's earliest recorded inn in 1338) and the Royal Oak (on old Kent Street, now renamed Tabard Street) guarantee that the George finds itself at the heart of a great pub crawl any night of the week.

And now such adventures are easy to plan, thanks to online pub-review websites. The George is reviewed on many of these, and against such stiff competition it doesn't always deliver. Reviews consistently revere the building, but one person has a problem with slow service, another one thinks the beers are boring, someone else thinks the beers are fine but doesn't like the food, and someone else again will say all the above are fine, but it's far too expensive. In other words, in many ways, it's just a typical pub.

The George today is managed by Greene King, which is the biggest British brewer, now all our huge lager manufacturing conglomerates are owned by foreign corporations. Greene King's regular beer range is middle of the road and can appear boring to those in search of huge bombs of hop flavour. Greene King IPA is pretty bland, but it's the largest cask-ale brand in the UK so it clearly does the job for a large number of people, if not for me. Some other Greene King beers are unfairly maligned: when I'm in the right mood and if it's perfectly kept, Abbot Ale can make it into my top ten. And I'm delighted to report that the George Inn's beers, whatever you think of the brands and the recipes, are perfectly kept – almost all the time.

So it's just a pub then. But given the right relationship and the right circumstances, any pub can form a bond as strong as marriage in a drinker's heart. The first one you managed to get served in when you were 16 or 17; the one where a big group of you used to hang out when you were 20, the one where you met and dated your partner; the one where you've done the quiz every Tuesday for the last ten years . . .

You don't have to have a history spanning at least five centuries. You don't have to count the three leading lights of English literature among your past regulars or near neighbours. And you don't have to have beautiful wooden galleries. But they all help.

I don't have an office outside my study at home, so when I have to have a business meeting I usually arrange it in a pub. Over the last year, I've arranged to have as many as I can in the George, and even if my meeting had no connection at all to this book, as the year went on I spent more and more time talking about the significance of the door, the inn sign or the weird little bar. I'd take people to look at the Parliament Clock or show them Dickens's life-insurance policy. I would have a feeling of desperate, anxious elation whenever I walked through the doors, as if I were carrying all these stories around with me and, having brought them back home, they had to be told.

I'm sad that the tall settles in the old coffee room and restaurant have disappeared, even though only the oldest visitors would remember them. I like the sense of reverence in the newly opened dining rooms at the far end. But I prefer to sit in the taproom, even as I worry that I'm missing the action when I do.

The refurbishment the George underwent in the summer of 2011 saw the kitchen moved and more seating and dining space made available. It was the year when, overall, British pubs started to take more money from food than drink, so even though the George still makes most of its money from drink, this increased focus on food is inevitable. The upstairs restaurant was turned into the gallery bar. Once the bedroom where H.V. Morton negotiated terms with the giant four-poster bed, it's now a quiet and softly creaking room that gently enforces a voluntary hush. Throughout the inn, the new colour scheme – a little softer than the old black and white – is more welcoming, and the National Trust, who suggested it, believe it to be more in keeping with the period of the building.

The George looks like a very old inn, and more importantly, it sounds like one too, from its tired creaks to the acoustics its low wooden ceilings create. Anyone who likes pubs can only love the place.

But it's not an unconditional love.

The George finds itself today not only in the pub industry, but also at the heart of the British heritage industry. It's funny how those two words go together – heritage and industry. 'Preserving our heritage' sounds interchangeable with 'remembering our history'. But you could comfortably say 'heritage industry' whereas saying 'history industry' doesn't sound right. The two ideas are different. History is history: it changes as it is studied, it is used for political ends, it creates arguments, and it is certainly open to interpretation. But it feels fixed and solid to all but those who work closely with it.

Heritage, on the other hand, often involves *doing something to* history – interpreting it, brushing it up, and charging people admission to see it. Towards the end of *Bankside: London's Original District of Sin*, David Brandon and Alan Brooke argue that, with its fine eateries and luxury penthouses in complexes with names like Tea Trade Wharf, with its full-size replica sailing ships and its wine-drinking 'experience', and with people dressed as zombies chasing you around the London Bridge Experience, Southwark is a prime example of the past being repackaged as nothing more than yet another form of idle consumerism:

> Heritage itself is a large and clumsy term that has on the one hand been instrumental in providing a good deal of important historical preservation and in stimulating an interest in history. On the other hand there have been some spurious projects more concerned with money making than providing a faithful representation of the past. The development of Bankside provides an interesting mirror for these debates.

Thankfully there are no tri-corner-hatted coachmen in the George Inn yard welcoming you to ye olde hostelrye. The George has always insisted it is a living, working inn rather than a museum. But this gives it a slightly paradoxical air if you walk around on your own, examining the walls and the menus. If it were any other pub, you'd be impressed that there were genuine antiques in some of the wall-mounted cases, objects brought here by the Cheeryble brothers or the National Trust from Dickens's home in Gad's Hill, Kent, and framed panoramas of London from the days when the George was in its prime as a coaching inn. It might be unfair of me, but here in the George I expect more, because the George shouldn't have to buy stuff in. There are dates and snippets of history on the walls here and there, several of which are incorrect. You don't have to spend a year sniffing around archives to know that the George was documented well before Stow's 1598 *Survey of London*, for example, which one wooden beam cites as the inn's earliest mention – you only have to pick up the booklet on sale at the bar to find earlier ones. The menus are expensively printed and mass-produced, and there are no other beers apart from Greene King beers. So bits of it feel a little corporate and chain-like.

But then, there are those great photographs of the inn and its neighbours in the nineteenth century. And one of those Greene King beers is George Inn Ale, specially brewed for this one pub. And if they did get rid of the identikit heritage tat and turn the whole thing into an authentic celebration of the George's history (perhaps even paying a fat consultancy fee to an expert on the inn's history in the process?) would we then have lost the point of the George as just a pub, and turned it into a museum rather than a living, breathing boozer?

I don't know. And when I drink here and have my meetings here, most people seem delighted with the George just as it is.

So I asked John Longden for a second opinion. Longden is the brains behind a campaign called Pub is the Hub (Patron: HRH Prince Charles), which exists to preserve pubs not (just) for their historical value, but because in many rural communities, they are the community: get rid of the pub in some places, and all you have is a bunch of houses standing close to each other. The focus of the campaign is therefore very specifically rural, but it turns out the George has a special place in Longden's heart.

'The George is the best example in London of a pub that promotes itself as a tourist attraction, and I mean that in the best possible way,' he tells me. 'I remember it well from when I came down to London from the north as a student. One of the best pubs I'd ever been to. And let's just say after that, it fell into corporate hands. Sometimes it gets handed over to the marketing department who just brand it like another unit. But now it's back in good hands, being run by people who care. The key to it all is a good licensee, someone who recognizes the individuality of the place and doesn't just treat it like another number.'

Scott Masterson is the man who currently has this pressure on his shoulders. Tall, well built and fit, with short-cropped dark hair and a neat goatee beard, he radiates the no-nonsense confidence of a landlord straight from the Harry Bailly mould.

Before I began my research, I imagined the twenty-first century George would have a revolving door of managers, much like it did in the late seventies and early eighties under Whitbread, between Frederick Martin's departure and John Hall's arrival. But Scott proves me spectacularly wrong.

'I started under John Hall as a trainee at Whitbread,' he says. 'After he retired George Cunningham took over, and ran it for about eight or nine years. I took over from George about six years ago.'

It's doubtful anyone will ever match again the reign of the Murrays, but there's still something about the place that keeps people here long term.

Scott's description of the clientele gives a vivid depiction of how Borough has changed over the last twenty years. He tells me that from Monday to Friday the modern equivalents of the old seventies pin-striped city gents still pop in on their way home, and the yard in summer is a magnet for local office workers. But a lot of business now comes from tourists. Many historical walking tours end here, and Americans and Japanese come not just for the building, but also to try the unique British cask ales on the bar. 'We sell more ale than anything else, and drink makes up about 75 per cent of our turnover,' says Scott. 'The George Inn Ale is by far the biggest seller, and they all want to try it. Whether they like it or not, that's different. But they all want to try something they can't get at home.'

Thinking back to Churchill, Eisenhower and Princess Margaret, I ask if any famous people have enjoyed a pint in here on Scott's watch. He doesn't seem too fussed by the question, and frowns before he answers. 'Yeah, we've had Madonna and Guy Ritchie, they were here. Oh, and Beyoncé came in once.'

'And Donna out of *Two Pints of Lager and a Packet of Crisps!* calls over one of the girls behind the bar. 'And that comedian, you know, the tall one, that's taller than all the others.'

'Stephen Merchant?' I offer.

She frowns and shakes her head.

What about locals? I ask Scott.

'Nah, not really,' says Scott. 'There are a couple of old boys in their eighties – brothers who walk round the area every Sunday night, and this is their last stopping point. But locals mainly drink in the smaller boozers around the place.'

At some level, it feels as if a little of the old distinction between inn and alehouse remains here. And certain other traditions seem reluctant to die: the Four O'Clockers and the Brotherhood of the Rolling Stones may be long gone, but the Mudlarks (antiquarians looking for relics on the banks of the Thames), the Marlowe Society, and staff groups from Guy's keep the appointments book for the two meeting rooms upstairs fairly full.

The yard still sees plenty of action too, with plays, battle re-enactments, morris dancing and outdoor film screenings happening throughout the year, as often as the weather will allow. My chat with Scott takes place in early January, and he tells me that the previous Sunday there was a procession to mark the twelfth night of Christmas. Two hundred people walked here together from the Globe Theatre, and had a wassail in the yard when they arrived.

Sometimes, heritage gets on just fine without an industry.

The first time I arranged to meet Scott here on official book business, about nine months before we had this conversation, he was called away on urgent business and I ended up being shown around by an assistant who introduced herself as Amanda, the business-development manager. I'd hardly started my research by that point and knew very little, and she tried to fill me in with what she knew. Talk turned quickly – as you'd expect – to how old and characterful the building was. 'I don't believe in ghosts,' she had said, 'absolutely, totally. I don't believe in anything like that.'

I've noticed that when people start a conversation with this line, there's always a 'but' coming.

'But . . . there was one night when we were doing the stocktake and I had to stay really late. I decided to just try and get it done once the pub was shut and the rest of the staff had gone home. It was about one in the morning . . . and I know it's just that this is a very old building, and it shifts and settles. But the creaking and everything, and this sense of . . . I lasted about twenty minutes and then ran out of the place. I'd never do something like that again.'

I recount this story to Scott, who shakes his head. 'No, that can't have been Amanda, she's never stayed late to do a stocktake in her life. It sounds more like Natalie, she likes a good story. But I really don't believe in ghosts at all, so I don't follow all that side of it. The staff do say that there's one of the old landladies – Miss . . . Murray is it? And she messes with all the new technology. Every time we get a new till or something like that, it never, ever works the way it's supposed to. And the thing is, that's *true*! But it's just because the tills are crap. They don't make them properly. It's not ghosts.'

I'm delighted to hear this! Maybe it's not her ghost, I tell him, but if Agnes Murray was going to haunt the George, after running the place for thirty years without installing a telephone, electric lighting, bathrooms or any other modern convenience, screwing up the new tills sounds exactly like the thing she would do.

I ask Scott if he drinks in here much, and if he does, which is his favourite part of the building, secretly hoping he'll say the taproom. But he shakes his head again.

'I make a rule generally of not drinking in the place I work. You don't have to anyway when you live around here, there are so many other places. John Hall had this big Doberman called Toby, and Toby knew all the pubs in the area and knew the route around them too. John would usually end up in the King's Arms, which belongs to Harvey's in Sussex. On the other hand, Frank from the Royal Oak – he's been the tenant in there for years – he'll come up here. But if I ever do have a drink here, I stand just there.' He points to a spot at the end of the main bar, where the flap lifts to allow people through. 'Partly so I can keep an eye on what's going on. You know, being the good licensee. But mainly because when I first came here, that's where John Hall used to stand. And after him, that's where George Cunningham used to stand.'

And with that, I know the George Inn is in safe hands.

Scott may be adamant that he doesn't believe in ghosts, but he still can't avoid them.

With a building this old, any idly interested visitor will say, 'There must be some ghost stories.' It's usually nothing more than an interesting prompt for conversation, but it happens in here all the time.

John M. East once spoke to one old potman, retired after

years of service in the George, who apparently confirmed that the taproom was haunted by a ghostly figure in knee breeches. 'Oh yes, I've seen him,' said the old man, 'Sam Weller of course.'

Only East would have the brass neck to ask us not only to believe in a ghost, but also to believe that it was the ghost of a fictional character who never lived and breathed in the first place, and who, even in the realm of fiction, belonged in the pub next door.

Do I believe in ghosts? Sort of, but not really. Although if I did, I'm sure I'd find them here.

I find myself back in the taproom, with a pint of Abbott Ale and my treasured copy of *Inns of Old Southwark* by Rendle and Norman for company. I always prefer the taproom, and when I walk in I always find myself drawn to the same seat, a little curved affair right by the window, with a small table in front of it and a couple of stools on the far side. I sit here with my book, and turn to a drawing by Philip Norman titled 'Tap Room of George Inn'. It shows a man wearing an apron, so we can assume he's a local worker, someone from the market or one of the butchers, or maybe one of the factories. It looks like he has the room to himself, like I do now, and on the table before him sits an empty plate and a foaming tankard of ale. He seems to be eating a sandwich, and light pours in from the outside, so we can guess he's having lunch.

I've looked at this drawing a few times, back home or in the library, but it's the first time I've had it here, so I study it carefully to try to figure out exactly where this man was sitting. It's confusing, because Norman's depiction of the taproom doesn't look at all familiar. It's too small, for one thing. And then I remember the wall that used to divide this room in two, whose removal so upset the Cheeryble Brothers, and I realize that it must be the wall on the right of Norman's drawing. When I subtract this wall from the drawing the rest of it suddenly falls into familiar place, and I realize I'm sitting

Tap Room of the George Inn, *by Philip Norman, for Rendle and Norman's* Inns of Old Southwark, *1888.*

in the same spot as the man in the picture. Of course the table is different, but the bench, walls and window are just the same.

Having worked this out, I can have a pretty good guess where Norman must have been standing to get the angle of the drawing: just over there, right up against the small fireplace. I can almost see him, gazing at me, capturing my clothing with a few pencil strokes, shading in my shadow on the floor.

But Philip Norman isn't the main presence I feel whenever I'm in this room. He's not the reason I will not swear whenever I'm in this seat. And he's not the reason I keep glancing anxiously over at the door to the manager's office, especially if someone is a bit loud or makes an off-colour remark.

She's still sitting in there, reading her book, her high-necked black dress fastened at the throat with her favourite cameo brooch. She's not a ghost, let me make that very clear: I do not believe anyone is haunting the George. She's an imprint. She was here so long, and made her mark so deeply, that it will never go away. I need to mind my language. I need to be polite and courteous. I need to sit up straight. And I need to remember to bring my copy of *Pickwick* with me one of these days, so she can show me where Mr Perker wrote out the cheque to Mr Jingle, and point out the very spot where Sam Weller was introduced to Mr Pickwick.

And I share with H.V. Morton ninety years before me the feeling that the shadows are suspicious, that the old place is trying to say to me 'The time may come when you, and those who love London, may have to fight for all that is left of me!' And like Morton, the knowledge that I would indeed fight hard places me in sympathy with those shadows. I have made friends with this strange old place.

TIMELINE AND DRAMATIS PERSONAE

A story like this one features a great many names. A lot of them don't do anything that's particularly interesting, so they start to make the pace drag a bit. But this wouldn't be a complete history without them, so if you're the kind of person who arranges your music in alphabetical order (by catalogue number) this section is for you.

A ROUGH TIMELINE OF THE LANDLORDS AND LICENSEES OF THE GEORGE INN

1475–85   Thomas Dewe is named as owner of the George Inn, Southwark, in a legal dispute between his son and ex-wife.

1509   The George aka the 'Syrcote' is owned by Thomas Combes.

1555   The George is owned by Humphrey Collett, bowyer and citizen of London, MP for Southwark in 1553.

1558   Collet dies and leaves the George to his son, Thomas.

1558   Nicholas Marten is named landlord of the George in Humphrey Collett's will.

1558–1562   At some point during this period, the George comes into the ownership of Edward and Richard Sawyer, or Sayer. Later in this period, Edward Sayer is defending his claim to the inn against Richard Sayer. Later still, the inn becomes the property of John Sayer, who appears in legal documents during various wrangles for ownership over the next century. Either Christian names were very scarce in those days, or John Sayer was one of those immortal types who goes travelling for thirty years and then come back pretending to be his own son.

1596 William Grubbe takes over the running of the pub as tenant landlord, paying rent to various generations of John Sayers.

1621 When William Grubbe dies his wife Elizabeth takes over as tenant landlord.

1626 Henry Blundell takes over as licensee, and Elizabeth Grubbe moves out of the inn itself to one of the tenements on the property, which is now quite substantial. Blundell upsets the powerful Southwark churchwardens and 'makes scoff' at them.

1634 Churchwardens' records reveal the George is owned by a Mr Sayer and Thomas Stone.

1668–92 Records of John Sayer still as owner(s).

1668 Nicholas Andrews acquires the lease from Sayer, and sub-lets to Thomas Underwood, who promptly dies. Underwood's widow, Mary, marries Mark Weyland in 1670.

1670 The George suffers from a devastating fire. Weyland has to rebuild it. The Sayers are forced in court to compensate him for doing so.

1676 The George – along with most of Southwark this time – burns to the ground. Weyland rebuilds it again. The Sayers are forced to compensate him again. Everyone starts to wonder if it's worth the bother. They look at the thriving trade, and decide it is.

1692 The Sayers sell up to John Sweetapple, who swiftly sells it on to Daniel Wight – a distiller – for a tidy profit.

1706–29 Daniel Wight dies and his son – yep, you guessed it, Daniel – acquires the George. Daniel Jr marries

Valentina Malyn, the daughter of a Southwark
brewer. Their marriage is witnessed by John Halsey,
a phenomenally successful London brewer and, later,
MP for Southwark.

1706   Mark Weyland dies. His widow, Mary, who has now
outlasted two husbands, continues to run the inn
under its new owners, the Wights.

1729–33   Daniel and Valentina's Wight's daughter, also called
Valentina, married to Philip Aynscombe, inherits
ownership of the George.

1733–40   Philip Aynscombe suffers from ill health and from his
own financial ineptitude. He signs ownership over to
his father, Thomas Aynscombe, who holds it in trust
for Philip and Valentina's daughter, who is called –
yep – Valentina.

1732   The first stagecoach leaves the George Inn, bound
for the Old Ship Inn in Brighton (which, like the
George, is still there today).

1733   William Golding is recorded as licensee, though he
probably took over from the elderly Mary Wayland
sometime before now. The George is a thriving inn,
paying the highest poor rates in the parish.

1740–46   After Philip Aynscombe dies, trustees hold the
George for Valentina III.

1746–1785   Valentina III marries Lillie Smith (a bloke). Under
the conditions of Thomas Aynscombe's will Smith
has to hyphenate his name to Aynscombe-Smith to
get his hands on the inn, which requires an Act of
Parliament. They have three daughters, call one
Valentina yet again, and reluctantly call the others
something else to avoid confusion.

1757   John Sabb takes over as licensee.

1778   Thomas Green takes over as licensee.

1785–1849   The three daughters, having each married very nice
men and becoming very well to do, inherit the

George but have no interest in inn-keeping. They appoint trustees to oversee the business.

1803 John Green takes over as licensee.

1813 Westerman Scholefield takes over as licensee.

1836 Westerman Scholefield dies, and his widow Frances (who was the niece of John Green) carries on running the George as licensee.

1849–74 The trustees of the three Aynscombe families sell the George to Guy's Hospital, who want the land on which the by now defunct coaching inn stands in order to expand hospital facilities. Guy's demolishes a big chunk of the rear stable yard.

1859 George Grinslade takes over as licensee.

1870 George Grinslade dies. His widow, Mary Ann, moves to the Old Kent Road. The executors of his will run the lease.

1871 Agnes and Amelia Murray arrive at the George. Agnes, aged 18, is listed as a barmaid in that year's census.

1873 Richard Grinslade, trustee of George Grinslade's estate, listed as nominal licensee.

1874–1937 The Great North Railway Company (GNR), later the London and North East Railway Company (LNER) buys the George from Guy's to use the bulk of the property as railway warehousing.

1903 Amelia Murray dies aged 76. Her daughter Agnes, having already worked at the George for thirty-two years, takes over as licensee.

1934 Agnes Murray dies aged 81 (we think – various census data suggests she lied about her age at times – she was 18 in 1871, but somehow only 44 in the 1901 census).

1935 Leslie and Harold Staples, huge Dickens fans nicknamed 'The Cheeryble Brothers', take over the lease and begin making extensive improvements.

1937 LNER doesn't want to see the George disappear but can't afford the repairs. Donates the inn to the National Trust, who still own it today. The inn faces a long period of closure as essential repairs are carried out, so the Cheeryble Brothers give up the lease. The National Trust sublets the lease to Flower's Brewery of Stratford-upon-Avon, who run the inn and appoint its licensees, starting with Charles Griffith, who replaces the Staples brothers when they leave.

1955 Fred Martin takes over as licensee from Charles Griffith.

1962 Flower's Brewery is bought by Whitbread.

1967 Whitbread takes over formal responsibilities as leaseholder.

1976 When the George closes for much-needed repairs, Fred Martin retires.

1977–78 R. Pitman is licensee. (Despite its relative recentness, no records exist for the George during this period, having all been shredded by Whitbread.)

1979–80 P. Bowers is licensee.

1981–82 C. Bulford is licensee.

1982–85 Paul Davis is licensee.

1985 John Hall takes over as licensee.

1997 John Hall retires, and George Cunningham takes over as licensee.

2004 Whitbread sells the George as part of Laurel Pub Co. Greene King takes over the lease.

2005 Scott Masterson takes over as licensee when George Cunningham retires.

Some previous Chroniclers of The George Inn

Because there are so many Johns and Williams, this may be useful to refer back to.

John Taylor – 'The Water Poet', they called him. Actually, they didn't, but this eccentric traveller and self-publicist called himself it. Gave us a vital insight into the business of sevententh-century waggoning inns with his *Carriers' Cosmographie*.

Sir John Mennis – Leading exponent of Stuart-era fart poetry drinks a dodgy pint (of wine) in the George in 1656. Regrets it. Writes poem.

George R. Corner FSA – Compiler of the first serious history of Southwark's coaching inns, and the first to recognize their significance. Didn't like the George as much as its more famous neighbours.

Dr William Rendle – Kindly Victorian-era Southwark GP, looks a bit like Rex Harrison (in my imagination), becomes leading exponent of the history of Southwark and its inns in his (and their) dotage.

F. Hopkinson Smith – American who loved Charles Dickens so much, he came here to write a travel guide to Dickens's London in 1912. It's not his fault if he believed the lines the locals fed him about the George.

Bertram Waldrom Matz – Big noise in the Dickens Fellowship around 1920, created a delightful and engaging niche as a scholar of the role of inns in Dickens's work – particularly the George.

William Kent – Shakespeare conspiracy theorist who used later editions of his 1930s pamphlet about the George to publicize his Looney theories concerning the bard's true identity. Serious

Shakespeare academics ignored him – proof, in his eyes, that they had something to hide.

JOHN M. EAST – Descendant of an old waggoning family (and a more recent influential actor and theatrical impresario), relative of Agnes Murray, 1970s softcore porn star and possible inspiration for the *Viz* comic strip, 'Aldridge Prior, the Hopeless Liar'.

JUDITH HUNTER – Academic who unearthed the first new research about the George for over a century, published in a 1989 National Trust booklet still on sale behind the bar.

BIBLIOGRAPHY

To read is to fly: it is to soar to a point of vantage which gives a view over wide terrains of history, human variety, ideas, shared experience and the fruits of many inquiries.

(A.C. Grayling, *Financial Times*, review of
A History of Reading by Alberto Manguel)

PRIMARY SOURCES

Seventeenth and eighteenth century Burney Collection, British Library

Nineteenth century british newspapers, British Library

Nineteenth century UK periodicals, British Library

'The George, 77 Borough High Street, Southwark, London (NGR: TQ 3265 8009): Interpretive Historic Building Survey', The National Trust, 2009

The Times Digital Archive, British Library

Press-cuttings scrapbook, 'Inns', John Harvard Library, Southwark

Various archives of documents and photographs, London Metropolitan Archive, London

Various archives of documents and photographs, the National Monuments Record, Swindon

Various archives of documents, the National Archive, Kew

SECONDARY SOURCES

Anon., *A true narrative of the great and terrible fire in Southwark* (L'Estrange, 1676)

Aubrey, John, *History of the County of Surrey* (Gale Ecco, print-on-demand edition, 2012; first published 1718)

Barker, Theo and Gerhold, Dorian, *The Rise and Rise of Road Transport, 1700–1990* (Macmillan, 1993)

Bone, James, *London Echoing* (Jonathan Cape, 1948)

Boulton, Jeremy, *Neighbourhood and Society: A London Suburb in the Seventeenth Century* (Cambridge University Press, 1987)

Boym, Svetlana, *The Future of Nostalgia* (Basic, 2001)

Brand, Stewart, *How Buildings Learn: What Happens After They're Built* (Phoenix, 1994)

Brandon, D. and Brooke, A., *Bankside: London's Original District of Sin* (Amberley, 2011)

Brandon, David, *London Pubs* (Amberley, 2010)

Brandon, David, *Stand and Deliver! A History of Highway Robbery* (The History Press, 2010)

Brown, Pete, *Man Walks into a Pub, A Sociable History of Beer* (2nd edn., Macmillan, 2010)

Browner, Jessica A., 'Wrong Side of the River: London's Disreputable South Bank in the Sixteenth and Seventeenth Century', *Essays in History*, 6 (University of Virginia, 1994)

Bryson, Bill, *Shakespeare* (HarperPress, 2007)

Bryson, Bill, *At Home: A Short History of Private Life* (Black Swan, 2010)

Burford, E.J., *Bawds and Lodgings: A History of the London Bankside Brothels, 1600–1675* (Peter Owen, 1976)

Burke, Thomas (ed.), *The Book of the Inn* (Constable & Co, 1927)

Burke, Thomas, *English Inns* (Adprint, 1943)

Carlin, Martha, *The Urban Development of Southwark c1200–1550*, Ph.D thesis (University of Toronto, Southwark Library, 1983)

Carlin, Martha, *Medieval Southwark* (Hambledon Press, 1993)

Clark, Peter, *The English Alehouse: A Social History 1200–1830* (Longmans, 1983)

Concanen, M. and Morgan, A., *The History and Antiquities of the Parish of St. Saviour, Southwark* (J. Delahoy, 1795)

Cordle, Celia, *Out of the Hay and into the Hops, Studies in Regional and Local History*, vol. ix (University of Hertfordshire Press, 2011)

Corner, George, *On some of the ancient inns of Southwark* (Cox & Wyman, 1860)

Cox, B., *English Inn and Tavern Names* (Nottingham University Press, 1994)

Davies, Philip, *Lost London 1870–1945* (English Heritage, 2009)

de la Beyodere, Guy (ed.), *The Diary of John Evelyn* (Boydell, 1995)

Defoe, Daniel *A Tour Through the Whole Island of Great Britain* (Penguin, 1971)

Dickens, Cedric, *Drinking with Dickens* (New Amsterdam, 1980)

Dickens, Charles, *The Pickwick Papers* (Penguin, 1994)

Earnshaw, Stephen, *The Pub in Literature* (Manchester University Press, 2001)

East, John M., *'Neath the Mask: The Story of the East Family* (George Allen & Unwin, 1967)

Elwall, R., *Bricks and Beer* (British Architectural Library, 1983)

Everitt, A., 'The English Urban Inn 1560–1760', in Everitt (ed.), *Perspectives in English Urban History* (Macmillan, 1973)

Farnol, Jeffery, *The Amateur Gentleman* (Burt & Co, 1913)

Forgeng, Jeffrey L., *Daily Life in Stuart England* (Greenwood, 2007)

Groom, Arthur, *Old London Coaching Inns and Their Successors* (London Midlands & Scottish Railway Co., 1928)

Harris, Stanley, *Old Coaching Days* (Richard Bentley & Son, 1882)

Harrison, William, *Description of England* (Holinshed, 1577)

Hart, W.H., *Further remarks on some of the Ancient Inns of Southwark*, Surrey Archaeological Collections 3 (Surrey Archaeological Society, 1865)

Hunter, Judith, *George Inn – An illustrated souvenir* (The National Trust, 1989)

Hyde, Ralph (ed.), *The A–Z of Georgian London* [Basically John Rocque's incredible 1749 map] (London Topographical Society, 1982)

Kent, William, *The George Inn, Southwark* (A. Brown & Sons, 1970)

Keverne, Richard, *Tales of Old Inns* (Collins, 1939)

Kumin, B. and Tlusty B., *The World of the Tavern: Public Houses in Early Modern Europe* (Ashgate, 2002)

Larwood, J. and Hotten, J.C., *History of Sign-Boards* (Chatto & Windus, 1951)

Lucas, E.V., *Loiterer's Harvest* (Methuen & Co., 1913)

Matz, Bertram Waldrom, *The George Inn Southwark: A survival of the old coaching days* (Chapman & Hall, 1918)

Matz, Bertram Waldrom, *The Inns and Taverns of Pickwick* (Cecil Palmer, 1921)

Matz, Bertram Waldrom, *Dickensian Inns and Taverns* (Cecil Palmer, 1922)

Mennis, Sir John, *Musarum Deliciae, or The Muses' Delight* (John Camden Hotten, 1656)

Morton, H.V., *The Nights of London* (Methuen & Co., 1926)

Myers, A.R., *Chaucer's London* (Amberley, 2009)

Outram Tristram, W., *Coaching Days and Coaching Ways* (Macmillan, 1893)

Pantin, W.A., 'Medieval Inns', in E.M. Jope (ed.), *Studies in Building History* (Odhams Press Ltd, 1961)

Popham, H.E., *The Taverns of London* (Cecil Palmer, 1927)

Porter, Stephen, *Pepys's London* (Amberley, 2011)

Porter, Stephen, *Shakespeare's London* (Amberley, 2009)

Pudney, John, *A Draught of Contentment* (New English Library, 1971)

Reilly, Leonard, *Southwark: An Illustrated History* (London Borough of Southwark, 1998)

Reilly, Leonard, *The Story of the Borough* (London Borough of Southwark, 2009)

Rendle, William and Norman, Phillip, *The Inns of Old Southwark and their Associations* (Longman, 1888)

Rice, Matthew, *Rice's Architectural Primer* (Bloomsbury, 2009)

Richardson, A.E. and Eberlain, H.D., *The English Inn Past and Present: a review of its history and social life* (Batsford, 1925)

Richardson, A.E., *The Old Inns of England* (Batsford, 1934)

Roberts, Sir Howard and Godfrey, Walter H. (eds.), *Survey of London*, xxii: *Bankside* (London County Council, 1950)

Ross, Cathy and Clark, John, *London: The Illustrated History* (Penguin, 2011)

Saunders, Ann (ed.), *The London County Council Bomb Damage Maps, 1939–45* (London Topographical Society and LMA, 2005)

Smith, F. Hopkinson, *In Dickens's London* (Scribner, 1914)

Stanley, Louis, *The Old Inns of London* (Batsford, 1957)

Stow, John, *A Survey of London* (The History Press, 2005; first published 1598)

Stuart, Donald, *London's Historic Inns and Taverns* (Breedon Books, 2004)

Strype, John, *Survey of the Cities of London and Westminster* (Churchill, 1720)

Tames, Richard, *Southwark Past* (Historical Publications, 2001)

Taylor, John, *Carriers' Cosmographie* (self-published, 1637)

Timbs, John, *Curiosities of London* (Hotten, 1867)

Turner, T. Hudson, *Some account of domestic architecture in England* (John Henry Parker, 1851)

Wagner, Leopold, *London Inns and Taverns* (George Allen and Unwin, 1924)

Walford, Edward, 'Walford's History of Southwark Inns', in vol. vi, *Old and New London* (Cassell & Co., 1878)

Watson, Bruce, Birgham, Trevor and Dyson, Tony, *London Bridge: 2000 years of a river crossing* (Museum of London Archaeology Service, 2001)

Werner, Alex and Williams, Tony, *Dickens's Victorian London, 1839–1901* (Ebury, 2011)

Wolmar, Christian, *Fire & Steam: How the Railways Transformed Britain* (Atlantic, 2007)

ACKNOWLEDGEMENTS

I began writing this book in January 2011. In October 2011, my laptop was stolen from my local pub, and never recovered. It contained every word I'd written by that point, most of which was the detailed history of the George compiled from press cuttings, online newspaper searches and previous historical accounts.

'Did you have it backed up?' asked everyone I have ever met, and quite a few other people besides.

No, I didn't.

I lost everything, had four months left before my deadline, and had to start from scratch. And it normally takes me two or three years to write a book.

That I succeeded in recreating the book – or even had the will to do so – is thanks largely to the beer community on social media networks. My anguished tweets about my loss were met with concern, sympathy and support of both an emotional and practical flavour. People retweeted the description of my laptop. They told me where it might turn up. Once we'd ascertained that no, I hadn't backed up, they offered loads of advice to get me sorted out and prevent anything similar from happening again.

Special thanks to James Grinter and Laura Goodman – James got me back up and running, rescuing what data I had (none of it to do with this book) from knackered old external hard drives and sorting me out generally. And thanks to the staff and other punters at the Jolly Butchers (apart from the scumbag who nicked the laptop – I hope you spend an eternity in hell with nothing apart from Corona to drink) for all their help and support.

More generally, the story of the George was not an easy one to uncover. Thanks to Frances Brace, Katherine Bryson, Les Capon,

Martha Carlin, Stephen Earnshaw, Alan Ford, Tony Hodgson, Tim Holt, Lucy Inglis, Jo Kreckler, Scott Masterson, Chris Murray, Jim Packer, Ron Pattinson, Rupert Ponsonby, Roger Protz, Nick Redman, Alice Stacey, Tessa Wild and Steve Williams, for helping me reveal it.

This book was written at a time when the government felt it was morally acceptable to close down public libraries. But this, and other books like it, simply could not be written without libraries, archives and other resources. Thank you so much to the British Library, the National Monuments Record, the brilliant local-history guys at the John Harvard Library in Southwark, the London Metropolitan Archives, and everyone who is committed to funding, preserving and fighting for resources such as these in the face of such appalling philistinism. You guys rock. All of you. As a character in Neil Gaiman's *Sandman* series once said, 'A culture that doesn't value its librarians doesn't value ideas, and without ideas, well, where are we?'

Thanks to Jon Butler at Macmillan, whose name should arguably join mine on the front of this book, to Kate Hewson who carefully and thoughtfully edited it, Dusty Miller for the stuff she has to do at work and the stuff she doesn't have to do but does anyway outside work because she believes in me when I don't believe in myself, and to everyone else at Pan Macmillan who, by the time you read this, will have worked their butts off ensuring this book makes it into your hands.

Thanks to my agent, Jim Gill at United, for taking care of all the stuff I hate doing and helping create the conditions that actually allow me to write with a roof over my head.

Thanks to Chris Gittner and Liz Vater for being both my biggest fans and best friends, and to Liz especially for putting up with this yet again, and keeping me alive and sane in circumstances I hope never to repeat. And thanks to the makers of *America's Next Top Model* – if it weren't for you, she might have got bored and resentful.

PICTURE AND TEXT ACKNOWLEDGEMENTS

The author and publisher would like to thank the following for permission to reproduce the images and text used in this book:

Page x: The George Inn, circa 1870, reproduced courtesy of English Heritage.

Page xi: The George Inn, circa 2012 © Green King.

Page xii: The George Inn ground-floor plan, 1849, reproduced courtesy of English Heritage.

Page xiii: The George Inn ground-floor plan, 2009, © National Trust.

Page 44. Map of Southwark, 1542, reproduced courtesy of the National Archives, English Heritage. Annotations © Martha Carlin, from *Medieval Southwark* (Hambledon Press, 1993).

Page 106: Chaucer's Pilgrims leaving the Tabard, taken from *The Works of Geoffrey Chaucer*, John Urry.

Page 153 and endpapers: Detail from 'Visscher's London', Visscher, Nicolaes (Claes) Jansz © Private Collection / The Bridgeman Art Library.

Page 168: *Southwark Fair*, 1733, Hogarth, William © Private Collection / The Bridgeman Art Library.

Page 208: *The George Inn Yard*, 1800, J.R. Weguelin, reproduced from *Inns of Old Southwark*, Rendle and Norman.

Page 223: Detail from John Rocque's map of London, 1749, reproduced from *The A-Z of Georgian London*, London Topographical Society, 1982.

Page 233: 'Coaches in Southwark', 1826, after an engraving by James Pollard.

Page 245: National Railway Company plans for the demolition of the George, 1879, reproduced courtesy of English Heritage.

Page 249: The George Inn, 1880s, reproduced courtesy of English Heritage; The Tabard, 1880s, reproduced courtesy of English Heritage.

Page 271: A postcard made by Agnes Murray, advertising the George. Author's own.

Page 284: Performance of Shakespeare at the George, taken from *The Times*, 11 February 1935, reproduced courtesy of the British Library Newspaper Archive.

Page 302: Plans from the London County Council survey of London, 1947, reproduced courtesy of English Heritage.

Page 333: *Tap Room of the George Inn*, 1888, Philip Norman, reproduced from *Inns of Old Southwark*.

Quotation on page 289 taken from *London: The Biography*, © Peter Ackroyd (Vintage, 2001)

Quotation on page 350 taken from *Sandman: The Kindly Ones*, © Neil Gaiman (Titan, 2012)